I0894383

HENRY'S ROSES

HENRY'S ROSES

THE LIVES OF ELIZABETH OF YORK, MARGARET OF SCOTLAND AND MARY OF FRANCE

AMANDA HARVEY PURSE

AMBERLEY

To Rosso. I read the book to him.

First published 2025

Amberley Publishing
The Hill, Stroud
Gloucestershire, GL5 4EP

www.amberley-books.com

ISBN 978 1 3981 2085 3 (hardback)
ISBN 978 1 3981 2086 0 (ebook)

British Library Cataloguing in Publication Data.
A catalogue record for this book is available from the British Library.

1 2 3 4 5 6 7 8 9 10

Typesetting by SJmagic DESIGN SERVICES, India.
Printed in the UK.

Appointed GPSR EU Representative: Easy Access System Europe Oü, 16879218
Address: Mustamäe tee 50, 10621, Tallinn, Estonia
Contact Details: gpsr.requests@easproject.com, +358 40 500 3575

CONTENTS

ACKNOWLEDGEMENTS

This project has in effect been fourteen years in the making, starting with a personal aim to publish a book on Elizabeth of York in 2025. Over those years of working on this assignment, I have felt the history twist and turn around itself and myself, like the stems of an unruly rose bush, to become something more than a book on Henry VIII's mother, Elizabeth of York, although she remains a powerful force behind it.

Elizabeth of York has always fascinated me because her story can reveal so much of her times, being a daughter, sister, niece, wife and mother to kings of England. She managed to survive through a particularly turbulent period of history, from the 'Princes in the Tower' and the beginnings of the new Tudor dynasty, giving birth to one of the most infamous monarchs ever, surviving it all but not having our hindsight with which to make decisions. Elizabeth never knew what was around the corner, she did not know how her actions were going to form the past we know today, but she did have her own family history to look back on, and formidable ladies such as her grandmother, Jacquetta of Luxembourg, and her mother, Elizabeth Woodville, to share their knowledge and experiences with her, which surely stood Elizabeth of York in good stead for what lay ahead. This is why I decided to add chapters on both Jacquetta and Elizabeth Woodville. A person's story doesn't always start from the moment they were born; it could be centuries in the making.

Although a major part of this book considers how the relationships Henry VIII had with his mother and two sisters could have formed and shaped the monarch he would become, I have tried also to shine a light on the lives of Elizabeth of York, Margaret of Scotland and Mary of France. In doing so, I hope their own characters will stand alongside, if not on a taller podium, than Henry VIII, who often overshadows everyone else.

The comparison between Margaret and Mary Tudor's lives and their relationship with their brother Henry was a stimulating by-product of the task originally planned. As we discover Elizabeth, Margaret and Mary together, I hope questions I have asked throughout are a way for us all to think about the situations, the actions and the people we are encountering. The majestic grandeur, the royal titles and the political arenas should not blind us to the real people they were.

Looking at the circumstances surrounding what has become known as the 'Princes in the Tower' through the eyes of Elizabeth of York is a good example. She was the sister of these boys. Whether or not she was closer to one more than the other, she was witness to her own mother's feelings; she was the niece of

Richard III and would become the wife of Henry VII. By the time Lambert Simnel and Perkin Warbeck arrive, Elizabeth is Queen Consort with her own children, her own heirs to the throne. What must she have been feeling?

With a subject matter so complex as the fate of the Princes in the Tower, Elizabeth of York's role can become a footnote. This was, more or less, at the beginning of her reign, when everything was new and unstable, when the mighty symbol of the Tudor Rose was just a bud. It is quite possible that her experiences made Elizabeth even stronger than she might have been through her own bloodline alone. This steeliness born of such events is important to history, as it can be identified in her children at certain points, as we shall see.

I could not have done this alone and I would like to take this opportunity to thank Connor Stait, Philip Dean, Shaun Barrington and all at Amberley Publishing. You allowed me to complete my rather specific mission by accepting this project and you put faith in me (while coping with the constant ideas I have for future books).

I would like to thank Sue Richardson, Elspeth Grey and all who work and volunteer their time at All Saints Church in Maidstone, Kent. They look after what could possibly be the only monument to an interesting royal lady, as we will discover in these pages. They were so helpful and considerate, allowing me time alone to respect and remember a fascinating woman.

I would like to thank The British Library, The Richard III Society, Lambeth Palace Library, The National Archives, The College of Arms in London, The Guildhall Library in London, The Royal Historical Society, Westminster Abbey Archives and the staff at Westminster Abbey, at Winchester Great Hall,

St Mary's Church, Bury St Edmunds, King James VI Hospital in Perth, Kinnoull Burial Ground, Perth and Kinross Heritage Trust, Enfield Archaeological Society, and all the magazines and websites I have sourced. I apologise if I have missed anyone.

It feels right, in a book about three influential women of the past, that I should thank three influential women of our time who have been an enormous inspiration to me. Firstly, the joint Chief Curator of Historic Royal Palaces, Tracy Borman OBE. Tracy's love for the Tudor period is infectious and I feel I am extremely lucky to have a person like her being supportive of my written work and of my aim to make history accessible to all. For this and much more, I will always call Tracy Borman an inspiration.

Secondly, I would like to thank Professor Turi King. She is best known for using forensic DNA methods to identify the remains of King Richard III. Her passion for her subject matter is an inspiration. Without Professor Turi King opening my eyes to her area of expertise, I would not have considered looking into DNA for pointers to the truth about other figures featured in the narrative.

Thirdly, I would like to thank Professor Janina Ramirez. She focuses on the medieval period and I have had the wonderful opportunity to study under Professor Janina Ramirez many times. I am a medievalist because of her. I would like to thank her for the time she spent in conversation with me at Canterbury, and for being so encouraging.

I would of course like to thank my family and friends, who have had to cope with me constantly distracted, stopping only to say, 'Isn't this amazing that… or 'Do you know these two are related?' I am extremely appreciative of your patience and support.

Henry VIII was and will always be, a fascinating monarch. He was the son of a king who had a weak claim to the English throne. In his mother and his sisters, the Queens of England, Scotland and France, Henry VIII was surrounded by women who arguably had stronger claims to the throne. They certainly had strong personalities, as hopefully we are about to discover.

Amanda Harvey Purse

2025

Introduction

HOW ROYAL WAS ELIZABETH OF YORK?

The chapter title perhaps asks a strange question. Being the daughter of King Edward IV made her royal, depending on your view of how legitimate Edward was. This alone could have been the reason why she was seen as an important match for her future husband, Henry Tudor. But did her royal blood come purely from her father's side of the family? Her mother Elizabeth Woodville has been described in many different ways over the years. Perhaps the most memorable descriptor is 'commoner'. So, if she was not of royal blood, the only royal blood in the veins Elizabeth of York came from her father. Is this true?

To answer this question, we need to understand the background of Elizabeth Woodville and to do this, we need to step back before she was born and discuss her mother. This is not as easy as it may sound, as Elizabeth's parents were Sir Richard Woodville (modern spelling of the surname) and Jacquetta of Luxembourg. Documentation on Jacquetta herself is, to date, hard to find. However, her importance cannot be denied, the fact that she was the great grandmother to King Henry VIII being just one of the many reasons.

We can start Jacquetta's family history with Waleran I, Lord of Ligny. He was the fourth grandfather to Jacquetta of Luxembourg, part of a family that had ruled the area of Ligny-en-Barrois in France since at least the 1240s. According to the French historian André Du Chesne, with Waleran I the French branch of the House of Luxembourg begins, the royal family of the Holy Roman Empire in the later Middle Ages.[1]

We can then travel down Jacquetta's family tree until we meet Waleran III. Waleran III was captured by the English in 1374 and taken to Windsor Castle. Amazingly enough, while imprisoned there, he married Maud Holland, Lady Courtenay. This was an important match, as Maud was Edward the Black Prince's stepdaughter and so was half-sister to King Richard II.[2] Being married to a powerful woman meant that Waleran III could negotiate his own ransom and be released, as it connected his royal French blood with the English royal family. Waleran III's brother, John, Lord of Luxembourg, was Jacquetta's grandfather. He would take the side of the English in the Hundred Years' War and under pressure from the English he sold them Joan of Arc for ten thousand libra, which would ultimately lead to her martyrdom. John II would marry Margaret, Countess of Brienre and together they would have five children, one of them being Peter of Luxembourg in 1390, who would be the father of Jacquetta. John II died on 5 January 1441 at Guise.[3]

From a brief look at Jacquetta's family tree, we can see that Jacquetta, and so her daughter and granddaughter, had a higher social standing than we may have been led to believe, but does having a distant relative marrying King Richard II's sister truly make Elizabeth of York royal enough from her mother's side of the family, or do we need something more? From Jacquetta's father, Peter of Luxembourg, we can travel further back to Guy I of Luxembourg. From Guy's wife, Mahaut of Chatillon, we trace back another fascinating branch of Jacquetta's family tree from Mahaut's parents, Jeanne de Fiennes and John – sometimes given as Jean Chatillon – Saint- Pol.

John was the son of Marie of Brittany and Guy IV, Count of Saint-Pol. Through Marie, we have a connection to Beatrice of England, as they were mother (Beatrice) and daughter (Marie). Beatrice of England was the daughter of King Henry III of England and the granddaughter of King John. This means that through Jacquetta's father's side of her family, Jacquetta was the six times granddaughter of King John. Pursuing this a little further, we discover that through her father, Jacquetta of Luxembourg was related to William the Conqueror and all his connections with the French royalty – and even further back to his connections to the Viking chieftains.

It is usually noted that Jacquetta was related to royalty through her first marriage, and as much as that is very important to know, it can seem to suggest that the bloodline of Elizabeth Woodville, as the daughter of Jacquetta's second marriage, was less exalted. However, now taking Jacquetta's family history into account, we can see that Elizabeth Woodville's bloodline, being a daughter of Jacquetta from whatever marriage, was royal in itself. These are interesting concepts to bear in mind as we try to get to know the background of Elizabeth Woodville, the mother of Elizabeth of York, through the lineage of her mother Jacquetta of

Luxembourg – and the connections to the English royal family do not end there.

Jacquetta's mother was Margaret of Baux, the daughter to Sueva Orsini. Sueva herself was the daughter of Nicolo Orsini, the son of Robert Orsini. Robert was the son of Anastas la de Montfort, Countess of Nola, the daughter to Guy de Montfort. (Try to keep up!) Guy de Montfort was the son of Simon de Montfort and Eleanor of England, daughter to King John of England.

To sum up what this all means with a hopefully manageable conclusion, this means astonishingly, Jacquetta of Luxembourg was the six times granddaughter of King John of England from her mother's side of her family, too. Jacquetta of Luxembourg was related to King John from both her father's side of the family and from her mother's; which means that her and – perhaps more importantly, for this work – any of Jacquetta's children, grandchildren and great grandchildren, Henry VIII and his sisters, for example, were related to William the Conqueror in not just one way, but in two, from one woman, Jacquetta of Luxembourg.

So, we return to the question laid before us at the beginning. How royal was Elizabeth of York, considering she was the daughter of Elizabeth Woodville, who was classed as a 'commoner', though the daughter of King Edward IV? It is fascinating how the royal family tree grows and entwines itself around so that on one branch, a woman could be the daughter to a king but on another branch the same woman may also be the eight times granddaughter of a much earlier King of England. These thought-provoking facts certainly provide an interesting introduction to the family background of Henry VIII's first Tudor rose, his mother, Elizabeth of York.

1

LEARNING FROM THE SHADOWS – JACQUETTA OF LUXEMBOURG

It is frustrating for a historian or researcher that the beginnings of Jacquetta's life are unknown to us to date, through lack in documentation. Still, perhaps with someone as intriguing as Jacquetta, she may just pop up here and there and if we are quick, we may be able to catch a glimpse of her, and if we dig a little deeper, we may be able to find a hidden monument to her.

The year of Jacquetta's birth seems to have been around 1415 or 1416. However, for a female it would then have been unusual to record the event. Using resources from the French chronicler, Monstrelet, who states Jacquetta was around the age of seventeen when she married for the first time[1] and knowing the date of that marriage because of the importance of the groom, gives us her birth date in those years. The fact that Jacquetta was born at a time that was so important to her family, being the year of the Battle of Agincourt, when winning sides seemed to switch, if only briefly, could be seen as a sign of events to come for Jacquetta.

Her childhood to a certain point remains unknown, however, we can assume she had the normal upbringing of a woman of her status, with an extensive education. Jacquetta's well-known love of books later in life testifies to this. Jacquetta would have been partly, if not fully literate in a few languages deemed important for her later responsibilities. This would presumably have included English and French, perhaps others. During the Hundred Years' War and considering the many castles the family owned, her childhood was probably spent moving from place to place. This may also be one of the reasons why her name rarely appears in documents.

The French chronicler Monstrelet tells us that it was Jacquetta's uncle, Louis, who planned Jacquetta's marriage at an early stage.[2] The negotiations for her marriage may have started when Louis, the Bishop of Therouanne, travelled to England to visit the new young King of England. The person Louis had in mind for his young niece was John, Duke of Bedford, one of the Lord Protectors of the King. It is interesting to note that while it is well known that Jacquetta's second marriage caused a scandal and political problems, so did her first.

The scandal was that John had only been widowed for a short time before he remarried. John's first wife was Anne of Burgundy. This marriage alliance was vital to the continued success of the English armies in France.[3] Anne died of the plague on 13 November 1432 at the Hôtel de Bourbon adjoining the Louvre Palace in Paris.[4] Just five months after her death, John married the young Jacquetta of Luxembourg on 20 April 1433 at Therouanne Palace.

Philip III, Duke of Burgundy considered the speed with which his erstwhile brother-in-law had remarried was insulting to the memory of his sister and family. Not only did this cause rancour within the family, it also caused a much larger political problem, as it led to the fracturing of the alliance between Burgundy and England. England lost the support of Burgundy at a time that the English needed that help the most[5].

The marriage technically made Jacquetta the first Lady of France, second only to the King's mother in England. One would imagine Jacquetta knew what this meant, she was to gain higher status but this brought her closer to the dangers of the political situation. For example, on his way to marrying Jacquetta, John had to stop a mutiny in a garrison in Calais. This particular mutiny was over pay, and although such mutinies had normally ended peacefully, John had decided to have the ring leaders executed. This was not enough for John, as on his way back from his wedding accompanied by his bride, he revisited the garrison to make sure all was still in order and to reinforce discipline. Deciding all was not right, John then dismissed eight more soldiers, who had to return home to England unpaid.[6] This would be a political lesson Jacquetta would learn from quickly.

The newly married couple continued on to Paris, where Jacquetta became the mistress of the palace of Hôtel de Bourbon. Jacquetta was introduced to her husband's famous library that was full of hand copied manuscripts and religious texts. However, the couple did not stay long in Paris as Jacquetta's husband had to visit England a few months into their marriage to meet Henry VI. Jacquetta went with her husband[7] and what an extraordinary experience this must have been for Jacquetta, the pageants, pomp, the crowds, and being amongst the senior members of the English nobility who were all jockeying for power in the court of the child king.

While there, the news of what John had done in France reached the court, and for his service and loyalty he was given permission to retire from court life and it looked like he would do this and stay in England with his new wife. The couple's home was the 'H' shaped manor house, Penshurst Place in Kent. It had a great central hall and an octagonal hearth. John and Jacquetta added a new wing, now called the Buckingham Building, and like many a noble family, they placed their own coat of arms all around their new home.

Jacquetta received news that her father had died, and given the time and the area in which her father lived he may have died of the Plague. He was only forty-three years old. Her uncle may have arranged her marriage to the Duke of Bedford, but Jacquetta was the property of her father. All her training and education would have had to have the consent and approval of her father, as would her marriage. Whether Jacquetta liked her father or not, he would have played a major role in her early life, so although she was married and setting up her own home, news of his passing must have affected her strongly. Being so far away from her childhood home at that moment may have highlighted how isolated Jacquetta was without the support of a large family behind her. Perhaps not wanting this feeling for her own relations may have been one of the reasons why Jacquetta would have a large family herself.

All set for a quiet retirement at Penshurst Place, but the couple's plans were thwarted by events in France. With food not getting past the soldiers of the French king and a general lack of law and order, Paris begged John to return to help sort things out.

Back the couple went to Paris, just before Christmas. Jacquetta's uncle Louis, who had been left in charge during John's absence was surely relieved to have John back. However, there was a realisation that the tide was turning against the English in France, and so the couple began to move from place to place to feel safe. They settled for some time in the city of Rouen.

John's health was failing at this point, but he still continued to work, keeping the supply lines open in Paris. He had a powerful opponent to go up against in this. Charles VII, who had inherited a desperate situation for France when he became king in 1422, was rapidly gaining power, and because of John's own marriage to Jacquetta, the duke no longer had the support of Burgundy to rely upon. Losing this fight as well as the fight with his health, even from his sick bed John still tried to help by placing people he trusted in key positions. The duke placed a new lieutenant, Sir Richard Woodville, then thirty years old, in the garrison at Calais. This may have been the first time Jacquetta was introduced to the man who would become her second husband. John was still working on the problems in Paris when, on 14 September 1435, he passed away. He was buried in Rouen and he left Jacquetta a very rich woman, bequeathing her many lands, one-third of his main estates, and the famous library[8].

Jacquetta was only nineteen years old and yet a wealthy widow, which might lead one to conclude she could do as she wished, especially with her high status. But it was precisely that high status - she still held the title of the Duchess of Bedford – that meant she was a subject of the King of England, and as his subject, the king called her back to England.

Jacquetta was offered her widow's pension in February 1436 on the condition that she did not marry again without the king's permission. This was so that another marriage could be arranged for her by the royal council. Jacquetta would break the rules. To date, there is no record found of the date of Jacquetta's second marriage, but when she travelled back to England, she confessed to having married Sir Richard Woodville. Jacquetta was an intelligent woman; she would have known this would cause yet another scandal in her life and that she might be punished for her actions. Why did Jacquetta take the risk? Perhaps it was because she was pregnant, considering the rough date at which Jacquetta gave birth to her first child.

She did receive a fine of one thousand pounds, which may look like serious chastisement, but it seems the king really did like his aunt, as one thousand pounds was now small change to Jacquetta. the king's anger, if it existed at all, did not last that long: by October 1437 the couple were pardoned in time for the birth of Jacquetta's first child.

The famous symbol of the Tudor Rose, as everyone knows, came about through the marriage of Elizabeth of York (the White Rose) and Henry Tudor (the Red Rose). But the famous Tudor symbol came to be because the 'roses' were born of two scandals that happened in 1436, fifty years before the marriage of Elizabeth of York and Henry VII. At about the same time as Jacquetta's 'scandalous' marriage to Richard Woodville, which eventually led to the birth of Elizabeth of York (the White Rose), another 'scandalous' marriage was said to have taken place. This was the marriage between Henry V's widow to Owen Tudor, which led to the birth of Henry Tudor (the Red Rose).

During the winter of 1437-1438, Jacquetta with her new family divided her time between the court of Henry VI and her new country house at Grafton in Northamptonshire. Jacquetta was now lady of the manor. This came with certain responsibilities, such as making sure the lands were maintained, supervising the tenants, paying the taxes, supporting the local churches, maintaining law and order on her lands and collecting tolls. Richard would be in charge of road management within his lands and looking after the markets. In exchange for their 'protection' by Richard and Jacquetta, the tenants were expected, if the couple so wished it, to go to war for them. When Richard was absent, either because of war or being at court, Jacquetta would be expected to take on the management of her husband's estate as well as her own.

In 1438, Jacquetta and Richard had a son, whom they named Lewis, possibly after Jacquetta's famous uncle and bishop. As happened to so many medieval families at the time, high-born or low-born, the baby died. We do not know if this was their first child who did not survive into adulthood, as records do not always record the dates of birth or death in this time period. Perhaps more children passed away at an early age that may have slipped through the net overtime. Jacquetta was a very fertile woman.

The next time we know Jacquetta gave birth was in 1439. Richard was still serving away in the military at this point. This was a girl, who was named Anne. More children were to follow, their first son to have survived into adulthood was named Anthony, then Mary, Jacquetta, John, Richard, Eleanor, Lionel, Margaret, Edward and Katherine, who would later marry Henry Stafford, the second Duke of Buckingham.

Henry, Duke of Buckingham, would ally himself very closely to the throne, taking the advantage of having a royal bloodline, but also being a close friend to Richard, Duke of Gloucester,

King Edward IV's brother. He would first help Richard III to the throne but then switch sides, leading an unsuccessful rebellion in his own name against King Richard and was executed for treason on 2 November 1483.[9]

In 1452, Jacquetta and Richard arranged the marriage of their oldest child, Elizabeth Woodville, to Sir John Grey, the oldest son of Sir Edward Grey and Lady Elizabeth Ferrers of Groby Hall, the great-great-grandparents of Lady Jane Grey. This would be the same Grey family that Jacquetta's great granddaughter, Mary Tudor, arranges for her own daughter to be married into. But for now, this particular marriage could be viewed as a union of two Lancastrian families, seen as a sign of loyalty to the king. Elizabeth was fifteen and her new husband was twenty years old. It looked like Jacquetta and Richard had chosen their side in the Wars of the Roses at this moment, that they had elected to be loyal to the King of England, which meant opposing Richard, Duke of York. This might not seem important to us at first, it is obvious that by choosing one side in a war the family would logically go against the other side, but we have something the Woodvilles did not, we have hindsight. Richard, Duke of York would not be just the Woodville's foe, he would be the future father-in-law of Jacquetta and Richard's oldest child, Elizabeth Woodville, because Richard, Duke of York was the father of the future King Edward IV.

Although we have already discussed the family connections Jacquetta had to Henry VI, Jacquetta also had connections to the Queen of England, Henry VI's wife Margaret of Anjou. Jacquetta's younger sister, Isabelle de St-Pol had married Margaret's uncle, Charles du Maine. When Jacquetta became a lady in Margaret's court, this family tie may have helped to cement their friendship. Jacquetta's life as a lady to the Queen Consort of England meant that she and her husband Richard had a front row seat for the drama of the changing fortunes of the royal family. It must have highlighted the many dangers this world had, giving Jacquetta experience to pass on to her children and future grandchildren. Jacquetta would experience the highs and lows of the royal court from the shadows. For example, she would be at court when her mistress, Margaret of Anjou, finally gave birth to an heir, after seven years of trying, in the spring of 1453, when Jacquetta herself was also pregnant with her son Lionel. However, although the birth of Prince Edward would have normally helped to cool any simmering unrest, Jacquetta would have seen that having a single heir did not always mean stability, an experience she would have shared with her own daughter, when Elizabeth Woodville was in the same position.

Beginning in 1453, Henry had a series of mental breakdowns, rendering him unable to rule. Henry VI was not mentally well at the time of the birth of his heir, which was highlighted to the king's council when the child was taken to him. When the child was placed in the king's arms, the king gave no reaction at all.[10] This confirmed that the king was unfit to rule, and Richard, Duke of York was appointed Protector and Defender of the Kingdom on 27 March 1454, until the recovery of the King or until the King's son reached fourteen.

Richard chose immediately to banish Jacquetta's mistress, the Queen Consort of England, who had just given birth to the heir to the throne, to Windsor Castle. What a shock this must have been to Margaret of Anjou and her ladies, including Jacquetta. For Margaret had just performed the main duty of a queen, she had given birth to a healthy male heir, and yet still her position within the royal court was at risk. We can imagine that this experience seen by Jacquetta was shared with her own family when they were in a similar position. We can see the fear of the volatile reign of both Henry VI and Margaret of Anjou repeated in the reign of Elizabeth Woodville and King Edward IV and even at the start of the Tudor period under Henry VII and Jacquetta's granddaughter, Elizabeth of York.

At the time of Margaret's banishment, Jacquetta was pregnant again, and as a sign of loyalty she chose to name her child Margaret, after the queen Jacquetta had served so faithfully. At Christmas 1454, Jacquetta witnessed a brief improvement of her mistress's situation when Henry VI suddenly recovered from his illness.[11] However, the king then lost the Battle of St Albans and was captured. Margaret and her son fled to the safety of the Tower of London – an action that Jacquetta's granddaughter, Elizabeth of York, would repeat almost forty-two years later during the Cornish Rebellion of 1497.

Henry VI would regain control and this time the king wanted peace. He tried for unity by leading a procession through the streets of London, with Lancastrians and Yorkists walking side by side, which became known as the Loveday of 1458.[12] In this, Margaret of Anjou walked beside her rival, Richard, Duke of York and Jacquetta, who was probably pregnant with her last child, walked with her husband. Although, this was a great public celebration of unity, many had not forgiven the Yorkists for the number of people killed at the Battle of St Albans. The Loveday nevertheless did certainly put on a show for the public, and no doubt Jacquetta learned and shared with her future generations the power of public spectacle, no matter what was really going on behind the scenes.

Inevitably, war broke out again and Jacquetta added to her experiences of the royal court by witnessing the eventual downfall of her mistress, Margaret of Anjou. Although there would be moments of triumph for Margaret, King Henry and their son Prince Edward, such as the largely bloodless Rout of Ludford Bridge, the Yorkists kept fighting back. One occasion at Calais Castle affected Jacquetta and her family. Richard Woodville, Jacquetta and their son were openly mocked when they were captured by the Yorkist Earls of Warwick, Salisbury and the Earl of March, who would later become King Edward IV, future son-in-law of Richard and Jacquetta.[13] Although Richard, Duke of York, was eventually defeated, his head cut off and placed on a pike and displayed over Micklegate Bar in York,[14] it would be Richard's son, Edward, Earl of March, who would eventually win the day by having the people of London claim he was the rightful King of England and then, defeating the last remaining loyal Lancastrians, at the grim Battle of Towton. Through all this bloodshed, Jacquetta, her husband and her family had survived, but now they had to come to terms with the fact that England had a new Yorkist king.[15]

With the death of Elizabeth's husband, Sir John Grey, in these battles, Elizabeth was struggling to pay for her deceased husband's home at Groby Hall. She eventually went home to her parents at Grafton, while she tried to get the money owed to her and her sons through her deceased husband's estate. At this point Jacquetta and her husband had no access to the court, nor any real influence to help their daughter in her time of need. They were instead treated with suspicion, but they did gain a royal pardon. In 1463, Jacquetta's husband and son were summoned to the new king's council to advise, and they surely used this opportunity to gain the king's trust and favour.

A year later, Edward travelled north and may have stayed at Grafton, where he could have met Elizabeth Woodville. We know at some point Elizabeth was able successfully to appeal her case for getting her dowry land.[16] As it turned out, Elizabeth Woodville did not need her dowry from her marriage to Sir John Grey as she was to be married again within a few weeks, to the King of England himself. It would be stated later, because it was so incredible for a King of England to marry what was thought to be 'a commoner', that Edward must have been bewitched by Jacquetta.[17]

Her daughter's instant rise in the royal court meant Jacquetta and her family was even closer to the royal circle than they had been before, and Jacquetta would spend the rest of her life beside her daughter, the new Queen Consort. This must have been a bizarre outcome for Jacquetta. She had moved to England to become Duchess of Bedford and in doing so began many years of loyal service to the Lancastrian royal house, including those serving personally the Lancastrian Queen Consort of England, Margaret of Anjou. Now, she was serving another queen, who happened to be her own daughter, a Yorkist queen.

Jacquetta no doubt shared with her daughter all the knowledge and experiences that she had gained in her own time in the royal court. She would also have shared the ups and downs of court life and possibly helped with the birth of her daughter's royal heirs, including Elizabeth of York.

Jacquetta would pass away in 1472 at the age of fifty-six. She had been mourning the death of her husband, Richard Woodville, for three years, as Richard had been swiftly executed at Kenilworth Castle on 12 August 1469, with the couple's son John, after the Battle of Edgecote. There are records to suggest that Richard Woodville was buried at St James's Abbey in Northampton,[18] but after the Abbey was destroyed in 1538, it is unknown where exactly Richard was buried. In an archaeological dig of the site of the abbey in the latter part of 1999 and the early stages of the 2000s, three hundred bodies were found and underwent analysis to reveal the state of health of the people at their death and the burial practices of the medieval period, but there was no indication of who was who.[19]

Not much has often written of Jacquetta, possibly because of the lack of documentation, However, Jacquetta's interesting legacy has always been there, waiting for us to discover it as well as herself too. Take her love for books, for example, which could have been inherited by her granddaughter, Elizabeth of York. Elizabeth of York in turn could have used this love of the written word when teaching her son, the future King Henry VIII, and his sisters, Margaret and Mary. We might even be able to push this idea further, when we think of the famous Holbein portrait of a teenaged girl in a Tudor red dress, holding a book. Is that Jacquetta's love of books filtered down the family to Jacquetta's great-great-granddaughter, the renowned scholar that was Queen Elizabeth I? In any case, Jacquetta had certainly set up her bloodline to continue, but perhaps not always in the way she may have hoped.

The DNA of Jacquetta Woodville

Jacquetta was connected to witchcraft while she was alive and afterwards, a notion that has even been depicted in modern-day fiction. It seems to be an association that never quite leaves her, and modern scientific techniques can suggest that Jacquetta may well have set a 'curse' upon her family, but not through witchcraft.

Much has been made of the change in personality of Jacquetta's great grandson, Henry VIII during his reign, understandably so. There were almost two different kings from around the turning point of 1536. Henry VIII was described in his youth as charismatic and athletic, in stark contrast to the previous king. Henry VIII seemed almost jovial as a ruler, a personality trait that saw him being compared to his grandfather, the Yorkist King Edward IV. After 1536 and his near-death experience on the jousting field, a change began to be noticed within Henry. He was described as increasingly paranoid, less patient, less forgiving, and less athletic, turning into a brutal tyrant. Or perhaps he simply let the mask slip to reveal his real nature.

One thing that certainly did unite Henry VII and son was the mounting pressure to secure the Tudor dynasty. Henry VII had pinned all his hopes on his first-born son, the man that was the true embodiment of what the Tudor rose emblem stood for, the combined factions of both Lancaster and York, knowing that he had already a spare should anything happen. When that something did happen and Prince Arthur passed away, Henry VII's dynasty seemed fragile again, with only one son. The gravity of this situation must have laid heavily on both Henry VII and Elizabeth of York. This suggests why, knowing all the dangers of having a child and the fact that Elizabeth was considered to be too old to have any more children, the couple still tried for more. This would have dreadful consequences.

For Henry VIII, the near-death incident in 1536 only demonstrated even more emphatically to Henry how weak his own dynasty was. He still had no son, after over twenty years of marriage to his first wife and after marrying again. The pressure of succession returned to the Tudor reign as it had done one generation before and would continue to be something the family would struggle with throughout their entire era. Many motives for this change in Henry VIII, both mentally and physically, have been suggested, ranging from hypothyroidism (underactive thyroid), diabetes and even syphilis, but they would not be an answer as to why the reproduction of healthy males was a particular problem for this royal family. Could the answer have been found in the bloodline we have been describing?

It has been suggested that Jacquetta may have had the Kell blood group in her system, similar in characteristics to the more familiar ABO and Rhesus blood types, and this may have been passed down through her family.[20] This could have caused miscarriages, stillbirths or early deaths. It can also cause antibodies within the woman's womb that prevent her from having any more children, if she was successful the first time. The K antigen can often affect the males' chances of reproducing and their mortality rates, more than the females'.[21]. These are very interesting points when considering this particular royal family and knowing its famous history.

Richard Woodville had a number of children with Jacquetta, but if Jacquetta passed the K antigen down to her children, let us consider her sons first. Of the number of sons Richard and Jacquetta had, four we certainly know had no children and, to date, there were three other sons that have no records to suggest they did either. However, it must also be pointed out that in the medieval period, there was a high rate of infant deaths. Also, there may have been other factors at work here, for example John Woodville married a woman who could have possibly been postmenopausal at the time of their marriage.

To explore the suggestion further, we must consider Elizabeth Woodville's male children with Edward IV, to follow the bloodline to Henry VIII. But the fate of both their sons, Prince Edward and Richard, as the 'Princes in the Tower', leads us to a dead end. Stepping down the family tree we have Henry's brother, Prince Arthur, who died relatively young through illness. The way in which Henry's mother passed away could add weight to the theory, if it wasn't for the fact that dying from 'childbed fever' was common.

There are many 'what ifs'. The fact that childbirth mortality was extremely high, not only through illness and infections, but even through the possibility of political assassination, muddles the waters. However, it remains an interesting concept and if valid, the mutterings that Jacquetta used witchcraft to put a 'curse' upon her family are supremely ironic.

Jacquetta was the grandmother of Elizabeth of York and great grandmother of Margaret and Mary Tudor, the three women central to this narrative, but she was also so much more. Time and time again we have discussed moments and experiences in Jacquetta's life that may have helped prepare future generations of the royal family when it was their time. Jacquetta's importance to these stories then, cannot be denied. Having examined the very long life of Jacquetta of Luxembourg – Duchess of Bedford, Lady Rivers, six-time granddaughter of King John I, twice, mother of the Queen Consort of England Elizabeth Woodville, grandmother of the first Tudor queen, Elizabeth of York and great grandmother of Henry VIII, Mary Tudor and Margaret Tudor – it would be gratifying to have a place to go to remember her. But where?

It may appear as if there is nowhere to go, that such a fascinating woman left no physical mark upon our world for us to visit. The place she was born is unknown, her manor house in Grafton, Northamptonshire, has been built over and there is no record, to date, of her burial place. However, during research for this book, a place has been found. We need to return to the beginnings of Jacquetta's second husband's story, Richard Woodville. This may seem an odd place to start, considering we are trying to find a place for Jacquetta herself, but the outcome is marvellous for any history devotee.

For us, for Jacquetta and her husband, Maidstone in Kent holds a secret. All Saints Church in Maidstone is situated on the River Medway near the Archbishop's Palace on a busy main road, but once inside, the peace and tranquillity envelops you as you enter. Anne Boleyn's cousin John Ashley's memorial is within, along with the memorial for John's wife, the famous 'Kat' Ashley, the long-time devoted subject of Queen Elizabeth I. There is a stained-glass window above the door. This window survived Henry VIII's Reformation, perhaps the only stain-glassed window to have done so of the Tudor period. There are other histories within the church, such as evidence of the destruction of painted saints by Oliver Cromwell's men, you can still see the scratch marks made in the stone from their swords.

If you walk toward the High Altar, up the stairs and head to the left, you will see a memorial plaque, grey in colour, on the floor. Once the top part of a tomb, this memorial is placed by the altar. The placement is significant as it highlights the pre-eminence of the people memorialised. Sadly, as years have passed, the details of this memorial have faded but we can see still that the plaque has a family shield in all four corners, then in the centre there is a faint outline of two people, one is of a man and the other a woman, dressed in medieval clothing. This memorial is for Richard and Jacquetta Woodville. This maybe the only mark of them left anywhere in the world. All the history, all the meaning, all the events that we have just discussed in this chapter, end with this one plaque on the floor of a church in a busy town in Kent, the birthplace of Richard Woodville, the birthplace of the great grandfather of Henry VIII, Margaret of Scotland and Mary of France.

Today, this memorial is being looked after by Sue Richardson, Elspeth Grey and others at All Saints Church. If Jacquetta could know what her final monument in this world was going to be, she would be happy with it being cared for by such wonderful people.

2

LEARNING FROM THE QUEEN OF ENGLAND – ELIZABETH WOODVILLE

We have already described how Elizabeth Woodville's first marriage to Sir John Grey was organised by her parents in the early part of the 1450s, probably between 1452 and 1454.[1] In 1453, Elizabeth would have been around sixteen years old, her husband would have been twenty-one. Elizabeth's dowry was five hundred marks and from her husband's side of the family the couple were granted several manors that belonged to John Grey's parents, Lord and Lady Ferrers. These included lands in Nobottle and Brington in Northamptonshire, but from the start of their marriage it is believed the couple spent their time at Elizabeth's parent's home of Grafton, and also at Astley Castle in Warwickshire.

The first child from the marriage was Thomas Grey. It is suggested that Thomas Grey was born around 1455 in

Westminster, London.[2] Not only would his mother's future marriage to King Edward IV help to give Thomas several titles, such as the first Marquess of Dorset, but being the stepson of the King of England also meant Thomas could marry into the royal family himself, which he did, twice. His first marriage was to Anne Holland, the king's niece, and the second marriage was to the king's cousin Cecily Bonville, the wealthiest heiress in England at the time, as the niece of the Earl of Warwick, the 'Kingmaker'. This marriage brought Thomas the titles of Lord Harrington and Lord Bonville, and fourteen children, seven boys and seven girls. It is through Thomas Grey that the family tree connects Elizabeth Woodville, his mother, to Lady Jane Grey, the granddaughter of King Henry VII, for she would have been the great-great granddaughter of Elizabeth Woodville.

Elizabeth Woodville would have another son with her first husband, named Richard, possibly after Elizabeth's father, born around 1457.[3] This means he would have been around four years old when his father Sir John died at the Battle of St Albans and about seven when it is thought his mother married again to Edward, King of England. Staying with his mother for the early part of his life meant that he enjoyed all the benefits of growing up within court life, such as taking part in jousts. Richard would be knighted in 1475 and he began his political career by serving in the border counties of Wales on behalf of his half-brother, Edward (later Edward V). In doing so, Richard was given the role of Justice of the Peace in Herefordshire, sitting in sessions for Hereford and Ludlow.[4] In 1479, he became Chester Castle's constable and by 1482 he had proved himself to his mother and the King of England sufficiently to be tasked with helping to bring up the then Prince of Wales, Edward.[5]

After the death of Elizabeth's first husband, Elizabeth and her family believed that because the Woodvilles had paid her dowry in exchange for lands to be used by her husband and herself, now these lands should be passed to Elizabeth solely. However, her mother-in-law disagreed. Lady Ferrers believed her son and daughter-in-law were only tenants of the lands and Lady Ferrers could request them back at any time. It is believed that Lady Ferrers may have thought she had enough authority to win her case, as she had remarried to Sir John Bourchier, cousin to King Edward IV. The Lancastrians, who the Woodvilles were at this point, were on the losing side of the Wars of the Roses. However, Elizabeth Woodville, like her mother before her, was resourceful, a trait perhaps the future Tudor queen, Elizabeth of York, also displayed.

Elizabeth first went to William, Lord Hastings, a close friend and chamberlain to the new king. Elizabeth may have felt that she could do this because William had married into the Grey family to which she had once belonged. It has been suggested that through him, Elizabeth was able to ask the king for help with her side of the argument. Elizabeth had moved back to her parent's home at Grafton while this was being sorted out, so, it would have been logical for Lord Hastings to set up the meeting between the pair at Grafton.

For some people today, 'medieval' can mean medieval chivalry. So, it can be very tempting to think of Elizabeth and Edward's first meeting as one of instant attraction and as being romantic. Future writers would claim that Edward had fallen madly in love with Elizabeth on first sight. That the King of England had married her 'by blind affection and not by the rule of reason'.[6] Apparently Elizabeth waited under an oak tree near her parent's home at Grafton for Edward to pass by. When he did, so intrigued was he that he stopped and that is how Elizabeth managed to plead her case for her confiscated lands. This tree became known as the Queen's Oak and it stood between Potterspury and Paulerspury in Northamptonshire.[7] By 1879, this particular tree was almost nine metres wide and in celebration of the story, in 1937 a line of lime trees were planted leading up to the oak.[8] This oak caught on fire in 1994, badly damaging it.[9] It died in 1997, although its burnt stump remains. On Monday 4 September 2000, the then HRH the Prince of Wales, Prince Charles planted a tree at the nearby Royal Hermitage, naming it the 'Woodville Oak' in remembrance of the famous Queen's Oak. The shovel Prince Charles used to plant the tree was inscribed and placed in the nearby village hall.

Like a lot of good stories, this one is sadly lacking documentation. The original Queen's Oak had been tested in 1997 and its suggested age was three hundred and forty years, meaning that it was planted around 1650, not before 1464, for Edward and Elizabeth's tryst.[10] The meeting arranged by Lord Hastings is more practical if a little lacklustre. We also must remember that Elizabeth Woodville, being her mother's child, does not resemble a damsel in distress, although she could play one if it suited her purposes.

Elizabeth's background record as a Lancastrian was unblemished. She had lost her husband fighting against the man now before her, and thereby Elizabeth had lost her financial security and her sons had lost their father. It is perfectly possible that Elizabeth had been told of the mockery of her own family by him in the past. Elizabeth would not have wanted an audience with this new Yorkist king, if she believed she did not need his assistance. Although it is rarely mentioned, Elizabeth was not the only member of her family to seek an audience with this new king to ask for assistance. John Woodville, Elizabeth's brother, had needed money at the age of eighteen and at Pontefract Castle he was granted an audience with the king, who lent him six shillings and eight pence.[11] So, some kind of precedent had been set for the Woodville family, that gaining an audience with the new king was an option. The Woodvilles saw no issue in asking for help from this new Yorkist king, if there was no other way.

Elizabeth's first meeting with Edward may not have been as romantic as it has been portrayed and the same could be said for the first meeting between Elizabeth's daughter, Elizabeth of York and Henry VII. When they first met, Henry Tudor was more or less a complete stranger to Elizabeth of York, not to mention from the opposing clan. Perhaps Elizabeth of York had learned from her mother's experience that romance at the beginning of a royal relationship may not always be key.

Edward's history could suggest that there may have been something closer to love on his part. He had already experienced 'falling in love', with an attractive Lancastrian widow, so if there was any instant attraction between the pair on their first meeting it more likely was felt by Edward, not Elizabeth. The Lancastrian widow from Edward's past was Lady Eleanor Talbot, daughter of John Talbot, Earl of Shrewsbury. There was a suggestion that Edward had met Eleanor around 1460, marrying her secretly a year later on Monday 8 June 1461[12]. This apparent secret marriage would return to haunt Elizabeth Woodville, but perhaps more importantly it would affect her future sons, the Princes in the Tower.

However, Edward was an intelligent king. It is possible that he saw past Elizabeth Woodville's famed beauty and instead mapped out a way to complete one of his main aims as king at the beginning of his reign: unity. Elizabeth came from a Lancastrian family, she had married into another Lancastrian family and by doing so, she had Lancastrian sons; but their existence proved Elizabeth was fertile, the overriding advantage any Queen Consort of England had to have. By marrying someone so well connected to the opposite side of the Wars of the Roses, was Edward petitioning for peace?

This was something that Elizabeth Woodville would later achieve far more effectively than Edward did, in planning the union of their daughter, Elizabeth of York, to the Lancastrian Henry Tudor. But was it actually Edward IV who first attempted amalgamate the Houses of York and Lancaster, before the legendary symbol of the Tudor Rose was born?

No matter how much Edward may have wanted to join the Houses of Lancaster and York together, he would have known that this would not be an easy task to undertake. For a King of England to take an English wife from *any* stratum of society had not been done since the reign of Henry I, leaving aside Elizabeth's ostensibly lowly birth. Edward's idea of connecting the nobility risked alienating them. At this time, his cousin, Richard, Earl of Warwick, to whom Edward owed his crown, was working on behalf of the new King by negotiating an alliance with France through his marriage to King Louis XI of France's sister-in-law, Bona of Savoy. Edward must have known this was happening and yet still chose to marry Elizabeth Woodville before the Earl of Warwick had returned from his negotiations. Nevertheless, the idea of a king marrying for love and to an apparent 'commoner' too, only helped to enhance the chivalric ideal that this period of history seemed to adore. It was also helped along with commentators such as Thomas More, who wrote of 'Kindling his desire', of 'much wooing' and 'chastity'.[13] Edward and Elizabeth's relationship was so strong, so fast, that it gave the impression at the time that it had leaped from the pages of some chivalric tale into the real world and that is why the romantic first meeting between Edward and Elizabeth still gets an airing today.

Whatever the truth behind their first meeting and courtship, Edward and Elizabeth married secretly, probably on 1 May 1464, either in the church local to Elizabeth's parent's home in Grafton or within the manor's chapel, called the Hermitage. The site of the Hermitage was excavated in 1964-5 and it was found that the chapel's flooring once had tiles with the arms of the Woodvilles and the House of York. This can indicate the chapel was where they married,[14] as could the fact that Edward would have been in the area at the right time.[15]

Edward and Elizabeth kept their marriage a secret for a few months, but when the pressure became too great for Edward to marry Bona of Savoy at the Great Council meeting at Reading in the September 1464, Edward chose the moment to shock everyone, including the Earl of Warwick, by calmingly stating that he had already married Dame Elizabeth Grey.[16] It was beyond the pale for a king not to marry without benefit to his realm. Although we now know Elizabeth Woodville was not 'common' and she did give lands from her family to the King, this was nowhere near enough.

If the majority of the nobles were against this marriage, there was actually little that most could do about it without outright rebellion. It was around this time, as quoted later by writers such as More and Fabian, that rumours of Jacquetta's witchcraft began. For some, this was the only way to explain the king's astonishing course of action. One noble that certainly didn't shy away from expressing his disapproval, even if it came close to an act of rebellion, was Richard, Earl of Warwick. He, who fought beside Edward's father and by doing so had technically become the 'Kingmaker' to Edward himself, had been made a fool of in the King's Council and abroad by this marriage. Four years later, still nursing this grudge, the earl chose to raid the area now called Mote Park in Maidstone. This may not sound like much of a target, but it was in the Mote Estate that Richard Woodville, Elizabeth's father, was purported to have been born and so the lands passed down through the family to King Edward via Elizabeth.[17] The Earl of Warwick then went on to organise a full-scale revolt the following year, with drastic results for the Woodville family.

It is possible that Edward chose the council meeting at Reading to share his news because Elizabeth had told him that she was pregnant.[18] If this was the case, then Elizabeth must have miscarried, as her first recorded birth was of Elizabeth of York on 11 February 1466, two years after the announcement.

Now it was time for Elizabeth Woodville to become Queen Consort of England. On 24 May 1465, Elizabeth left Eltham Palace on her way to the Tower of London, the chair that she sat in as she travelled was covered in silk. Elizabeth must have looked every inch a queen, with jewels adorning her clothing. When the procession reached Southwark, Elizabeth was escorted across London Bridge by the Lord Mayor of London and the City's aldermen, all dressed in bright red outfits. A choir of twenty-five people then sang to Elizabeth as she reached the drawbridge of the Tower and, just as Elizabeth's grandson, Henry VIII, would do for his second wife, Anne Boleyn, Elizabeth was greeted at the entrance of the Tower by her husband. The couple would spend two nights at the Tower before she set out on another procession through the capital.

In her second procession through the streets of the capital from the Tower, Elizabeth, was this time escorted by the newly made Knights of the Bath riding in front of her, wearing their blue gowns and white silk hoods. As Elizabeth made her way through Cheapside to Westminster, she was greeted by actors playing two saints that were chosen to represent Elizabeth's family, St Elizabeth and St Paul, the latter a play on Jacquetta's maiden name of St-Pol.[19]

Inside Westminster Hall, George, Duke of Clarence rode on a horse to collect Elizabeth, and with the Earl of Arundel and the Duke of Norfolk, she travelled to the Palace of Westminster. Once entering the hall of the Abbey, with the door being opened by the Duke of Clarence, Elizabeth was escorted by the Bishop of Salisbury and the Bishop of Durham with a canopy above her head held by the Baron of Cinque Ports. Elizabeth was dressed in royal purple and her shoes were removed. The lady who held Elizabeth's train was the Duchess of Buckingham, the aunt of Edward IV, Anne Neville, and surrounding her were the Duchess of Suffolk, Margaret of York, Edward's sisters, and Elizabeth's mother, Jacquetta.[20] As Edward seems not to have appeared in the coronation list of people who attended, it is possible, like many kings after him, he was watching from a hidden space within Westminster Abbey.

At the altar, Elizabeth knelt before the Archbishop of Canterbury while he read to her before anointing her head, crowning her and guiding her to the throne. While the gospels were being read out, Elizabeth was given two sceptres to hold rather than an orb. This was because Elizabeth Woodville was not queen by birthright, so she would never hold an orb, something reserved for those who were. After the reading, the sceptres were given back to the abbot as Elizabeth made an offering at the altar.

After the coronation, there was a banquet in Westminster Hall, with three courses being served, trumpets playing for each course. The first comprised of seventeen dishes, the second course, nineteen and the last fifteen.[21] Elizabeth's brother Anthony had the honour of being the official cupbearer, from which he gave out Hippocras, a spiced wine. Music was provided by the King's Minstrels.

When the banquet was over, Elizabeth departed to her chambers with the Bishop of Durham and Salisbury either side of her. As was tradition, a tournament took place the next day, Monday 27 May, and alongside the jousting, other games were played on the green next to Westminster Abbey. Elizabeth Woodville was now Queen Consort of England and after that impressive display of wealth and pomp, everyone knew of her, her family and the fact that she was a Grey widow no more.[22] Considering what we have now learnt of Jacquetta, Elizabeth Woodville may have leant on her mother's knowledge and previous experiences as she assumed her role as Queen Consort. We can also speculate that this same knowledge was then shared with Elizabeth's own daughter, Elizabeth of York, when *her* moment to become Queen Consort of England came.

Elizabeth Woodville took on the care of Henry, Duke of Buckingham and his brother Humphrey, who had been given as wards to King Edward until they reached adulthood. Elizabeth was given money to cover their care as they had 'for some time been maintained at her expense'.[23] Elizabeth would also spend much time and money on saving educational establishments that were struggling financially. For example, she saved the Queen's College at Eton when Edward IV had planned to merge it with St George's Chapel at Windsor Castle[24], when Pope Pius II authorised the demolition of it with a 'licence to pull down and carry away'.[25] In honour of Elizabeth's involvement, the King ordered the badge of Queen's College to be replaced by the shield of Elizabeth. The couple would visit Eton several times. We can see Elizabeth's passion for education inherited from Jacquetta. In the next generation, Elizabeth of York was to have a great deal of influence over the education of her children, the future Henry VIII and his sisters Margaret and Mary.

Before the birth of Elizabeth of York, Elizabeth Woodville, as was tradition, took to her private chambers. The walls and ceiling were covered in tapestries to keep the room warm. Overlapping rugs covered the floor and there was a canopy over the bed in the hope that this would keep out the chill. Her windows might have been blocked as it was thought that sunlight may harm the child, but it was Elizabeth's choice.[26]

At the start of the labour pains, Elizabeth would have first gone to the chapel to receive communion and then returned to her chambers, accompanied by her mother and other female attendees. We have a record of the actual day of Elizabeth of York's birth in Robert Fabians' chronicles: 'This year, that is to say the 11th of the month of February, was Elizabeth Princess, and first child to King Edward born at Westminster, whose christening was done in the abbey with most solemnity; and the more because the King was assured of his physician that the Queen was conceived with a Prince.'[27] Although in the chaos or excitement, the king was first told he had a healthy baby boy, not a girl;

Edward still welcomed his daughter with love and all the rites fitting for a royal baby.

The child was the first born into the English royal family to be christened Elizabeth. The christening was conducted by the Archbishop of York, George Neville, brother to the Earl of Warwick, while the Duchess of York, Edward's sister, and Jacquetta were made godmothers. A month later, Elizabeth Woodville's churching took place. This was an important ritual, where the mother of the newly born child would be 'cleansed of any sin'. The mother had to wear a veil to 'hide her shame' and kneel at the altar to make an offering. Once this was done, the mother was then allowed 'back into society' and to her duties as Queen Consort.

3

DAUGHTER TO A KING – ELIZABETH OF YORK

At Princess Elizabeth's birth, her father was just twenty-three years old and five years into his reign. Edward had brought prosperity to England, or at the very least, brought stability after the many years of war leading up to the Battle of Towton on 29 March 1461. His next most pressing need was for an heir.

There was much anticipation surrounding the birth. The king was expecting a son, something that most kings did, but for Edward this may have not been just wishful thinking, because his wife had already given birth to two healthy boys with her first husband. Also, Edward's physician, Dominic de Serigo, had assured him that 'the queen was conceived with a prince'.[1]

Any disappointment notwithstanding when a princess arrived, she was brought up with exceptional care, which would be true of her own children. Elizabeth Woodville would often have her children around her as she carried out her queenly duties, which would have given Elizabeth of York invaluable insight into the role she would later take on. A good example of the closeness between mother and daughter was during a trip to Norwich in 1469. Elizabeth Woodville travelled without the king, as he was fighting the northern rebels at the time. Instead, she travelled with her two daughters, Mary aged two years old and the three-year-old Princess Elizabeth. This was a kind of mini progress, with all the attendant glitter and pageantry. They were greeted with full ceremony as they entered Norwich through the Westwick Gate. There were figures of angels and giants upon a stage of red and green fabric. All across the city, there were banners displaying the King's and Queen's arms. A pageant called 'The Salutation of Mary and Elizabeth' was presented, with songs, speeches and music. This was probably the first pageant Elizabeth of York would remember, and it may have inspired Elizabeth's love for such things that would survive throughout her whole life.

From Westwick Gate, they travelled to Friars Preachers where there was another stage built for the royal party to watch a performance, the queen sitting in the Great Chair of St Luke's Guild. Rain stopped the performance and the royal party went into their temporary lodgings at Friars Preachers. Sadly, this trip would not be all pleasure, as it was while at Norwich the royal party learnt the northern rebellion that Edward had gone off to meet, was led by the Earl of Warwick and Edward's brother, George, Duke of Clarence. Both men had been angry over Elizabeth Woodville's rise and their own loss of power. In this rebellion, Edward was caught off guard and was imprisoned, while Elizabeth Woodville's father and brother, the Earl Rivers and Sir John Woodville, were captured and beheaded on 12 August 1469, without trial.[2]

Upon receiving this news, Elizabeth fled with her two daughters back to London, all pomp and pageantry gone, they were running in fear of their lives. Children can often pick up on danger even when very young, and Elizabeth of York could have sensed the anxious atmosphere in her family. Not only were her grandfather and uncle executed without trial, but her grandmother Jacquetta had been arrested on the charge of witchcraft at this point. This charge could lead to a death sentence. Jacquetta and her family would have known of this, as Jacquetta's sister-in-law, Eleanor Cobham, Duchess of Gloucester, was convicted and imprisoned for the rest of her life on the same charge. At the age of three, Elizabeth of York could not have understood the nature of her family's terrifying position, but she may have been able to sense the stress her mother, Elizabeth Woodville, must have been under.

Luckily for Elizabeth's family, the northern rebels' plan failed when support for Warwick or Edward's brother, George, melted away, so Edward was released. Once this was done, Edward was able to commission a council to exonerate his mother-in-law, Jacquetta, of all the charges of witchcraft by January 1470. For now, Edward's actions were still conciliatory, confirmed by the fact that at the age of four years old Elizabeth of York was betrothed to George Neville, the Earl of Warwick's nephew and heir. To celebrate the family being united, they travelled to Canterbury to give thanks for their survival.[3] Elizabeth Woodville now started to introduce her children to the roles they would later play in the royal court, a moment in Elizabeth of York's life that she would learn from and never forget.

The harmony within the royal family was not to last. Warwick and George, Duke of Clarence, began plotting once again. This time, the betrayal was so much worse, as they had decided to work with Margaret of Anjou, who was an implacable enemy of the Yorkist throne. Her orders could once have resulted in the death of Richard, Duke of York, the father of George, Duke of Clarence. George nevertheless coped with an alliance with this woman, for his own gain. George's motivation could have been multiple: he coveted the throne, or simply hated the Woodvilles, or he trusted Warwick so much that he agreed to go ahead with the rebellion against his own brother and family. Margaret held out the possibility of Warwick and George attacking Edward with an army funded by Louis XI of France, through her connections with him. So dangerous was this confrontation that it forced the King of England into exile, to the Netherlands. Elizabeth Woodville and her children fled to the sanctuary of Westminster Abbey.

Elizabeth of York was now four years old. She was with her sisters, Mary now aged three and Cecily, who was just eighteen months old. They were now trapped in the stone-cold building of Westminster Abbey and her mother probably could not hide her panic in the situation they had all found themselves in. This building would not have been as quiet or as peaceful as one might think. Although this was a place of worship, their sanctuary was full of people of all classes mixing together, including heretics, beggars, thieves and even people who had found themselves bankrupt, all trying to evade the law. The space Elizabeth of York found herself in with her family was dark, cramped and possibly smelly, a far cry from the palaces she had known.[4] Not only was Elizabeth of York's mother panicked, but she was also heavily pregnant. Elizabeth Woodville was no longer Queen Consort of England anymore and Elizabeth of York was not a princess, so it was quite possible that they were not treated with any special favour. The upcoming labour would then have been quite different to any other birth Elizabeth Woodville would have had with King Edward. This would have only added to the panic and fear the whole family would have had, as childbirth was still very dangerous for mother and child.

One wonders what memories Elizabeth of York had at this time: was it the grim surroundings, did she remember the fear in her mother's eyes? Or was it being so close to her mother giving birth, without the ritual and pomp of a royal birth? What did this experience of what was happening to her mother do to Elizabeth of York's understanding of her and her family's role in society at this young point in her life? Did this cause an apprehension in Elizabeth, something that played heavily in the back of her mind for the rest of her life and in doing so, affect later actions?

Elizabeth Woodville gave birth on 2 November 1470 to a healthy baby boy that was christened Edward, named after his father. Elizabeth Woodville and her growing family would spend more than six months claiming sanctuary until suddenly, Elizabeth of York's father came back into their lives. He appears to have rescued them. Edward had finally got the backing and funds from the Duke of Burgundy to return to England and regain his throne. However, Edward would first have to make sure his wife and children were safe, so he arrived at Westminster Abbey on 12 April 1471 to take them away to his mother's home at Baynard's Castle. His family had grown in his absence, his longed-for son and heir had been born. This must have spurred Edward on in winning back his throne and so Edward rode out to meet Warwick at the Battle of Barnet. Warwick was killed there, the man who had worked with

Edward's father, the man who helped Edward himself to become King of England and had been a constant thorn in Edward's side thereafter, was dead. Three weeks later, Edward defeated the remaining Lancastrian forces at Tewkesbury. Edward had returned as King of England and his family were restored to royal life, including the young Princess Elizabeth of York. With the death of Warwick there was no more need for Elizabeth's betrothal to George Neville. Elizabeth was back to the splendour of the palaces and the royal parties she had once known and loved. At the age of six, Elizabeth of York's love for dancing was already apparent. Lord Gruuthyse of Bruge visited the royal family at Windsor Castle in September 1472 and noted: 'When they had supped, my lady Elizabeth the King's eldest daughter, danced with the Duke of Buckingham.'[5]

Elizabeth would not have enjoyed quite the same level of education that her new brother, Edward, would, as she was no longer the king's heir. We know, however, like her grandmother before her, she would have been educated as a princess should be. She could read and speak French, we know this because of the books she owned that have survived, mostly in the British Library today. For example, there is a copy of a manuscript entitled *Testament de Amyra Sultan Nichhemedy, Empereur des Turcus* dated inside '12 Sept. 1481', with the ownership being confirmed by 'Elysabeth the Kyngys dowghter' written within it.[6]

Elizabeth of York's library also included her own Book of Hours.[7] Such books often illustrate the personality and knowledge of their owner. No two are the same, owing to the fact that they can be adapted to the owner's particular wishes. They were usually written in Latin and were often given to women on their wedding day or at other important events. So important were these books that they were often passed down through the family.[8] It is interesting then, that when Elizabeth of York passes away, this book falls into the hands of Edward Stafford, Duke of Buckingham, rather than her son and heir, the future Henry VIII.[9]. We know that Edward Stafford is eventually executed by order of Henry VIII,[10] but before that they were close. Were they, however, close enough for Henry to give his beloved mother's Book of Hours to him? Or was it not a choice for Henry to make? We know Henry was very close to his mother and with a book so personal to her, it is strange that it did not stay with the family.

Elizabeth had also gained, possibly from her grandmother's first husband, John, Duke of Bedford's famous library in France, a book entitled *Estoire des Saint Graal; La Queste del Saint Graal La Morte le roi Artu, c.1315-1325.*[11] This was a romantic French Arthurian tale of the quest to find the Holy Grail. It was once owned by Elizabeth's mother before it went from Jane or Joan Grey, Elizabeth of York's aunt, to Eleanor Haunte, and then came to Elizabeth of York herself, by the 1480s at the latest.[12] Elizabeth of York also had books in her library from her father, such as a book of poems by Charles d'Orleans entitled *Epistres de Pseudo-Heloise; Les demands d'amours; Le Livre dit grace entiere, c.1483.*[13] It is marked by the coat of arms of Edward IV. It also contains the coat of arms of Elizabeth of York's future husband, Henry VII, suggesting that Elizabeth may have passed down her books to her husband to read, as well as using the knowledge she found within, to help teach her children.[14]

As well as literature, Elizabeth of York enjoyed singing, dancing and music. Her father had at least thirteen minstrels, who would play instruments at the many court festivals, so Elizabeth would have been surrounded by the minstrel's musical trumpets, stringed instruments and small pipes from a young age[15]. This would have been an education that she would have remembered and used in future teaching as once she became Queen Consort of England herself, she had her own band of minstrels, separate from her husband's band, and her children would play the virginal, clavichord, organ and lute.[16] Elizabeth of York also enjoyed horses and was often seen riding beside her mother in parades and royal processions. She would also have learned needlework, we can see the fruits of this when in 1502 Elizabeth made Henry VII's Garter mantle out of lace paid for from her own privy purse.[17] Elizabeth would have played games like dice and backgammon, games deemed fitting for a princess to know.

All this education, in its various forms, produced a child able to fulfil her father's ambitions. It made his daughter a high card to play in any future negotiations with other countries. A sign that her father was thinking this way was that in 1474, when Edward was planning to invade France to recapture the lands lost by Henry VI, he prepared his will before setting off, in which he carefully made sure each of his children were provided for. Elizabeth of York was bequeathed ten thousand marks for her dowry in any future marriage. As it turns out, no battle was joined. Instead, Elizabeth of York was betrothed to the French king's son and heir, Charles, to help cement the new peace treaty between the two countries.[18] Elizabeth was nine years old and could probably understand a little better the importance of this betrothal than her earlier one.

From this point on, Elizabeth of York believed that she would become Queen Consort of France, a role that in fact her daughter, Mary, would take on, rather than the famous Queen Consort of England we know her to have been today. This was the first time an English-born princess would have been considered for the role of a future Queen Consort of France, adding no doubt to the already mounting pressure at Elizabeth's door. The King of France, Louis XI, even agreed to pay for the trip Elizabeth would take to France, as well as providing her with an annual dowry of sixty thousand pounds as soon as Elizabeth became of marriageable age.[19] Despite her tender years, Elizabeth would no doubt have sensed the change in her circumstances, as now she was being addressed as 'my lady, the Dauphine'.[20]

At the age of ten, Elizabeth was with her family attending the high Mass for her grandfather, Richard, Duke of York, when his body was reburied at Fotheringhay in 1476.[21] This would not be the only royal occasion Elizabeth would be involved in at this age. At the Feast of St George at Windsor Castle, Elizabeth rode out with her mother wearing a plum-coloured outfit that matched her parent's clothing in the Garter Procession.[22]

Two years later, Elizabeth attended the royal wedding of her brother Richard at St Stephen's Chapel within Westminster Palace, who was four years old. His five-year-old bride was Anne Mowbray. However, all did not go exactly to plan as the bride and groom were related, so the royal group were stopped at the chapel door. Finally, the papal bull that had allowed the marriage to take place was found and the wedding went ahead.[23] A tournament was held in celebration of this marriage at Westminster tilting field, which would have been roughly situated within New Palace Yard, a part of the Houses of Parliament that is not open to the public today.[24] It would have been from here that Elizabeth would have watch the jousting on 22 January 1478[25] where many of her family members took part, including her half-brother Thomas Grey, Marquess of Dorset, and the Duke of Buckingham, Elizabeth's paternal cousin as well as her maternal uncle.[26] Elizabeth would have also seen her other stepbrother, Sir Richard Grey, and her uncle, Anthony Woodville, playing a role within the festivities.[27]

As Elizabeth grew older, she assumed more responsibilities. At fourteen, she was made godmother to her younger sister Bridget at her christening. However, there was an uncomfortable family situation brewing underneath all these royal family occasions, as Elizabeth was now of marrying age. In line with the peace treaty with France, Edward demanded the sixty thousand pounds of annual dowry from the King of France, Louis XI, as was agreed. This money was not forthcoming, so Edward sent his ambassadors to France with a message that Edward still wished his daughter to marry the heir to the French throne and so wished to have Elizabeth's dowry paid.[28] This started a disagreement between the two kings, as Louis tried to reduce the agreed amount and suggested other offers instead. Meanwhile, Elizabeth was now old enough to understand the role she was to play and she may have started to realise her own wishes may not count, she was always to be a pawn in a much larger game.

While Elizabeth waited to see what the outcome was to be, death and grief hit the royal family. Anne Mowbray, the child bride of Elizabeth's brother Richard, died on 19 November 1481, and six months later Elizabeth would lose her sister Mary, whom Elizabeth had grown up with for most of her life, on 23 May 1482. Not allowing much time for these two events to sink in, Elizabeth's life was then to change dramatically, and not for the last time. On 23 December 1482, Louis XI of France signed a treaty with Burgundy and in the process married his son and heir, Charles, to the daughter of the Holy Roman Emperor, Maximilian. Princess Elizabeth of York was now sixteen years old and had been jilted. The life that would have been drummed into her from the age of nine years old had gone, she would no longer be the future Queen Consort of France. Sadly, we know that life for Elizabeth was not going to improve for her anytime soon. If Elizabeth had thought her life had changed significantly in her short existence so far, she would be in for a far greater shock in the coming years.

The year 1483 started well enough for the sixteen-year-old Elizabeth of York, although the fact that Elizabeth had been rejected by the French had not been forgotten, as her father had started making plans to take his revenge on Louis XI. The Scottish border had been stabilised enough to allow Edward to focus his energies on the French, so apart from this, all seemed well as he and his queen took the lead in the procession from St Stephen's Chapel to Westminster Hall on Candlemas Day, 2 February, but unbeknown to the family their lives were about to change forever.

On 25 March 1483, Edward travelled from Windsor Castle to Westminster Palace. While there, Edward was suddenly seized with violent chest pains, which apparently lasted for five days. The fact that there were several theories that began to emerge at the time and afterwards suggests that no one quite knew what was happening to the king. It has been suggested that Edward had been poisoned, mainly because of the suddenness of his symptoms. Recently, it has been proposed that Edward had caught a sexual disease due to the number of mistresses he had in the latter part of his reign, with the term 'fishing' described what the king had been doing before he fell ill.[29] Perhaps he had caught a cold while actually fishing in the Thames, but there have been suggestions that the king had caught malaria or, because of his growing weight, that diabetes was his undoing.[30]

The statement that the king had recently gone fishing rather than just stating he had caught a cold gives us an extraneous detail that may indicate the king really had gone fishing, but had returned with a cold, perhaps thinking nothing of it at the time. If the attack was as severe as it was described, it may have been pneumonia that caused Edward's quick death. It looks as if the king's death came as a surprise to many at court, possibly even to his own family; but were there signs beforehand of Edward's failing health?

By 1480, Edward had changed physically, he was no longer the healthy young soldier he once was. The trials and tribulations of fighting for his throne and his love of food and wine were beginning to show. In 1481, Edward was meant to have travelled with his brother Richard to attack Scotland, but he did not. This was the first time Edward had let his brother down in battle. How noticeable would this have been to the last two sons of York, who had always been soldiers above all else? Did this highlight to both brothers that Edward was an aging king? If so, in the aftermath of Edward's death, perhaps instead of everyone being in shock at the death of the king, maybe both the king and his brother were expecting it. With this in mind, we can posit a conversation between the brothers, with the outcome that Richard was made protector of Edward's son and heir, rather than the boy's mother. Did Edward tell Elizabeth Woodville of this conversation and could this be why there is no record found to date of Elizabeth Woodville telling Richard of his brother's death, because she knew he detested the Woodvilles and Richard would, by being made protector, have all the power?

Most agree that Edward IV died on 9 April 1483. This date seems to have originally come from the *Crowland Chronicle*, that states Edward had died on that Wednesday, and this has been accepted ever since.[31] For example, this date was given in the *Great Chronicle*, in *Fabian's Chronicle* and in *Edward Hall's Chronicle*; but there is a possibility the date is wrong.

The City of York's records imply that Edward may have died either on the 1st or the 5th, depending on whether his York Requiem Mass was held on the third or seventh day after his passing.[32] In this, it seems to suggest the Archbishop Rotherham of York, who was at Westminster Abbey at the time, sent a quick dispatch to the Dean of York telling him of the king's death, in order that his cathedral in York could arrange timely prayers for the soul of the King of York. The dean certainly seemed to know of the king's death according to this record by the evening of 6 April 1483, and if so, it would suggest King Edward passed away some time before 6 April rather than on the 9 April.

Also, Dominic Mancini, writing six months after the event, stated that Edward IV died on Monday 7 April. This may suggest there may have been a delay between the actual death and when the royal council was told of it. This has led some to speculate the holding back of information was according to the wishes of Elizabeth Woodville, as she tried to plan the future for her and her children before it became public knowledge. However, the Dean of York's actions after receiving the news may have undermined the now Queen dowager's plans.[33] If this was a true description of what happened, what effect did seeing her mother hold onto secrets have on her daughter? Did Elizabeth of York watch how her mother conducted herself, with speed and authority, and learn that sometimes a Queen Consort had to act fast to survive while being the possessor of certain information?

The official announcement of the king's death came from the Royal Council early on the morning of 9 April 1483 and from this, there may be the simpler explanation for the alternative dates. Perhaps, the date of the official announcement was taken to be the date of the king's death in later chronicles. Still, in the full official account it did state that the king had actually died the night before this announcement was made public.[34]

By convention, the king's body was covered with a cloth from the navel to the knees, so that all might see that the body showed no signs of evidence of violence. This public viewing lasted for at least twelve hours, before the body was taken away, to be prepared for burial by being embalmed, wrapped in cloth and finally encased in Lead. Followed, was a period of lying in state before the body, in a coffin, was placed in the Palace of Westminster, St. Stephen's Chapel. On Wednesday 17 April 1483, the king travelled to Windsor for the last time, with the service being conducted by the Archbishop of York, Thomas Rotherham. After the funeral, Edward's coffin was lowered down in its permanent resting place.

When Edward had planned for his daughter's marriage back in the 1470s, he had also recorded where he wished to be buried. The place chosen was not Westminster Abbey, like most of the earlier Plantagenet kings. Edward had instead chosen the splendid new chapel of St George that he had begun to construct in the lower ward of Windsor in 1475. Although Henry VI is also buried there, he was reburied at Windsor much later, making Edward IV the first king to be buried at Windsor Castle.

When Edward died, neither his tomb nor the chapel had been completed. Although it was thought that a tomb carrying a magnificent golden effigy was to be placed at the upper level of the as yet uncompleted chantry, at the end of the funeral the outcome of this unfinished work meant both the king and then his consort were buried in a vault below the chapel floor, the spot now marked with a simple black stone slab.[35] With this, King Edward IV's reign had come to an end and Elizabeth of York was no longer the daughter of the King of England.

4

SISTER AND NIECE TO A KING

With the death of her father, Elizabeth of York's life would change very quickly. In the coming months Elizabeth would have to deal with a lot of adjustments – to her surroundings, her titles, her fortune, and even as to whom she could trust. A lesser woman might have crumbled. Elizabeth was made of stronger stuff.

Elizabeth of York and her family were now, once again, in sanctuary at Westminster Abbey, but there were two main differences to their earlier time there. The first was that the family had grown. Elizabeth Woodville had with her five daughters and her youngest son, Richard, Duke of York. The second was that Elizabeth Woodville had moved her family to the abbey knowing that her husband would not be able to rescue them, as he had done before.

At the age of seventeen, Elizabeth of York was living with the family at the abbot's home above the entrance of the cloisters, named Cheyneygates, in the Westminster Abbey complex. Interestingly, Elizabeth of York's future husband, Henry VII would often dine with Abbot Islip in these same rooms and it would be where Thomas More, the author of *The History of King Richard III* (in which he writes of Elizabeth of York's staying there with her family) was held in custody before he was taken to the Tower of London. Elizabeth must have known she was safe within the confinement of Westminster Abbey, but she must have also sensed the danger she could be in if events kept on changing the way they were going. Her future was unknown and her life was at risk, but what life was she going to have stuck inside the abbey?

Subsequently, actions beyond Elizabeth's control started to happen very quickly. On 7 May 1483, Richard, Duke of Gloucester, Elizabeth's uncle, dealt Elizabeth's family another blow when he took over the late king's property. By doing so, he made Elizabeth and her family paupers.[1] A few days later, he was made the official protector of the new king, Elizabeth's brother. This meant that Richard, Duke of Gloucester was now the governing authority. Around 10 June, a letter written by Richard was shown to the royal council. In it, he stated that Elizabeth Woodville was plotting to murder him and through that, he managed to convince the council that Richard, Duke of York should be taken from his mother's protection and given to him, for him to place the boy with his brother in the Tower of London. By 16 June, this is exactly what happened, and the young Duke of York went to join his brother Edward V.

Envisaging all this unfold through Elizabeth of York's eyes is a new perspective on these events to most. We cannot know how she was feeling at this time, again there is no documentation, but here was a seventeen-year-old girl who had just lost her father and her and her family's lives were once again in danger, possibly by the orders of another uncle. Her father would not be coming to rescue them as he had done before. Their finances were in disarray because of the actions of the same uncle, and now her youngest brother had been taken from his family, people that he personally would have known a lot better than he did the brother he was joining. Surely an animus against her uncle, Richard, Duke of Gloucester, was growing inside Elizabeth, especially as she was not privy to all the motivations of his actions, being confined in the abbey rather than being at court.

More damaging news was to come, as a rumour began to circulate that Elizabeth of York's father had married someone else before he had married her mother, making the marriage between Edward IV and Elizabeth Woodville null and void. This would mean that the children of that marriage were illegitimate, that Elizabeth of York was not a princess, but it would have more serious ramifications for Elizabeth of York's brothers, for they would not be the heir and the spare to the throne anymore, the heir would then be Elizabeth's uncle Richard, who happened to have the boys under his protection rather than their mother's. On 22 June 1483, Doctor of Divinity Ralph Shaa made the suggestion of the illegal marriage between Edward IV and Elizabeth Woodville public in a sermon at St Paul's Cross. This claim was repeated two days later in a speech by the Duke of Buckingham at the Guildhall in the City of London. The claim was gaining traction.

The woman in question was Eleanor Talbot, but she had died in 1468, so she could not confirm or deny it. This proposition originally came from Robert Stillington, Bishop of Bath and Wells, who apparently went to Richard, Duke of Gloucester to tell him of it and that he had performed the marriage ceremony.[2] Robert Stillington's actions are questionable. For example, it has been suggested that while the bishop was imprisoned as a result of his friendship with Edward IV's brother, George, Duke of Clarence, he told George of Edward's association with Eleanor Talbot, which at the time could have helped George's own claim to the throne.[3] He then repeats the story when it suits Richard, Duke of Gloucester's claim to the throne. It looks like a case of telling people what they want to hear at the right time.

What is not often mentioned is that at the time of both of Elizabeth of York's brother's births, Eleanor had already passed away. So technically, even if we were to believe that Edward had married before Elizabeth Woodville, he would not have been bigamously married at the time he had gained his heir and spare. To marry someone during this period was not always as official as it is today. You could marry someone by openly admitting it in public, in this case to nobles and lords at court, and by consummating the union. Openly declaring Elizabeth Woodville to be Edward's Queen Consort to the court could have completed the first action in marrying someone. The fact that Edward and Elizabeth continued to have children also confirmed the marriage. This could in itself make Edward V and Richard, Duke of York legitimate.

On 25 June 1483, more bad news. Anthony Woodville, Elizabeth's uncle, and Sir Richard Grey, her half-brother, who had been held prisoner in the north, had been executed on the orders of Richard, Duke of Gloucester.[4] There was no escape from this long nightmare. Being away from court and hearing one-sided information through drips and drabs, it would be no surprise if Elizabeth began to hate her uncle Richard. His orders seemed to be killing off not just the friends and associates of her family but also her family members as well. Did she fear for her own life and the lives of her brothers who were in the care of her uncle Richard at this point?

After the death of Anthony Woodville and Richard Grey, Richard, Duke of Gloucester accepted the decision of the royal council that he become King of England in place of the now illegitimate boy prince. He sat on the royal chair in the court of the King's Bench at Westminster Hall on 26 June 1483, though he was not crowned until 6 July 1483. Elizabeth of York and her family must have heard the coronation bells ring out at Westminster Abbey. Elizabeth of York could not have known the fate of her two brothers, still believed to be in the Tower of London at this point, but by the sound of those coronation bells, she would have known she was no longer the sister of a king, but a niece.

At this point and before we leave the subject of Elizabeth of York as the sister to a king, the sister to the Princes in the Tower, it could seem a little odd not to approach the circumstances around this still hotly debated subject, however, sadly we cannot analyse every aspect here, due to the space needed to discuss the rest of Elizabeth's life.

First of all, it is fascinating how history can imprint an image in our minds. Later fictional portraits of these two boys, clinging together, almost as if they are looking for their murderers, suggests that these boys had a very close relationship. However, due to their different childhoods, surroundings and the different persons within their short lives, they may not have been very close at all. The heir, Edward, as Prince of Wales, would have been sent to Ludlow Castle in Wales under the wardship of Anthony Woodville and Sir Richard Grey at a very young age to learn the requisite skills to become the future King of England. He would have possibly viewed these men with more affection than his own mother and father. Richard, Duke of York would have grown up within the busy environment of the royal court in London, with his mother, father and other siblings. This could very well suggest that these boys were practically strangers to one another when they were placed in the Tower of London together.

The label of the 'Princes in the Tower' can bring to mind an image of these boys being in a dark, cold, lonely prison. This is a popular perception of the Tower of London as being a fortress, a prison, something it would become during the Tudor dynasty. The Tower was in fact so much more than that when Elizabeth of York's brothers stayed there. It was a royal palace, hence why Edward V had originally been placed there to prepare for his coronation, it was an armoury, it had a zoo and its own marketplace. In many ways, it was a mini town within its own walls and would have been far busier than we think. This viewpoint may help us, as we consider the events that ensued.

When Edward IV died, his son Edward was living at Ludlow Castle under the guardianship of his uncle on his mother's side, Anthony Woodville and his half-brother, Sir Richard Grey. Edward's brother, Richard, Duke of York was living with his mother and sisters at Westminster Palace, knowing far more of the impact and aftermath of his father's death than his brother. Elizabeth Woodville wanted her son, now Edward V, to be taken from Ludlow Castle and delivered to London as quickly as possible, to be crowned king. She had made plans for his coronation to happen on Sunday 4 May 1483.[5] This would have been just twenty-five days after the official announcement of Edward IV's death. Either Elizabeth Woodville was very forward-thinking and organised to have already planned for such an important occasion beforehand, or as has been suggested, Elizabeth had more time to plan her actions. It is probable that Elizabeth Woodville, perhaps with her mother's guidance and awareness of the sudden changes in court life, planned ahead and was very organised during her reign as Queen Consort.

However, if there was a rush on Elizabeth Woodville's part to have her son crowned king, there didn't seem to be any urgency on the part of Edward V or his guardians. It had been suggested the news of the death of Edward IV reached Ludlow Castle on 14 April 1483 but the royal party did not set off for London immediately, choosing instead to celebrate the feast of St George there, setting off the next day on 24 April 1483.[6] This could suggest that there was no trepidation about any threat towards the boy at this time.

En route from Ludlow Castle to London via Northampton, the travelling royal party met up with Richard, Duke of Gloucester, who, according to Edward IV's last wishes and following a precedent seen during the early reigns of Kings Edward III, Richard II and Henry VI, was Edward V's official Lord Protector of the realm, owing to the fact that the boy was deemed too young to rule and Richard was the closest male royal relative. Richard, Duke of Gloucester then dined with Anthony Woodville and Sir Richard Grey, where 'they passed the whole time in very pleasant conversation. Eventually, Henry, Duke of Buckingham also arrived and because it was very late, they went off to their various lodgings.'[7] All seemed well until the following day when

Anthony Woodville, Sir Richard Grey and Thomas Vaughan were arrested and sent north to the home of Richard, Duke of Gloucester at Pontefract Castle, while Richard himself rode out to Stony Stratford where Edward V was staying.[8] On 30 April 1483, it seems that instead of travelling further south with the boy, Richard decided to take the young king north and back to Northampton, staying there overnight and into the next morning. We know this because Edward V writes a letter to the Archbishop of Canterbury, the boy's cousin, from Northampton, dating it 2 May 1483.[9] It was about then that Elizabeth Woodville and her family heard of the arrest of Anthony Woodville and Richard Grey, and this led to the family moving from the Tower to the sanctuary of Westminster Abbey, as we described earlier.

On 4 May 1483, the day of the coronation suggested by Elizabeth Woodville and agreed originally by the council, Edward V was still travelling south towards London with his uncle Richard and had reached St Albans Abbey, setting off from there for the last stage of their journey.[10] They reached London the same day and were welcomed into the city by dignitaries.[11] Edward V was then taken to the Bishop of London's Palace and it is here that Richard, Duke of Gloucester gave his oaths of loyalty and asked others to do so.[12] Here Edward V stayed until 9 May 1483, with most believing Edward V was the newly established King of England.

It was the Duke of Buckingham who suggested the boy king should now be moved to the Tower of London, to prepare for his coronation, as most kings had done before[13]. It was also the Duke of Buckingham who travelled by boat to Westminster Abbey with Cardinal Bourchier, the Archbishop of Canterbury, to try and persuade Elizabeth Woodville to release her son Richard from sanctuary on 16 June, so he could be with his brother at the tower in preparation for Edward's coronation. Dominic Mancini writes that Elizabeth Woodville seemed to trust the word of the Cardinal that her son would be safe, but he also mentions there was an armed force sent to surround her at the sanctuary[14] – so did she have really any choice but to trust him?

From 16 June 1483, the boys were together at the tower. This was while the rumours of Edward IV's marriage to Elizabeth Woodville being invalid were still floating around. Richard, Duke of Gloucester was feeling anxious over what to do about these rumours, as he writes a letter to the Mayor of York saying so.[15] The *Calendar of Patent Rolls* considers that by 20 June, it was considered by many that Edward V's 'reign' had come to an end, because of the allegation of illegitimacy.[16] This was just four days after Elizabeth Woodville had handed over her second son to the care of Richard, Duke of Gloucester. According to these *Patent Rolls,* Elizabeth of York had now lost her status as sister to a king and would have to wait six more days before she became niece to a sovereign. On 26 June 1483, Elizabeth's uncle accepted the crown.

Now, we turn to the matter of the disappearance of the Princes in the Tower. The first and most famous outcome for Elizabeth of York's brothers was that they were murdered. If this was the case who were the main suggested suspects in this crime?

Richard, their uncle

Both boys were in the care of Richard, Duke of Gloucester, and he had the most to gain from their deaths. Richard never explained where they had gone or produced them publicly in his two-year reign, even at the height of the rumours that he was a child killer.

He did not give them a burial, which would have been expected if they had died innocently, and he had a history of ordering the deaths of members of their family.

Thomas More provides a damning report of Richard III in *The History of King Richard III*, written, according to the nephew of the publisher, in around 1513.[17] You can get the mood of this work within the first few pages. Thomas writes of the passing of King Edward IV:

> There was never any prince of this land attaining the Crown by battle so heartily beloved with the substance of the people; nor he himself so specially in any part of his life as at the time of his death. Which favour and affection, yet after his decease, by the cruelty, mischief and trouble of the tempestuous world that followed.[18]

Simply put, this could mean Edward IV was good in all ways and the actions of the next male in control were all bad. However, what may be missed here is a sarcastic undertone showing through. Thomas, we know, was clever with his words in later life, so much so that Henry VIII or at least his advisors, had to work very hard to find a reason to execute him, failing on several occasions. However, this was written when Henry VIII was on the throne and his father Henry VII had gained the crown by force of arms, and yet Edward IV was the best who had attained the Crown 'by battle'. Is there a possibility that Thomas was obliquely stating Henry VII wasn't as 'beloved' as Edward IV? The query is raised here because More's book has often been put forward as part of the famous Tudor propaganda machine; that More deprecated Richard III because he was writing during the dynasty that had replaced him. When Henry VIII wanted Thomas to take the Oath of Supremacy, however, accepting Henry VIII as the Head of the Church of England, on pain of death, Thomas refused.

Does this sound like a man who would fear the Tudors and describe Richard III in the way they wanted? If not, then this could suggest that this 'bad' version of Richard III, the inspiration behind William Shakespeare's play, was correct. However, it could also mean that Thomas believed what he was told happened and he believed in the people who told him, as he would have been only five years old at the time of the disappearance of the princes. This still does not make his account of what happened true, it just shows us that he believed it to be true at the time of writing. It is worth noting this possibility as we read: 'And forasmuch as his mind gave him that, his nephews living, men would not reckon that he could have right to the realm, he thought therefore without delay to rid them.'[19] With this in mind, Richard apparently gets John Green to travel to the Tower of London with a message to the Constable of the Tower, Robert Brackenbury. In it, he asks Robert to 'put the two children to death'.[20] Robert refuses, so Richard, on the advice of a page, chose Sir James Tyrell and his brother Sir Thomas to do the deed, after Richard III had apparently handed them the keys to the tower.[21] Although the details of this account is always worth a read, it can still make us question, was there any physical evidence then or even now, of Richard III doing away with his nephews, that we could bring to a modern-day court?

Henry, Duke of Buckingham

The reason Richard's right-hand man, for a time at least, the Duke of Buckingham, has been suggested as a suspect is because he wanted to boost Richard's claim to the throne. Or possibly, he was planning to make his own claim to the throne as he, too, had a bloodline linked to the royal family. If the latter was true, then the duke would have had to murder Richard III, his son, the Earl of Warwick and many more. However, could the Duke of Buckingham have thought that the murder of the boys in the tower would tarnish Richard III's reign enough to bring him down?

Richard never blamed the Duke of Buckingham for the children's deaths, even after Buckingham's own rebellion against him, when he could have used him as a scapegoat. The duke remains a strong suspect as only he and Richard III had been accused of the murder of the princes in contemporary sources. In a collection of 126 folios of heraldry belonging to Christopher Barker written in the early 1500s, it is stated that 'the sons of Edward IV were put to death by the vice of the Duke of Buckingham.'[22] Vice is an interesting word. In the medieval period it could mean 'advice'. This then means that the Duke of Buckingham advised someone to murder the boys or advised, how to murder them. However, the word 'vice' could also have meant 'devise', suggesting a plot, one involving the Duke of Buckingham.

Henry VII

This suggestion relies on the boys still being alive in 1485 when Henry VII took the throne. Henry VII had to counter the claim that the children were illegitimate, so that he could marry Elizabeth of York and strengthen his claim to the throne. This made both boys legitimate and so was a threat to Henry VII's reign. However, the boys were thought to be dead by the autumn of 1483 by many, including, some have suggested, their own mother. This may have been because of the large number of people working within the tower noticing that food was no longer being sent to the boy's rooms, and the fact that the boys could no longer be seen at the windows. Whatever was done, however it was done, was done before Henry VII could get hold of them himself. Henry VII never produced the bodies at the beginning of his reign, when he could have blamed their deaths on the 'evil' Richard instead of himself. If he had them killed as soon as he was made king, he could have blamed their deaths on Richard, but he does not.

Margaret Beaufort

The mother of Henry VII is a relatively new suspect for this crime and seems to have only been accused in fiction, she was never accused at the time. If she was involved, why didn't Richard use her as a scapegoat? Would she have had access to the boys? It is very tempting to think of Margaret always wanting her son to become king, because we have hindsight on our side, but equally Margaret might have only wanted her son to have the titles and lands originally given to him as the son of Edmund Tudor. Fighting for kingship was a very risky business. Just about everyone involved in the Battle of Bosworth was surprised by the outcome. In hindsight it is easy to forget this. Would his mother have really wanted Henry, her only child, to risk so much to gain the crown? And would Elizabeth Woodville really have worked with Margaret Beaufort at the end, if there was the slightest notion that Margaret's orders may have killed her boys?

An earlier lesson

One of the major questions is why did neither of the Kings of England, Richard III or Henry VII, produce the bodies of the boys, dead or alive, within their reigns to prove the boys were not a threat? Henry VII had a history of showing off prisoners to prove that he had them in his keeping, Edward, the Earl of Warwick being a perfect example of this. Why did Henry VII not do the same with both boys of Edward IV? Did he not know where the boys were?

With Richard, the answer maybe even more intriguing. There is always the possibility that Richard did not know where the boys were, that someone else had taken them or had given orders for their deaths and because of this Richard could not produce them. However, there are other possibilities, if the boys were alive and Richard decided to show them, then every person unhappy with Richard's reign would know where another claimant to the throne was and if rescued, they could become a figurehead for rebellion. Interestingly, Richard may also have been working with a template already set up and that he may have known very well, because believe it or not, the circumstances of the Princes in the Tower were not so unique.

To discuss this template, we need to go back to King Henry VI's grandfather, Henry IV, Henry Bolingbroke. Richard II was on the throne, the son of Edward, Prince of Wales, otherwise known as the Black Prince, but when Edward died in 1376, Richard II became heir apparent to King Edward III's throne. Richard II's reign was considered tyrannous and misgoverned, leading many to believe that Richard II was an untrustworthy king, so Henry Bolingbroke stepped up as a possible rival to the throne.[23] But Henry Bolingbroke was not the next heir to the throne. Henry came from the line of Edward III's third son, John of Gaunt, but there were two young boys who were closer to the throne than Henry, for they came from the line of Edward III's second son, Lionel. They were Edmund and Roger Mortimer. Not only were the circumstances similar to that of the Princes in the Tower, but Richard III came from the same royal family line as the Mortimer boys, his grandmother being Anne Mortimer, the boys' sister.

Edmund Mortimer was just eight years old when Richard II was deposed by Henry Bolingbroke, who became Henry IV, and his son would later become King Henry V. What was the King of England to do with the two young Mortimer boys? Firstly, Henry IV placed the boys in the custody of Sir Hugh Waterton at Windsor and then at Berkhamsted Castle. They were treated honourably and even brought up with Henry IV's children, John and Philippa.[24] However, on 13 February 1405, the boys were abducted and quickly recaptured, Constance of York was held responsible and was arrested.[25] Following this abduction the boys were kept under tighter conditions at Pevensey Castle until on 1 February 1409, they were put in the charge of the king's son, the future Henry V, who at this time was only five years older than Edmund Mortimer.[26]

Being looked after and cared for by the members of the family that were on the throne, a bond formed and when Henry V came to the throne, he freed the Mortimer boys, believing they were no threat, and even made them Knights of the Bath.[27] They were given lands, and although Edmund chose to marry Anne Stafford, which displeased the king because Anne was related to King Edward III, they retained a close relationship with Henry V and to some extent, with his son Henry VI, when Edmund was appointed to be part of the Regency Council for the then boy king.[28] Edmund left no heir and so his estates, titles and claim to the throne went to his sister, Anne, and her son, Richard, Duke of York, the father of Edward IV, George, Duke of Clarence and the future Richard III.

We could suggest that keeping the young boys who had claims to the throne imprisoned, out of sight but still close to the royal family, created a bond, so that the boys became loyal and never chose to rebel. Could this have been Richard III's plan for his own nephews, in the hope that they would become loyal to him over time? However, Richard III would also have known that by keeping the Mortimer line alive, eventually led to Henry VI being overthrown by a claimant from that family and so was the reason he, Richard III, was upon the throne. Knowing this, could he run the risk of history repeating itself?

Survival

The concept of the Princes in the Tower surviving is just as intriguing. What if the most famous royal murder case wasn't a murder at all? What if the two little boys were rescued and survived? Do we actually have any undisputable evidence from the time to suggest a murder had taken place at all? There have been many stories throughout the years about how the boys had escaped and what had happened to them. One of which is close to this author's heart as she first wrote about it way back in 1991 for a writing competition. This is the story of Richard of Eastwell: was he just a well-read bricklayer, the illegitimate son of King Richard III, or the younger of the Princes in the Tower?

The tale begins with King Richard III travelling north for his summer procession and during Buckingham's Rebellion, an opportunity arose to take one of the princes out of Richard's care. This was done by Sir John Fogge of Ashford in Kent, he knew the boys and was related to them through their mother, the Woodville's side. He apparently only had enough time to get to one boy, Richard, and he takes him to live out the rest of his days as a bricklayer in Ashford. Eventually, the boy works on the grounds of Eastwell Manor and it is noticed that although this bricklayer keeps himself to himself, he reads a lot and can even read Latin. Did he have a princely education? A church burial record states that on Monday 22 December 1550 a man named 'Rychard Plantagenet' was buried at Eastwell Church, near Ashford in Kent. There is a tomb, weathered over the years, within the ruins of the church, inscribed 'Reputed to be the tomb of Richard Plantagenet, 22nd December 1550'.[29] Now we have the DNA of the Woodville family and also Richard III's, due to the discovery of Richard in 2012, it would be fascinating to know whether there is a trace of DNA left inside the tomb at Eastwell Church. Although this story was known at least as early as the 1700s, a rather better known one is the story of Lambert Simnel.

Richard Simon, an Oxford priest, believed that a ten-year-old pupil in his care looked extremely like the sons of Edward IV. However, when he heard false rumours that Edward, Earl of Warwick had died imprisoned in the Tower of London, due to the ages being more plausible, he decided to claim this boy to be Edward Plantagenet, the Earl of Warwick, son to George, Duke of Clarence, instead.[30]

He took the boy to Ireland and presented him to the Lord Deputy of Ireland and the Earl of Kildare, then paraded the boy in the streets as the Earl of Warwick, the Yorkist claimant to the English throne. When Henry VII heard of this, he instantly paraded the real Earl of Warwick, still in his charge.[31]

On 24 May 1487, Lambert was crowned as 'King Edward VI' at Christ Church Cathedral in Dublin. Lambert gained many powerful supporters including John de la Pole, Earl of Lincoln, a relation of the princes and Margaret of York, sister of Richard

III, threw her lot in with Lambert and collected two thousand mercenaries to fight against Henry VII. The boy's army clashed with the king's on 16 June 1487 at the Battle of Stoke Field, and Henry VII was the victor. He pardoned Lambert, purportedly because he recognised the boy was being used as a puppet and gave him work in the royal kitchens, later he becomes a falconer. It is suggested he was father to Richard Simnel, a canon of St Osyth's Priory in Essex.[32]

However, what if the boy that was crowned in Ireland was actually the true King Edward V? Edward V was proclaimed king, he did have men swear their loyalty to him, however he was missing one thing, a coronation. Is this why so many people went to the trouble of crowning this boy, because they knew he was the true Edward V? Is this why his aunt, Margaret of York, organised an army? Would the mercenaries really have fought at the Battle of Stoke Field for the Earl of Warwick, or for someone they believed was the rightful King of England?

In May 2020, Albert Jan de Rooij of the Dutch Research Group, found a document in an archive in Lille, France. It was a receipt of 16 December 1487 for some four hundred pikes from Maximilian I, the King of the Romans (who would become the Holy Roman Emperor) to 'serve her nephew – son of King Edward, later her brother (may God save his soul), expelled from his dominion' for the German and Swiss army that had been gathered to fight. The woman is Margaret of York, sister to Edward IV and Richard III but also stepmother-in-law to Maximilian I. Although Maximilian would be involved within the next pretender's story, the date of this letter tends to suggest this was for the boy later known as Lambert Simnel.

The words 'expelled from his dominion' and the fact that this was just a receipt, not a document by anyone of importance, make this a very exciting find. Edward V, if still alive in 1487, would have indeed been 'expelled from his dominion' and the date of December 1487, could suggest that Edward had survived the Battle of Stoke Field, which happened in the June that year.[33]

But the document doesn't name the nephew. This could cause more problems than originally thought, as Margaret of York had another nephew who was not a son of King Edward IV but who had travelled to Ireland around this time with a German and Swiss army, the one the receipt claimed the pikes were for. This was John de la Pole.[34] This is nevertheless an intriguing document to have been found after all these years.

From 1491 to 1497, Perkin Warbeck travelled around Europe claiming he was the younger of Edward IV's sons, Richard, Duke of York. He managed to gain strong support from Charles VIII of France, Margaret of York and Maximilian I and it is said that the boy attended Maximilian's father's funeral. It was while there that he was recognised as King Richard IV.[35]

On 3 July 1495, the boy landed with a small army in Deal, Kent, but faced strong opposition from the locals and was forced to retreat, ending up in Scotland, were he gained support from James IV, the future husband of Henry VIII's sister Margaret. The boy would spend Christmas as the King of Scotland's guest at Linlithgow Palace.[36] Having a boy claiming to have been Richard, Duke of York was a major coup for James IV, as he knew Henry VII was seeking backing from Ferdinand and Isabella of Spain to help boost the English forces in France, Scotland's ally. Ferdinand and Isabella of Spain would not ally themselves to Henry VII if he was not the true sovereign.

With help from James IV, this boy was married into the French nobility, to Lady Catherine Gordon. James gave the boy clothes for his wedding in the purple colour that only royals were allowed to wear.[37] James IV had tried to invade England with the boy, but support for him was not forthcoming and the Scots quickly retreated by 25 September 1496.[38]

The boy moved on to Cornwall and there he was proclaimed Richard IV on Bodmin Moor. He gained an army of six thousand and they marched through Exeter, heading towards Taunton. Henry VII sent an army to face them. When the news of this reached the boy, he was said to have panicked and deserted his army, running to the sanctuary of Beaulieu Abbey. It is interesting that the boy claiming to have been the son of Edward IV and Elizabeth Woodville chose, when he thought his life was at risk, the sanctuary of a holy building. It was possibly a common act to take at the time, but one cannot help but imagine that this may have been something little Richard may have learnt from his mother in the times she and her family did the same thing.

This boy was then captured at the abbey and taken to London to be paraded through the streets before being taken to the Tower of London. If this was the real Richard, Duke of York, what must he have been feeling to walk back inside the place he had escaped from all those years before? The boy was initially treated well by Henry VII when he confessed to being Perkin Warbeck while in the tower but when later he was joined by the purported 17th Earl of Warwick, they apparently tried to escape in 1499. This led to the boy being hanged at Tyburn on 23 November 1499[39] and he was later said to have been buried at Austin Friars[40] in London. But there is no record of the specific location, which could be suggested as being deliberately unhelpful. This would also be the burial place of Sir James Tyrell in 1502, the man who murdered the Princes in the Tower on the orders of King Richard III in Thomas More's account.

Another document that has recently come to light was found by Nathalie Nijman-Bliekendaal of the Dutch Research group in the Gelderland archive in Arnhem. It is purportedly a firsthand account of Richard, Duke of York's life and how he escaped the Tower of London. It is unclear how this come to be in a Dutch archive, and it is not the original document, but a copy written in middle Dutch. It states that Richard left the Tower of London soon after seeing his brother and with the help of Lord Howard, who had dismissed the guards, and was taken in by John and Henry Percy. Here his story seems to entwine with Perkin Warbeck's. How long was Richard, Duke of York in the Tower of London? This document suggests not very long at all, but that wouldn't sit well with the contemporary accounts, stating that the boys were seen playing on the green with bows and arrows many weeks afterwards. Why did no one who worked within the Tower of London, including the guards who were apparently dismissed, say that Lord Howard and the Percys were the last ones to be seen with the boys?[41]

There is also another receipt found in February 2019 by Nathalie Nijman-Bliekendaal of the Dutch Research Group, in which 'Richard of England' pledges thirty thousand florins to Duke Albert of Saxony if he helps Richard gain the throne of England. It is signed, 'Richard of England' and has a beautiful royal seal attached. How would the young Richard, Duke of York have gained his own seal and taken it away with him, considering he and his family had to run to the safety of Westminster Abbey in fear of their lives, before he ended up in the Tower of London?

If he had not taken his seal with him and had his seal made later, do we know that it was actually on the orders of the real Richard, Duke of York? The signature upon this document is wonderful to see, but considering the age of the boy and his location before his disappearance, we have no handwriting by the real Richard, Duke of York with which to compare this document.[42] Whether you believe in one, both or none of the theories of the pretenders to the throne of England, it is interesting that there were two missing young boys and only two 'boy pretenders' to Henry VII's throne.

If the pretenders were who they first claimed they were, Elizabeth of York, now Queen Consort of England, was their sister. Lambert Simnel who may have been Elizabeth's brother Edward, was meant to have been working within the royal kitchens at one point. Perkin Warbeck was allowed to be at the same royal court as Elizabeth from 1497 to into 1498 and she would have had 'Perkin's' wife, Catherine Gordon, in her household.

Although Elizabeth of York would have seen his wife on a regular basis, there is no record that Elizabeth of York ever met 'Perkin Warbeck', who had been claiming to be her brother.[43] This is despite Perkin being allowed to be at the royal court, so that everyone could see Henry VII had the young pretender in his keep. One would imagine that if Elizabeth had met Perkin, it would have been a noteworthy event. It is not known if Elizabeth deliberately kept away from the boy, or whether she had any choice in this matter. A Spanish ambassador once observed that he thought Elizabeth to be 'powerless' at court.[44] But why not place Elizabeth in the same room as him, for what better hand could Henry VII play than to have his wife, sister of the real Richard, Duke of York, dismiss 'Perkin' publicly? Yet, Henry seems not to have done this. Was this for fear of how she would act?

This must have been a strange and tormenting time for Elizabeth. She was now a mother herself, with an heir and spare for the new Tudor dynasty, so many questions must have been running privately through her mind. What if Perkin looked similar to how she remembered her brother? What if he said something, did something that only the siblings of Edward IV and Elizabeth Woodville would know? What if Perkin made Elizabeth doubt her husband?

This pretender would have been different to the previous one for Elizabeth. Lambert's claims were that he was either Edward, Earl of Warwick, Elizabeth's cousin or Edward V. Although Edward V was also Elizabeth's brother, he was also the Prince of Wales and so was sent at a young age to Ludlow Castle in Wales. Elizabeth would not have known Edward V very well. However, Perkin as the younger Richard would have spent his childhood at the royal court. This meant that Elizabeth would have known the true Richard, Duke of York, if she saw him. Did this then mean that Elizabeth was obliged to put her own family first regardless of who 'Perkin' actually was? Did this create a feeling of guilt that Elizabeth never quite forgot?

***

However, Perkin Warbeck would be a character for the future for Elizabeth of York, let us return to her narrative, as she went from being a sister to a king to being a niece to a king.

It was around the time of King Richard III's coronation that rumours of Elizabeth of York's brothers not being seen anymore were circulating.[45] Richard, Duke of York, would have just turned ten. The fear for Edward IV's children was starting to take hold.

As the *Crowland Chronicle* reports, some wished the daughters would 'leave Westminster in disguise and go overseas so that if any human fate inside the Tower were to befall the male children, nevertheless through the saving of the persons of the daughters, the kingdom might someday return to the rightful heirs.'[46] It was because of these suggestions that it was insinuated that to prevent this from happening, Richard III sends troops to surround Elizabeth Woodville and her daughters at Westminster Abbey.[47] If Elizabeth of York desired a reconciliation with her uncle Richard now that he was King of England, his first action towards her and her family was making it harder. Perhaps these troops surrounding Westminster Abbey made Richard III feel more secure about leaving the capital so soon after his coronation. His progress took him to Windsor, Reading, Oxford and Gloucester, on his way to York, where Richard III invested his son, Edward of Middleham, as the Prince of Wales on 8 September 1483.

This is an interesting action. Firstly, it suggests that Richard worked fast to give his son the title of Prince of Wales, as this enhanced Richard's own position as king, highlighting the fact that he already had his heir. Secondly, by choosing York to do it in was not only in the heartlands of the people that were loyal to Richard, but suggested to them they had another 'son of York' to follow. However, it can also imply that Richard III knew the title of the Prince of Wales was free for him to give to his son, because he was already aware that the Princes in the Tower were dead. Though we have to bear in mind that as Edward V was classed as illegitimate, he would not be classed as the heir to the throne and so the title of the Prince of Wales was vacant anyway.

Richard III did not sit comfortably on the throne of England. Rebellions shot up from the likes of Richard's one-time right-hand man, the Duke of Buckingham and from France, in the name of one Henry Tudor. Henry Tudor, Earl of Richmond, gave the country a Lancastrian claim to the throne of England and at this time of rebellion, it did not seem to hugely matter how weak that claim was. Henry was indeed a descendant from King Edward III, via John of Gaunt, but it was through his mother's side of the family, Margaret Beaufort. Through his father, Edmund Tudor, who was half-brother to Henry VI; he could perhaps have a minor claim to the royal bloodline of France rather than of England.

Henry Tudor had been in exile for some time in France but now, at the age of twenty-six, he would claim the English throne. From August 1483, Elizabeth Woodville began to side with Henry Tudor via his mother, Margaret Beaufort. This could indicate that from this time she knew her boys had been done away with, possibly on the orders of Richard III. However, do her actions actually confirm this?

It was around this time that Margaret Beaufort and Elizabeth Woodville, via Margaret's Welsh physician, Lewis Caerleon, who was permitted to visit Elizabeth Woodville in sanctuary, planned for Elizabeth of York to marry Henry Tudor. Polydore Vergil writes that if Elizabeth of York died before the marriage took place, then Elizabeth Woodville had also given her consent for Henry Tudor to marry her other daughter, Cecily.[48] So, rather than Elizabeth Woodville's actions pointing towards a hatred of Richard III, that this may have been just a political move, to keep her and Edward IV's bloodline on the throne, no matter what. Was actually Elizabeth Woodville hedging her bets, rather than suspecting Richard III of anything malicious?

Whatever her true intentions were, messengers were now being sent to Henry Tudor to tell him of the plan, while more financial support was given to help Henry invade England. Although Henry's first attempt was delayed by storms, ironically, he had landed at Plymouth on the same day as the Duke of Buckingham's execution, after the duke's own rebellion had failed, on 2 November 1483. It may have been because of this news that Henry decided to head back to Brittany to plan a better attack, and this time he gained the knowledge and experience of Sir Edward Woodville, a naval commander, and Sir Thomas Grey, who both went to France with him, both members of Elizabeth of York's family.

On Christmas day 1483, Henry Tudor made a solemn oath of betrothal to Elizabeth of York at Rennes Cathedral in France, at the same time that a papal penitentiary for a dispensation for them to marry was sent to Rome.[49] For Elizabeth, this was her third betrothal, the first two ending in disaster. She must have questioned how could Henry Tudor possibly win a battle against a son and soldier of York, her father's brother? The years spent in exile meant that Henry Tudor was unknown in England and thus unknown to Elizabeth of York and her family. He had no real battle experience, no army or money of his own and did not know the ways of royal life, all Henry Tudor must have been to Elizabeth was an alternative to the life she presently led.

In January 1484, Richard III's Parliament issued the now famous *Titulus Regius: An Act for the Settlement of the Crown upon the King and his issue, with a recapitulation of his Title.* This document made Elizabeth of York a bastard. Elizabeth was nearly turning eighteen and already so much had happened in her short life but, as she was the daughter of King Edward IV and being betrothed to Henry Tudor, it meant that, whether she was classed as illegitimate or not, she was a threat to her uncle, King Richard III.

This may have been why the *Crowland Chronicle* describes Westminster Abbey being turned into a prison, with Richard constantly making 'dire threats' against Elizabeth Woodville and her daughters to force them to leave sanctuary.[50] Sensing no other way out, Elizabeth Woodville agreed to leave sanctuary if Richard III swore an oath to protect her children. This is an odd request if Elizabeth Woodville acted with Margaret Beaufort because she believed Richard had murdered her boys. If she had thought this, what would she have to gain from asking Richard to swear he would look after her daughters; would she have believed him the second time around? Would his words have meant anything to her? How could she trust this man if she believed him to be the murderer of her sons? Perhaps Elizabeth Woodville did not believe truly Richard had done so. Either way, such an oath Richard III did make on 1 March 1484:

> I, Richard by Grace of God King of England and of France and Lord of Ireland, in the presence of you, my lords spiritual and temporal and you, Mayor and Aldermen of my City of London, promise and swear verto regio upon these holy Evangels of God by me personally touched, that if the daughters of dame Elizabeth Grey, late called herself Queen of England, that is to wit Elizabeth, Cecily, Anne, Katherine and Bridget, will come unto me out of sanctuary of Westminster and be guided, ruled and demeaned after me, then I shall see that they shall be surety of their lives and also not suffer any manner hurt by any manner person or persons to them or any of them or their bodies or persons, to be done by way of ravishment or defiling contrary their wills, nor them or any of them imprison within the Tower of London.[51]

The last phrase is particularly interesting. Why mention 'imprison within the Tower of London'? With a guilty conscience Richard would not have wanted to remind Elizabeth Woodville of the Tower of London and yet, here these words are. With the oath taken, the children of Elizabeth Woodville left sanctuary and Elizabeth of York joined the court of Richard III and his Queen Consort, Anne Neville. Within a month of Elizabeth rejoining the royal court, Richard III's son and heir, Edward of Middleham, died on 9 April 1484, on the first anniversary of the suggested death of Edward IV. Queen Consort Anne, who was already ill, possibly with tuberculosis, was made worse by this news of her son's death. With the ill health of Richard's Queen Consort and the fact that she might not be able to bear any more children, rumours began at court that Richard was paying the much younger Elizabeth of York more attention, especially around the Christmas of 1484. 'It was said by many that the king was applying his mind in every way to contracting a marriage with Elizabeth, either after the death of the queen or by means of a divorce for which he believed he had sufficient grounds.'[52]

When Richard's Queen Consort did pass away on 16 March 1485, this only energised the rumours of a marriage between Richard and Elizabeth, so much so that Richard felt the need to openly deny it, saying that 'such a thing had never entered his mind'.[53] Shortly after this statement, Richard sent Elizabeth away from the royal court to his castle, Sheriff Hutton in Yorkshire. There she joined her cousin, Edward, Earl of Warwick, held there to stop claims that being the son of Richard's brother George, he could take the throne instead of Richard. Being out of the public's view, especially out of the view of the court, it is curious that no accident befell Edward, Earl of Warwick at this time, if indeed he was seen as a threat to the throne. Instead, he was executed for allegedly trying to escape the Tower of London with the pretender Perkin Warbeck, during the reign of Henry VII.

As to Elizabeth of York's own view of the possibility of marrying her uncle Richard, we have Polydore Vergil writing twenty-six years after the event that at this point Elizabeth was still in 'great grief' and because of that and the trouble within her own family, she had remarked: 'I will not thus be married, but, unhappy creature that I am, will rather suffer all the torments which St. Catherine is said to have endured for the love of Christ than be united with a man who is the enemy of my family.'[54] If she did say those words in response to her possible marriage to Richard, then after everything that was done to her close family after the death of her father, they are perfectly understandable. However, no names are mentioned, and at this point Elizabeth was betrothed to Henry Tudor, with or without her own agreement. Henry Tudor was a man she hardly knew and was a Lancastrian claimant to the Yorkist throne of England, so the words 'united with a man who is the enemy of my family' could have another meaning. A letter purported to be written by Elizabeth to Sir John Howard in February 1485 was précised in George Buck's 1619 book, *The History of Richard the Third*. It can imply that Elizabeth may have had a fondness for Richard. It apparently states:

> She prayed him (Thomas Howard) as before to be a mediator for her in this cause of "the marriage" to the "king" who, as she wrote, was her only joy and maker in "this" world and that she was his heart and in thought, in "body" and in all.[55]

However, there are problems with this letter. Firstly, the intentions of George Buck have been called into question. George was a defender of Richard III and has been accused of 'suppressing evidence and altering records' to prove his case.[56] Secondly, George Buck's original manuscript was fire damaged and there were parts of the letter that were missing and could have been edited by someone else (these particular words are highlighted with double quotation marks here).

How Elizabeth truly felt about her uncle did not matter however, as on Monday 1 August 1485, Henry Tudor, Earl of Richmond, set sail with two thousand men for England. Within just a few weeks, Elizabeth of York's future would be decided for her at the Battle of Bosworth.

5

WIFE AND MOTHER TO A KING

Henry Tudor had no real battle experience, whereas Richard III had fought in many well-known battles including those at Barnet and Tewkesbury, and had fought against Scotland. Richard III knew the lay of the land at the battlefield, Henry Tudor was fighting on unknown territory. This is why Richard managed to gain the higher ground, and with Richard's men far outnumbering Henry's, Richard III should have won the Battle of Bosworth.

However, in the middle of the many scrimmages within the overall battle, Richard made a risky decision in the hope of finishing the threat to his throne in one blow. He saw that Henry Tudor was cut off from the rest of the army, so he decided to bring together a troop to charge at Henry to kill him. Richard did get close to completing this task, he managed to kill Henry's standard bearer, William Brandon, who would have been standing close to Henry. In an odd turn of events, William was the father to one Charles Brandon, who would be the future husband of Mary Tudor, sister to the future King Henry VIII.

Richard did not know a change was in the air. Thomas Stanley finally chose which side to fight for, choosing his stepson Henry over his king and the safety of his own son, whom Richard was holding hostage. Richard was soon surrounded by Thomas Stanley's men, crushed and killed.

Although he seems to have been lucky to have won the Battle of Bosworth, Henry soon exhibited his own intelligence. One of the first actions Henry took was to date his reign from 21 August 1485, not from 22 August, when the battle actually happened. This meant that everyone who had fought against him at Bosworth was considered a traitor to the crown. Parliament could then pass judgment on them. Henry then turned his attention to Elizabeth of York by sending Sir Robert Willoughby to Sheriff Hutton to collect her and escort her 'attended by noble ladies' to the home of her mother in London.[1]

Before Henry could marry Elizabeth, Parliament had to withdraw her bastardy, and for that to happen, Parliament had to meet. This meant they needed Henry to be crowned and anointed, so that he could preside over the meeting as England's sovereign. This also was advantageous to Henry as it meant he would be crowned in his own right without Elizabeth, even though it was the heritage of Elizabeth that had placed him on the throne of England in many ways. Henry was crowned King of England on 30 October 1485.[2]

Henry's coronation echoed that of King Richard III's. Henry was able to do this because of the protocol book, known as the 'little Device', written at the time of Richard III's coronation with Anne Neville.[3] It was important to match Richard III's extravagance in his coronation, as display of finery and wealth was display of power. Five hundred yards of scarlet fine wool decorated Westminster Hall, the abbey and the Tower of London, ten yards of purple cloth of gold tissue was ordered to make one of Henry's outfits, eleven yards of crimson Cloth of Gold were ordered to make another outfit. His gloves were made of Holland silk, while his stomachers and doublets were made of satin. The king's horse had a trapper made from twelve yards of crimson damask.[4]

This would have been the first time most of his subjects would have seen Henry and in a way familiar to us with hindsight, knowing of the Tudor propaganda machine, Henry wanted to look his best – and to look like he belonged there. His coronation procession went from the Tower of London to Westminster Abbey. This was normal, Anne Boleyn's coronation procession travelled the same route, for example,[5] but were the two boys, the brothers of Elizabeth of York, still inside the Tower of London at this point? Would they have seen Henry leave the tower to become King Henry VII? It is an extraordinary thought.

Riding with Henry was his uncle, Jasper Tudor, who had been given the title that once belonged to Jacquetta Woodville's first husband, the Duke of Bedford. With them was John de la Pole, Duke of Suffolk and six henchmen on horses with arms and badges belonging to the new king.[6] Henry was anointed and crowned by Thomas Bourchier, Archbishop of Canterbury. This now eighty-year-old man had once convinced Elizabeth Woodville to hand over her second son to Richard III. Did he feel guilty about the part he played, no matter how innocent he may have been? Thomas was also cousin to the Princes in the Tower, now he was crowning a Lancastrian king.

After the coronation, Henry reversed the attainder 'of queen dowager Elizabeth, mother of Henry's betrothed' so that she regained her 'estate, dignity, prominence and name'.[7] With that, Richard III's *Titulus Regius* was 'cancelled, destroyed and ... the said act, record, and enrolling shall be taken and avoided out of the roll and records of said Parliament of the late King and burnt and utterly destroyed'.[8] Elizabeth of York was now legally a princess again.

After gaining the second dispensation to allow the marriage to take place, Henry married Elizabeth of York at Westminster Abbey on 18 January 1486 and the price of her ring was twenty-three shillings, four pence.[9] Not satisfied with having two dispensations from Rome to allow two people who were distantly related to marry, Henry asked for another from Pope Innocent VIII in March 1486.

The Pope affirmed the right of succession of Henry's heirs with the threat to excommunicate any challengers, and on 23 July 1486, a papal bull publicly proclaimed the legitimacy of Henry and Elizabeth's marriage.[10] Henry was preparing himself legally for what the future may hold for his succession. The acceptance by the pope signalled, Henry had hoped, that God had intervened to bring about the end of the Wars of the Roses with this union of the White Rose mixed with the Red Rose. With that, the Tudor rose, the symbol of this union, began to appear in architecture and art.

Although Edward IV had used the symbolism of the white rose to mean York occasionally, the Lancastrians had never actually used the red rose as their symbol. This myth may have come from the famous but fictional scene in William Shakespeare's *Henry VI,* in which the Duke of Somerset picks a red rose from the garden at Temple, London, to protest against Richard, Duke of York.[11] However, Henry understood the meaning and power behind symbolism and by adding a red rose, the colour of the Welsh red dragon called Cadwalader of his birthplace, to the white rose of York, he could create the most evocative of symbols. The Tudor rose symbol was meant to suggest the end of the decades of bloodshed of the Wars of the Roses, but we know that this was not completely the case, as these wars did not end with the Battle of Bosworth, they carried on for at least a few more years. However, as the new wife to the King of England, Elizabeth of York had one major task to complete, she needed to produce an heir to the Tudor throne.

Mother to a King

Knowing that Elizabeth of York was now pregnant, Henry moved Elizabeth to Winchester. This site was carefully chosen. It had once been the capital to the Anglo-Saxon kings and Winchester was thought to be associated with the court of King Arthur, whose knights were said to have gathered around the large round table that was displayed in the Great Hall of Winchester Castle.[12] Elizabeth had settled in St Swithin's Priory, now the Deanery, the Great Hall becoming the Queen's chamber.[13] Henry then attended to his role as King of England. Elizabeth waited for her labour to begin surrounded by her family, including her mother, Margaret Beaufort and Elizabeth's sisters. In the early hours of 20 September 1486, Elizabeth gave birth to a son. Within Margaret Beaufort's Book of Hours, it was suggested that this son was born just after midnight.[14] It has been suggested that because this boy was born eight months after Elizabeth's marriage to Henry, that the child was born premature. Certainly, his future health problems may suggest a weakness in his immune system which could suggest this was the case. On the other hand, he had bows and arrows and other sporting equipment sent to him, which could signify he may have been a healthy boy. If he was then, Elizabeth may have been a pregnant bride.

When the child was born, the entire city of Winchester celebrated with bonfires in the streets, bells ringing in churches and with messengers riding to important estates to tell them the news of the birth of the Tudor heir.[15] It is mainly due to Margaret Beaufort's detailed *Ordinance,* that we know how Winchester Cathedral was decorated for the baptism of the child. The walls were covered with rich tapestries and the floor in carpets. The font, which had been moved from Canterbury Cathedral to Winchester, was lined with soft linen. There were seven steps built inside the cathedral to form a stage, so that everyone attending would have a good view.[16]

Everything did not run smoothly however; the baptism was delayed for more than three hours due to bad weather. Finally, the ceremony went ahead with a baptism procession from the Queen's Great Chamber to the cathedral, with gentlemen of the court carrying unlighted torches and walking two by two.[17] John Alcock, the Bishop of Worcester, baptised the baby with the name of Arthur, named after the King Arthur of legend. The torches were lit and Elizabeth Woodville, now godmother to the child, carried the baby to the high altar, where she laid him down as a symbol of an offering.[18] One wonders, how Elizabeth Woodville felt at this time, carrying the little boy, the new heir to the throne, so soon after losing her own boys, the previous heirs to the same throne. Elizabeth of York's sister Cecily, with the Earl of Lincoln, John de la Pole, carried the baby back to the Queen's Chamber, where he was blessed by his father and mother. In a similar way to her own future daughter, Margaret, Elizabeth of York was ill after the birth of her first child, causing the royal court to remain at Winchester while she recovered and through the period of churching. By the Feast of All Hallows, the queen felt finally able to travel to Greenwich Palace.[19]

Six weeks after the birth of Prince Arthur, his nursery was set up in Farnham, Surrey. Arthur was taken away from his parents and given his own members of staff, mainly governed by Thomas, Lord Maltravers. The reason for this may have been through Henry VII's own choosing, as he may have believed being taken away from his own mother, Margaret Beaufort, at a young age, helped him to become the king he was. Elizabeth may still have had a hand in the organising of her son's care, even if she could not see him every day. This was because the governess that was chosen for Prince Arthur was Dame Elizabeth Darcey, who had been governess to Elizabeth's brothers Edward and Richard, as well as to Elizabeth herself.[20] Her wage was forty marks a year and she was assisted by Agnes Butler, Evelyn Hobbes and Alice Bywymble.[21] Although little Arthur would not have seen his parents that much, just like Prince Edward, Elizabeth's brother, Farnham was only nine miles from Woking Palace, one of the main residences of his grandmother, Margaret Beaufort. Being so close to her grandson, Margaret was able to visit him a lot more than his parents, and one would imagine Margaret keeping an eye on his education.

Arthur would have been expected to read French, Latin and Greek, have good grammar skills, knowledge of history and of the Bible. His first tutor was the former head of Winchester College, John Rede, later he would be taught by the poet and historian Bernard André from 1496 to 1500, and when Thomas Linacre returned from Italy, he became Arthur's principal tutor.

While establishing Arthur's nursery, Henry VII organised a separate income for Elizabeth of York. How Elizabeth gained this income, like so many events in her life, is still hotly debated today. Henry had taken lands and money from Elizabeth's mother to do this. There are a few reasons suggested for Henry commandeering his mother-in-law's estate. One of them was the simple fact that King Henry was a Lancastrian king, so his Queen Consort should receive her income from the duchy of Lancaster. However, when Henry restored Elizabeth Woodville's titles and estates, he had made the Lancastrian income severely limited. By giving the estates over to her daughter, Henry was rewriting an answer to a financial problem. The other suggestion has been that Henry had decided to punish Elizabeth Woodville, as set out by Polydore Vergil:

> Elizabeth the widow of King Edward was deprived by the decree of the same council of all her possessions. This was done because she had made her peace with King Richard; had placed her daughters at his disposal; and had, by leaving sanctuary, broken her promise to those [mainly of the nobility] who had, at her own most urgent entreaty, forsaken their own English property and fled to Henry in Brittany. The latter having pledged himself to marry her elder daughter Elizabeth.[22]

This can seem a little too late for punishing Elizabeth Woodville for actions taken before the Battle of Bosworth. Why would Henry wait until after he made Elizabeth Woodville godmother to his heir? Perhaps something happened after the baptism of Prince Arthur. Had Elizabeth, for example, participated in some activity that may have caused the forfeiture of her estates? Had she been involved in what was known as the Warwick Rebellion, the Lambert Simnel affair? The fact that her son by her first marriage, Sir Thomas Grey, Marquess of Dorset, was imprisoned in the Tower until after the Battle of Stoke, where the 'imposter' was captured could suggest there may have thought there was some Woodville/Grey involvement. However, Elizabeth's possible involvement only makes sense if Elizabeth Woodville believed Lambert to be her son Edward, rather than Edward, Earl of Warwick, the son of the Duke of Clarence. Elizabeth Woodville did not like the Duke of Clarence, her husband's brother for he had worked with Richard, Earl of Warwick and by doing so, had set in motion actions that killed her brother and father. However, if she truly believed Lambert was her son, would she have chosen him over her own daughter, while knowing her daughter had an heir to the throne as well? It would indeed be a hard decision for a mother to make, considering it was Elizabeth Woodville who had put her daughter in that position in the first place.

Elizabeth Woodville entered Bermondsey Abbey as a 'boarder' around 12 February 1487, just after her daughter's birthday. She was given free hospitality as the widow of a descendant of the abbey's founder. After all she had endured as Queen Consort, perhaps she just wanted to walk away from court life and live out the rest of her life in peace. On 3 February 1487, Elizabeth of York received an annuity of one hundred pounds and on 20 February, the lordships and manors of Waltham Magna, Badewe, Masshbury, Dunmore, Lighes and Farham in Essex.[23] Finally, at Easter 1487, Elizabeth of York gained 'all the profits and issues of all the land, honours and castles lately belonging to Elizabeth, late wife of Edward the Fourth'.[24]

Henry would soon face another rebellion from his wife's family, the organiser of which was John de la Pole, the same man who had carried the young Prince Arthur at his baptism. If Elizabeth of York had thought the Wars of the Roses had ended with her union to Henry VII, she would be sadly mistaken. Despite all the 'profits and issues', 1487, the year of the Lambert Simnel affair, would be a difficult one for Elizabeth in many ways.

We touched upon how Elizabeth may have felt towards whoever 'Lambert' was, however, what we had not discussed was what Elizabeth thought about so many of her own family standing against her by siding with these rebellions. Margaret, Dowager Duchess of Burgundy was Elizabeth's aunt, and in standing by Lambert and then later with Perkin Warbeck, Margaret was plotting against her own niece. How must this have felt for Elizabeth?

Once again, by no fault of her own, a family member seemed to have turned against her. She had already seen, at such a young age, how her life was endangered through the actions of her uncle George, Duke of Clarence. Richard III, another uncle, seemed from a certain point of view and in certain actions, to have also done her and her family harm. Now Elizabeth was on the throne of England herself, a mother to an heir and yet here was another family member out to harm her, with Elizabeth having done nothing against the Yorkist family that she came from.

However, Margaret of York was not the only family member that stood against Elizabeth and her newly made family. John de la Pole was the son of another 'Elizabeth of York', this one was the sister of Edward IV, George, Duke of Clarence and Richard III. This made John Elizabeth's cousin. John, as the oldest nephew of Richard III, was considered to be his heir after Richard's own son passed away. Certainly, Richard had begun appointing John to roles that might have helped in any future kingship, for example as the Lieutenant of Ireland.[25] By serving as President to Richard III's council in the north, he would have gained skills, knowledge and experience to rule.[26]. With all this experience gained and the fact that John had a good claim to the throne of England, it may have been surprising that John professed an allegiance to Henry VII when the time came, being at the baptism of Prince Arthur. He was even recorded as attending Henry VII's council at Sheen on 2 February 1487.[27] However, something happens and John is willing to change tack. He flees to Flanders and joins the army forming under his aunt's orders against Henry VII. He travels with the army of Germans and Swiss to Ireland, where he watches the purported coronation of either Edward VI (Edward, Earl of Warwick) or Edward V, Elizabeth's brother, in Dublin and by doing so, puts his full weight behind someone who threatens Elizabeth, for they could harm her, her husband or child.

Elizabeth must have felt devastated and betrayed by this family member. She had no choice in marrying Henry VII, it was her own family that had placed her in this position and now this same family were plotting against her, all because they suddenly had a 'better option' than Elizabeth was to them now. How did Elizabeth feel within this moment? She was a Yorkist Queen Consort of England, no role for a female could be higher; she must have felt she had done her duty to her father when his boys could not. But in doing so, she had no real family support, unlike many of the Yorkist rulers before her. Elizabeth of York was on her own. She was too new to become Henry VII's trusted adviser, but unable to fall back into the fold of her York family.

With the rebellion of 1487 apparently quashed, Henry turned his attention to his wife and the fact that she had not been crowned Queen Consort yet. The date chosen for Elizabeth of York's coronation was St Catherine's Day, 25 November 1487. The choice of date could be significant: after all, the man at the centre of these coronation plans, Elizabeth's husband Henry VII, was known to be a man who understood the power of symbolic actions.

We have already quoted Polydore Vergil's record of her words, that she would never marry 'a man who is the enemy of my family',[28] with the younger Elizabeth stating she 'would rather suffer all the torments which St. Catherine is said to have endured' than do so. Now, Elizabeth of York was being made Queen Consort of England on the same saint's day. Was this simply a coincidence? Or was this an indication that she had *not* married a man that was the enemy of her family? Or did this suggest that she *did* marry a man who was her family's enemy and that the trials and tribulations leading up to Elizabeth's coronation were compared to the 'torments' this saint is said to have 'endured'? When Polydore Vergil wrote his account, Elizabeth of York's coronation had already happened. Was this then simply a writer using later factual events to imbue more significance into earlier ones?

The queen's procession moved from Greenwich by water, travelling along the Thames with crowds of people watching from the banks. Boats that surrounded Elizabeth's barge were all displaying their personal badges with vivid coloured banners and the mayor, sheriffs and aldermen on the craft were dressed in their livery. One barge called *The Bachelor* must have caught most people's attention because on it was a 'great red Dragon spouting flames of fire into the Thames'.[29] The red dragon would have reminded the public to whom Elizabeth was married.

There were pageants along the way, with trumpets, clarions and minstrels. One wonders if this reminded Elizabeth of happier times with her family, when she was a child. The queen landed at the Tower Wharf and was greeted by her husband inside the Tower. These actions were famously repeated forty-six years later by Elizabeth's son, Henry VIII after the coronation of his second wife, Anne Boleyn. The repetition suggests that Elizabeth of York was being remembered, respectfully, by her son. The love Henry had for his mother and the relationship he may have seen between his mother and father was something he may have wanted to repeat with Anne Boleyn, perhaps more than any of his other wives. Famously, it has been claimed that Henry VIII saw something in Anne that was different, perhaps this difference was personal to him. Did he believe that in Anne he had found his own Elizabeth of York, the one woman he respected more than any other? Was the love of his mother so powerful that Henry would change the world to capture Anne? Was this why Henry pushed for a marriage with Anne Boleyn far more strongly than any other, because regardless of who Anne Boleyn was, or even how she looked, in her Henry saw the magnificence and wonder that he saw in his own mother, that he had lost at a tender age? Did no one match up to his mother, until he had found Anne?

It has often been asked what attracted Henry to Anne, some saying that she was not classed at the time as being 'good looking'. Some believe Anne's appeal may have been through her charm, wit, intelligence and knowledge instead. But did these traits also remind Henry of his mother? Did Anne challenge Henry in a way that his mother had once challenged his father, with her wit, charm, knowledge of the royal court and her learning? Was Elizabeth of York Henry VIII's first beloved and respected 'Tudor rose', one in whose image others were meant to follow?

While at the Tower of London, as was tradition, Knights of the Bath celebrated the coronation. The ceremony began the evening Elizabeth arrived, and it started with the ritualistic cleaning of the body and soul. Beards were shaved and the knights had their hair cut, before they were immersed in a bath. Then, the dressing of said knight begun, in a blue robe with straight sleeves and a white lace of silk on the left shoulder.[30] For Elizabeth's procession from the tower, she wore a kirtle of white Cloth of Gold with an ermine-trimmed mantle, a net-like headdress covered her hair, which was hanging down plain behind her back.[31] Again, this takes us to Anne Boleyn's coronation, for which she was dressed and wore her hair in a very similar way. For Elizabeth, the freshly cleaned streets were covered in tapestries and many people hung out of their windows to see their new queen. For the actual coronation, Elizabeth wore a kirtle and mantle of purple velvet. Her husband watched the ceremony from an elevated stage, concealed by a latticework, built on the right side of the abbey. He was there with his mother and Lady Margaret Pole, the daughter of George, Duke of Clarence. Elizabeth of York's mother was not in attendance.

Elizabeth of York must have had some heartache at the coronation, a feeling highlighted by the absence of her mother, Elizabeth Woodville. It had been only a short while ago that Elizabeth heard the same coronation bells ringing out for her uncle Richard III, from sanctuary in part of the building she was now in. Would this have stirred memories of the fear she must have had for her own life and the lives of her brothers, as she heard these same bells ring out for her?

One of the meals served at the coronation was 'shields of Brawne in Armour'.[32] This could have been boar, decorated in a knight's armour or the arms of Elizabeth of York herself. The boar was famously the symbol of King Richard III and yet here, a boar makes an appearance at the coronation meal, which seems odd. Boar was not an uncommon meat to have on such occasions, but with the countless alternatives – venison, deer, pheasant, swan, rooster, goat, rabbit, mutton, chicken – there was no need to make a feature of boar, especially because of what that animal would have meant to so many sitting at this feast, including Elizabeth of York herself. Was this deliberate on the part of Henry VII?

The next morning, Elizabeth attended Mass at St Stephen's Chapel in the abbey with her mother-in-law Margaret Beaufort and eighty gentlewomen. Afterwards, she moved on to Greenwich, where the king and queen spent the Christmas of 1487 and into the new year. By Easter 1488, the court had moved to Windsor Castle and would be there for St George's Day, 23 April 1488. This would have been a celebration that Elizabeth would have known well as she had taken part in it at the age of ten. During the procession, Elizabeth and her mother-in-law rode in a chair covered in Cloth of Gold carried by six horses, wearing matching garter gowns. This must surely have reminded Elizabeth of events when she dressed in the same outfits as her mother and rode out beside her.

In the first years of their reigns, Henry VII and Elizabeth of York spent a lot of time together, no doubt to promulgate the power of the new dynasty and the new symbol of the Tudor rose in public appearances.[33] They also turned their attentions to protecting their son, Prince Arthur, by gaining an spare to their heir, so when on 28 November 1489 Elizabeth gave birth, it was thought that this task was completed, however it turned out to be a girl. The family named the new child after Elizabeth's mother-in-law, Margaret Beaufort. The next day, on 29 November, Prince Arthur was made Prince of Wales, Earl of Chester and Knight of the Bath. He was only three years old.[34] On 30 November 1489, St Andrew's Day, Margaret Tudor was baptised at Westminster Abbey, where the font again had been borrowed from Canterbury Cathedral. The Marchioness of Berkeley carried the baby from the Queen's Chambers in Whitehall to Westminster, where the baby was received by John Alcock, Bishop of Ely.[35]

Christmas 1489 was spent at Westminster Palace, but an outbreak of measles caused the celebrations to be cut short. The epidemic meant the queen's churching was held privately on 27 December, before the royal party moved to Greenwich, where they celebrated New Year. By Candlemas day, the epidemic had subsided. Spanish ambassadors were continuously present in England at this point, due to negotiations over the marriage of Prince Arthur to Princess Katherine of Aragon. The negotiations had not been easy. The parents of Princess Katherine, Ferdinand and Isabella, had doubts. There had been a challenger for the throne of England, a young boy claiming to be the brother of Elizabeth of York – why would Spain make alliances with England's Tudor rose, if a Tudor rose was not meant to be on the English throne in the first place?

After Arthur became the Prince of Wales but before he moved to Ludlow Castle to continue his training to become King, for a short time Arthur's nursery was set up near Ashford in Kent.[36] Ashford is seventy miles from London, even further away from Wales, Arthur's future seat. There seemed to be nothing to warrant bringing the future heir's nursery to this place and then only for a brief time. We have mentioned Ashford in Kent before, the place Richard of Eastwell was meant to have lived, worked and died. Richard of Eastwell, as we have discussed, could have been a bricklayer, or the illegitimate son of Richard III or the younger Prince in the Tower.

If the latter was true, Richard of Eastwell was Elizabeth of York's brother. If Elizabeth of York or anyone else knew that Richard had actually survived the Tower of London and was living a quiet life in Ashford in Kent, would Elizabeth have wanted to show her first-born to her brother, the brother she had known so well as she had grown up with him? This may or may not give us an answer as to why Arthur was moved to Ashford in Kent for only the briefest time, but it is an interesting possibility. Arthur was then moved on to Ludlow Castle.

Elizabeth gave birth to her second son on 28 June 1491 at Greenwich Palace. This son was named after his father at his baptism, the location of which is very much debated. The only primary source we have on this subject states Henry was baptised in the Church of the Observant Friars at Greenwich, next to the palace the child was born in.[37] This source is from the bishop who performed the baptism, Richard Fox, Bishop of Exeter, however, the bishop gave the information at the divorce hearing of Henry VIII and Katherine of Aragon, many years after the said event. He may have made a mistake as the friary may not have been finished until after the baptism date. Two eighteenth-century works, *The Environs of London* by Daniel Lysons *1796* and *A Genealogical History of the Kings and Queens of England 1707* by Sandford and Stebbing, both locate Henry VIII's baptism at St Alfege Church in Greenwich instead.[38] After the baptism, Henry was given to his wet nurse, Anne Uxbridge, who would be in Henry's household for at least the next two years.[39]

Henry's older sister Margaret's nursery can be assumed to have travelled with Elizabeth of York as she moved from palace to palace. This would mean Margaret was at Greenwich when her mother gave birth to Henry. Looking into later accounts, it seems that Margaret was in the company of her new younger brother soon after his birth, and she had to share her staff with him.[40] This may well have formed a bond between the siblings, but how much like the bond between Henry VIII's own children it will become to be, we will discover in later chapters.

Elizabeth Woodville passed away on the night or early morning of 7/8 June 1492 at Bermondsey Abbey. This brought about an end of an era and, no doubt, sadness to Elizabeth of York. Her body was transported by barge to Windsor Castle, pass the Tower of London, where she knew with all certainty, her son and heirs were last seen alive, to where she was buried next to her husband, Edward IV. No bells rang and she was not received by the dean. At the burial were her three daughters, Anne, Katherine and Bridget, and her son from her first marriage, Thomas Grey, the Marquess of Dorset. Elizabeth of York was heavily pregnant again so could not attend and one wonders if the same could be said for her sister Cecily. Why Elizabeth Woodville was buried so simply, when she was the Queen Consort of England, is moot. Was this a sign of enmity within the royal family? Or could the speed of the burial suggest that Elizabeth Woodville died from the plague?

Elizabeth of York gave birth to another child on 2 July 1492, a girl they named Elizabeth. This may have been after her mother or the recently departed Elizabeth Woodville. From the *Privy Purse Records*, we know this child was dressed very finely and we can imagine that much like her other siblings she looked every inch a Woodville/Tudor.[41] Young Elizabeth joined the nursery of her older sister Margaret and brother Henry, while Prince Arthur was still at Ludlow Castle.

One wonders how Elizabeth of York was feeling about having her son at Ludlow Castle at this point? Ludlow Castle was the place that a Prince of Wales should be, but not only was it the place where Elizabeth's brother had been before he was taken to London for a coronation that was to never occur, it was the castle that her own father had rebuilt for her brother. Edward V and Prince Arthur would share the same staff too. Dr Argentine, the last person known to have seen Edward V alive in the tower, was also Prince Arthur's doctor.[42] What memories could this have conjured up for the young mother, Elizabeth?

Prince Arthur was doing well in his studies, Margaret had already been weaned off her wet nurse and by 1493, so was young Prince Henry, who was walking and riding.[43] There are hints that whenever she could Elizabeth of York stayed close to her children at Eltham. For example, when Henry VII left to fight in France, Elizabeth chose to stay with her children. Greenwich, her favourite palace, was not far from Eltham, a short boat ride. Eltham to Elizabeth may have also held some sentimental draw as a favourite palace of Elizabeth's father, and it was he who built the Great Hall that still survives.

In 1495, young Princess Elizabeth died. It was the first time Elizabeth of York and Henry VII suffered the grief of losing a child that is recorded, and it would not be the last. For Princess Elizabeth's funeral, the sum of three hundred and eighteen pounds was spent. A monument was erected in the Chapter House inside Westminster Abbey for her.[44] Elizabeth of York was again pregnant at this time which must have put an added stress upon her. Not only did the year 1495 mark a death in the family, but trusts were broken, too. Sir William Stanley, Henry VII's step-uncle and chamberlain, who was responsible for the access to the king's private chambers, was executed on 16 January for his alleged support for Perkin Warbeck. This misuse of trust may have finally pushed the royal couple to marry off the remaining sisters of Elizabeth of York to people who were loyal to Henry VII to presumably to stop any further claimants to the throne from emerging.

Elizabeth of York gave birth on 18 March 1496 to Mary, who we will discuss in more detail later. Royal life was not to settle with this birth however, as in May 1497, Cornish rebels rose up against Henry VII's new taxes to help fund his wars with France. Once again, Henry went off to fight and one wonders if he knew the situation he was placing Elizabeth of York in and what memories it might evoke. She had to move into the Tower of London with her children for their safety. Not only would this have reminded Elizabeth of all those times she had to run for her life with her mother, who happened to have been in the same role as she was now, but she was also running to a place where her brothers were last seen alive. She also had her own Duke of York, her son Henry with her, for Henry had only just been given the title that once belonged to Elizabeth's youngest brother. What a frenzy of conflicting emotions this must have evoked.[45]

Henry won the battle and was soon back in London, only to face Perkin Warbeck as we have read, Elizabeth soon gave birth to another son on 21 February 1499. They named him Edmund and later made him Duke of Somerset. Elizabeth had recovered well from this birth and was soon travelling with Henry VII to France to meet with Philip, the Archduke of Burgundy, the son in law of Isabella and Ferdinand of Spain, to continue talks on the future marriage between Prince Arthur and Princess Katherine of Aragon.

Back at home, the other children's education continued with music. The children were surrounded by players of bagpipes, trumpets, fiddles, organs, harps, horns and recorders.[46] They also must have heard local music; many songs were written about the royal family at this time. One of them, about Elizabeth of York, has the lines, 'In that garden be flowers hue, the gillyflower gent that she well knew, the fleur-de-lis she did rue, and said the white rose is most true, this garden to rule by righteous law,' the lily-white rose me thought I saw, and ever she sang.'[47]

The family would receive another blow with the death of Edmund at Hatfield on 19 June 1500. The child was only sixteen months old and may have succumbed to the contemporary plague epidemic. The body was transported through Fleet Street and buried next to the shrine of St Edward in Westminster Abbey on 22 June 1500, at the cost of two hundred and forty-two pounds, eleven shillings and eight pence (over £160,000 today).[48] There was a possibility that Elizabeth gave birth to another child named Edward and this child died young too, being buried in Westminster Abbey, but the dates of birth and death are still unknown, investigations are ongoing.

Now, the family began to focus their minds on planning the wedding of Prince Arthur and Princess Katherine of Aragon. Henry VII spent huge amounts on Katherine's procession. London probably still remembered the procession of Elizabeth Woodville and Henry's own Queen Consort, Elizabeth of York, but Henry wanted Katherine's to be far more lavish. There was a wedding tournament, banquets and gifts for all the guests. Elizabeth of York helped with the plans, organising three of her own henchmen from the Queen's horses to follow Katherine into London. There were five chariots, one 'richly apparelled and garnished' for the princess and four for the ladies appointed by Elizabeth's chamberlain.[49]

This marriage had been a long time in the making, for Elizabeth of York and Henry VII, let alone the bride and groom. This union was meant to be yet another step in the fortification of the Tudor rose. The negotiations had started in 1487 and there had been a treaty of marriage in 1496 and a formal betrothal at Woodstock in 1497, near Blenheim Palace today. Finally, after many delays, a Spanish princess was in England to marry Henry VII's heir. It is tempting to think that Henry VIII, who would become known for his flamboyant displays and the many court events within his reign, had learned how to plan these events from his father and his mother's planning of them.

Katherine made her grand entrance into the capital on Friday 12 November 1501, escorted by the Archbishop of York, Henry, Duke of York, the future King Henry VIII, the Duke of Buckingham and many other nobles. They passed through Southwark, seeing the first pageant on London Bridge.[50] The procession carried on to Gracechurch Street, where Katherine would have seen a structure of a castle with a portcullis and a Tudor rose symbol at its centre. In Cheapside, as it went passed the home of William Geoffrey, the procession was watched by the king, Prince Arthur, Margaret Beaufort, Princess Margaret and Princess Mary Tudor.[51] Elizabeth of York met her daughter-in-law for the first time on Saturday 13 November 1501 at Baynard's Castle.[52]

Elizabeth of York observed the wedding of her son to Princess Katherine on Sunday 14 November 1501 from a latticed closet constructed above the consistory of St Paul's Cathedral. She stood beside her husband. They had moved into a residence adjoining the cathedral the night before, so that they could enter the cathedral unseen. The groom had left his lodgings at the King's Wardrobe around nine in the morning to go through the secret chamber into the Bishop's Palace. Here, he changed into his white satin wedding outfit. Katherine had entered the cathedral escorted by Henry, Duke of York and she, too, wore an outfit of white satin, her train being carried by Cecily.[53] At the entrance to the choir, Prince Arthur and Princess Katherine walked hand in hand, turned south and then to the north, so that everyone there could have an opportunity to see the couple.[54]

After the ceremony, which took two hours, Henry, Duke of York took the princess back to Bishop's Palace to prepare for the wedding feast, which continued until five o'clock in the afternoon. Behind the scenes, the preparation of the wedding bed was going ahead, which needed to be blessed. No marriage was valid unless it was consummated. This moment would be famously brought up publicly in the divorce proceedings at Blackfriars in London, when Katherine's second husband, King Henry VIII, wanted a solution to his 'Great Matter'.

The wedding feast moved on to dancing with Prince Arthur dancing with his aunt, Cecily, Princess Katherine dancing with one of her ladies and Henry dancing flamboyantly with his older sister, Margaret, in 'so goodly and pleasant manner that it was to the King and Queen right great and singular pleasure'.[55] The wedding party moved on to the newly rebuilt and renamed Richmond Palace and the celebrations continued with hunting, dancing and even a Spanish tightrope walker. Prince Arthur and his new wife departed for Ludlow Castle to begin life together; they would not have known how short a time this would be.

In early 1502, the royal party was still recovering from the celebration of Prince Arthur and Princess Katherine's wedding, followed by celebrations of Christmas and New Years when there was another wedding. This time it was Princess Margaret, who was marrying James IV of Scotland on 25 January 1502. We will discuss this in more detail from the viewpoint of Margaret in a later chapter, however from the viewpoint of Elizabeth of York, how did she feel at this moment, with two of her children married off to secure the English throne, as she had once been? She had realised at a young age that her role as a Queen Consort of England was to build alliances, so she must have felt that she had done her duty and completed her role. However, as a mother, perhaps her natural worry for her children, for the many unknowns that Elizabeth would have experienced herself, was there; an underlining stress that she may have not noticed, nor possibly noticed the effect this may have had on her health.

For Henry VII, this was his second attempt to use marriage to calm the conflict between England and Scotland. He had previously tried to marry his mother-in-law, Elizabeth Woodville, to James III of Scotland with the future James IV having the pick of Elizabeth of York's sisters. This had come to nothing when James III died. Margaret had first been intended in part to undercut Perkin Warbeck's influence in Scotland, so it was first purposed that she should marry the King of Scotland in 1495, however Margaret was deemed too young at that time by both Margaret Beaufort and Elizabeth of York. Now, it was finalised, with hopes of peace between the two countries.

On 2 April 1502, Prince Arthur passed away, possibly from the Sweating Sickness. It was less than four months since his marriage. Henry VII and Elizabeth of York received the news at Greenwich and both were in terrible shock. Elizabeth of York had tried her best to comfort her husband, and she was quoted as saying to him, 'we are both young enough' to have more children.[56] Elizabeth perhaps realised what may be going through her husband's mind, a mind that may have been always forward-thinking to the problems that may lay ahead. Elizabeth was unable to suppress her grief for long: 'After she was departed and come to her own chamber, natural and motherly remembrance of that great loss smote her so sorrowful to the heart that those that were about her were pain to send for the king to comfort her.'[57] When looking at the relationship between Henry VII and Elizabeth of York, as much as we possibly can by using documents, in this moment of great sadness Henry and Elizabeth were there for each other. It could be so easy to see them as the backgrounds, roles, titles, and symbols that they were to history and in doing so believe there was no care or even love between them. Perhaps this isn't true, the fact that Henry VII never seemed to have had a mistress while he was King of England, when it would have been considered odd not to have done, may also add to the notion of it being an eventual love match between them.

Arthur was buried at Worcester Cathedral and the court went into mourning. There were no pageants and tournaments in 1502. Elizabeth of York was particularly kind to the young and now widowed Princess Katherine after the death of Prince Arthur, as she paid off any debts Katherine had taken on with the wedding and afterwards at Ludlow Castle, as well as paying for the black velvet to cover her dress and litter that took Katherine back to London.[58] They kept in contact with each other via messengers going back and forth between the pair when Princess Katherine stayed at Croydon.[59] Elizabeth also sent her children gifts, with Margaret receiving a black velvet gown, several sets of sleeves, furs for gowns and perhaps knowing her own daughter and trying to keep her mind busy through this upsetting time, Elizabeth also sent Margaret some strings for her lute.[60] Elizabeth was true to her word with her husband, even though she must have known the risks to her own health. Elizabeth was soon pregnant again, with hopes no doubt that this would be another boy.

There were signs that all was not well with this pregnancy however, as Elizabeth was visited by two nurses in November 1502, one visiting her at Westminster Palace and the other at Baynard's castle.[61] Elizabeth spent Christmas at Richmond, where Henry gave his wife money for furs before she moved to Hampton Court in January 1503 for a week.[62] She then took to her chambers at the Tower of London. The fact that she only did this a month before the birth implies the labour was not planned to be at the tower and the child was premature. Elizabeth gave birth to a girl, on 2 February 1503 and they named her Katherine, perhaps after the Spanish princess. Elizabeth had given birth many times, but this had happened in the Tower of London, a place that held so many memories for her. Did the act of giving birth make her think of the two young children, her younger brothers who had disappeared from the tower? Did this birth provoke an extra feeling of dread for her?

The child was baptised within the tower,[63] but all was not well with mother and child, causing Dr Hallysworth was summoned from Kent.[64] Sadly to no avail for on 11 February 1503 Elizabeth of York passed away, on her thirty seventh birthday. If you believe the Princes in the Tower died at the Tower of London, then so did their sister Elizabeth. The fact that her death happened nine days after giving birth indicates that Elizabeth had died from an infection during childbirth. Katherine was to pass away soon after on 18 February 1503.

Henry VII was devastated by the death of his wife. He ordered his council to prepare for her funeral, putting Thomas Howard and Sir Richard Guilford in charge, before immediately going into seclusion[65]. Elizabeth's body was wrapped in linen, she was enclosed in a lead coffin and placed in a wooden chest covered in black velvet and Cloth of Gold[66]. The coffin was taken from her chambers to the tower's chapel where it rested for ten days, very close to where the bones of two boys would be later found, purported to be the bones of her brothers that were later buried, as Elizabeth was, in Westminster Abbey.

Her funeral procession from the Tower of London to Westminster Abbey was lit with five thousand torches. The citizens of London lined Cheap Street, with all the church bells ringing. Near Charing Cross, torchbearers of different crafts stood in gowns and hoods of white cloth and on the bridge the abbots of Westminster and Bermondsey censed the body and accompanied Elizabeth to the Churchyard of St Margaret's, Westminster. The interment of Elizabeth of York cost two thousand four hundred pounds (over £2m today).

Elizabeth of York was uniquely placed to be a daughter, sister, niece, wife and a mother to Kings of England. Her legacy ran strong in her children. One was Queen of Scotland; one would be Queen of France and the other would become perhaps the most famous of all English kings. We can catch glimpses of his mother in Henry VIII's reign: in his love of music and his organisation of lavish events, including the coronation plans for Anne Boleyn. But perhaps sadly, Elizabeth's last lesson for her son was the way she died. That Elizabeth of York died through giving birth meant that Henry VIII would have understood what was happening to his wife Jane Seymour, when she passed away under the same circumstances' decades later. Elizabeth of York was Henry VIII's first Tudor rose, no woman could ever replace or live up to her, but it could be said this much-married monarch continued to look for his own version of her throughout his reign nevertheless.

6

FROM AN ENGLISH ROSE… – MARGARET TUDOR

On 28 November 1489, the Queen Consort of England was in labour at the Palace of Westminster, four years after the Battle of Bosworth. There were still loyalties to the past, and this new House of Tudor had to manufacture links to what had gone before, it had to wind itself like a vine around the roots of the English royal family tree to make its foundations more secure. To do this, firstly, King Henry VII married Elizabeth of York, daughter to Elizabeth Woodville and Edward IV and niece to Richard III. The next requirement was obvious: an heir. Arthur, Prince of Wales was born in September 1486, just one year into King Henry's reign. Now, they needed the spare. However, the second child, although healthy, wasn't a male.

Margaret Tudor was named after her grandmother on her father's side, Margaret Beaufort.[1] Although King Henry's second son, the future King Henry VIII, would famously be unhappy with having daughters, his father could see the potential in everything and that Margaret could be useful, even if she wasn't his 'spare'.

Margaret was baptised on St Andrew's day, 30 November, in St Margaret's Church, Westminster.[2] Being next to Westminster Abbey in the beating heart of the capital, St Margaret's Church would host many famous weddings, funerals and baptisms over the years, including, the baptism of Barbara Villiers, the future mistress of Margaret's three times grandson, King Charles II. It was also the place where many of the supporters of Oliver Cromwell, who signed the death warrant of Margaret's great-great-grandson King Charles I, were buried, such as John Milton. This judicial execution of a king may indeed have been made possible in part because of the beheading of Mary, Queen of Scots in 1587, Margaret's granddaughter.

Margaret spent most of her early childhood away from her older sibling. Although Prince Arthur was only three years older than Margaret, as the Prince of Wales and future heir, he already had his own household at Farnham Palace in Surrey. Margaret was to have her first nursery at the Palace of Sheen by the River Thames. This was a favourite place for her father, so Margaret would have seen more of her father and his side of the family than her brother did. It was Lady Margaret Beaufort, her namesake, who organised Margaret's care and education at times when her mother could not, as once again Elizabeth of York was to be in confinement for the upcoming birth of her next child.

On 28 June 1491, Elizabeth of York would give birth to her most famous child, Henry Tudor, the future King Henry VIII and he would have his nursery set up for him at Eltham Palace, joining his sister Margaret, whose nursery had been moved there.

Margaret's younger brother was the star of the family from birth. Henry was loved and adored by anyone that came into contact with him, and consequently he was spoilt, getting away with most things, including annoying his older siblings.[3]

Did Margaret feel that she was being treated unfairly, and would this feeling continue into adulthood? Or did she, like her mother before her, accept her fate and realise her role early on? Perhaps Margaret was thankful that her younger brother was demanding all the attention. With all the attention on young Henry, was Margaret allowed to be more herself, did it allow her to have some peace? Margaret would continue to want peace all throughout her later life, perhaps the desire started early. Margaret fulfilled her duties with great success, even at a young age. In the three-day celebrations to honour Henry Tudor becoming Duke of York in 1494, Margaret gave out prizes to the knights involved in the joust. These knights took their prizes with 'pleasure of their redoubted lady and fairest young Princess'.[4]

The nursery at Eltham Palace must have been lively, as a younger sister, Elizabeth, arrived there soon after the birth of Henry. Sadly, it was not to last, and Margaret and her brother were soon to deal with their first brush with death. On 14 September 1495, little Elizabeth Tudor, who was named after her mother and grandmother, passed away, reasons unknown. Aged three years and two months, she died at Eltham Palace. This was a shocking event that both siblings would remember, and maybe it drew them closer together in their childhoods.

Elizabeth Tudor's body was covered in a pall of Cloth of Gold with her coat of arms on it, while she lay within the King's Chapel for eleven days. Her hearse pulled by six horses carried her across the river to Westminster Abbey, where her coffin, covered in a cloth of red and white roses, was placed in the choir for her to be buried in her grave the next day. She was buried inside the chapel of St Edward the Confessor in a small tomb of black marble.[5]

Although it may have been situated elsewhere within the chapel, the tomb is now near Henry III's tomb. It can easily be overlooked because Elizabeth's gilt effigy that lay upon the black marble has gone. It was said to have had a plate at her feet that stated: 'Here after Death has a royal offspring in this Viz the young and noble Elizabeth daughter of that illustrious prince, Henry the Seventh, who swayed the Sceptre of two kingdoms. Atropos, the most severe messenger of Death, snatched her away but may she have eternal life in Heaven.' The inscription upon the black marble has disappeared over time and was certainly not there by the 1700s. It would have read 'Elizabeth, who was born on the second day of the month of July in the year of Our Lord 1492 and died on the 14th day of the month of September in the year of Our Lord 1495, upon whose soul may God have mercy. Amen.' Without these two inscriptions, Elizabeth Tudor's tomb sadly looks no more than a black box attached to other tombs.[6]

This was not the only child of King Henry VII and Elizabeth of York to die. As we mentioned earlier, Edmund Tudor died on 19 June 1500 and was buried in the same chapel as Elizabeth Tudor, but has no monument. There was also Katherine Tudor, who was born and died shortly afterwards in 1503, she, too, was interred in the same chapel and has no monument of her own.[7] These deaths must have affected the surviving siblings in some way, whether for a time it brought them closer or not we cannot say, but if it did, it can make the deteriorating relationship between Henry and Margaret in later life seem even more troubling. Arthur, Margaret and Henry would have one more sibling who would survive into adulthood, another girl, named Mary. The birth of another female may well have helped Margaret, as it balanced the family unit between genders.

Margaret did not only have the education of the nursery, she also had a teacher in her grandmother, Margaret Beaufort. Margaret Tudor would be taught how to be a lady by her grandmother, while her mother taught the young Princess how to read and write. If Henry as a male had superiors, Margaret might have taken the opportunity to listen in on her brother's lessons, too. However, according to the *Lives of the Princesses of England* by Agnes Strickland, Margaret was 'neither a learned nor an educated Princess'[8]. If this was the case, this would not have been seen as a serious failing, as Tudor princesses were not expected to rule, so their education could be limited. All Margaret would have been expected to be was a Tudor lady who would present herself well for a good marriage opportunity to a prince of another land, and in this, Margaret was a success.

In 1495, Margaret's marriage negotiations provided some kind of solution to one of the problems her father had, settling peace with Scotland. Margaret was to marry King James IV of Scotland. This was originally the idea of Margaret's father alone, as Henry VII's counsellors were not enthusiastic. Henry had to convince his own counsellors and he did this with an astute argument: 'Supposing that all my male's progeny should become extinct, and the kingdom devoted by law to Margaret's heirs, will England be damaged thereby and not rather benefited?'

How does one king keep another king wanting peace? Kinship though marriage is one answer. There was a slight problem however, in that James believed Margaret was too young to be mother to his heirs. King Henry may have been told of his own horrific birth because his mother was too young, so Henry delayed Margaret's marriage until she was deemed old enough to bear children.

A papal dispensation for the marriage was required, as Margaret and James were distant cousins. This was eventually given by Pope Alexander VI: ' ...by our apostolic authority and certain knowledge, by the tenor of these present letters, as a gift of special favour, [I] grant a dispensation to you and the said King James, freely and lawfully to contract matrimony together from this time forth and to remain therein when it shall have been contracted.'[9]

After the wedding of Prince Arthur and Katherine of Aragon on 14 November 1501, minds turned to Margaret's wedding and it began to be organised by the English councillors the Archbishop of Canterbury, Bishop of Winchester and the Earl of Surrey, and the Scottish councillors the Archbishop of Glasgow, the Earl of Bothwell and Bishop of Moray. The wedding was to be held on 1 September 1503. The negotiations would cover which palace or lands would become Margaret's, which would include places such as Linlithgow Palace and Stirling Castle and the rents from the Ettrick Estate. Margaret's dowry would be five hundred pounds per year and she would gain a household of twenty-four servants.[10] Margaret's husband would have thirty thousand golden nobles. The marriage treaty was signed on 24 January 1502, with the couple being betrothed the very next day at Richmond Palace. The Scottish King was not there, the Earl of Bothwell stood in for him. The Earl stated:

> I, Patrick, Earl of Bothwell, procurator of the right excellent, right high and mighty prince, James, by the grace of God King of

> Scotland, my Sovereign lord, having sufficient authority, power and commandment to contract matrimony per verba de presenti, in the name of and for my said sovereign lord, with thee Margaret, the first begotten daughter of the right excellent, right high and mighty prince, Henry by the grace of God King of England, and Elizabeth, queen of the same, as by the procuratory of my said Sovereign Lord, at the present time openly read and published, more plainly appears by the virtue of the same procuratory and as procurator of my said Sovereign Lord, James, King of Scotland and in his name and behalf and by his special commandment, contract matrimony with thee Margaret and take thee into and for the wife and spouse of my said Sovereign Lord, James King of Scotland and all other for thee (as procurator foresaid) forsake, during his and thine lives natural and thereto, as procurator foresaid, I plight and give thee his faith and truth, by power and authority foresaid, committed and given to me.[11]

Margaret replied in like manner before trumpets were played to signify that the ceremony was complete.[12] This was followed by a huge feast and now, as future Queen of Scotland, Margaret had achieved the same dignity as her mother, so she was allowed to sit at the top table. This purportedly did not go down well with a sibling of Margaret's, a certain Prince Henry. Henry was used to being the star of the family and used to lovingly but with some rivalry tease his elder sister in the nursery at Elham Palace. However, Margaret was now classed higher than Henry and the young prince was not happy.

Soon after the celebration, Margaret and her family had to deal with a shocking and sudden death, one that not only meant a great deal to the family personally, but politically, too, for this death changed the order of the Tudor heirs. This was the sudden death of Prince Arthur. As a sign of how close Arthur was to Margaret, although Henry was now the new heir to the throne, it is Margaret that Arthur mentions more in his will. He gave her his jewels, gowns, robes and plate.

Almost a year after the death of Prince Arthur, on 2 February 1503, Elizabeth of York gave Margaret, Henry and Mary another sibling while in the Tower of London. This was a premature birth and caught Elizabeth by surprise. She had attended church that morning and although she had sensed something was amiss, she had tried to ignore it. However, by the afternoon, it was becoming more and more painful. This ruined all the plans Elizabeth and Henry had made for bringing their eighth child into the world. The queen was not in the right royal palace, as the birth was planned to have been at Richmond, Henry VII's favourite, but there was no time to travel, the tower would have to do. The queen's midwife was at hand, but this would be Elizabeth's most painful labour. She eventually gave birth to a baby daughter. As we have seen, Elizabeth was to pass away soon after the birth of this child, probably due to an infection she caught while in labour.

In a space of a year, King Henry and his children had lost Prince Arthur, the Queen Consort of England and a newborn. In the midst of all this, Margaret was due to leave her country and her family to become Queen Consort of Scotland. If anything, Margaret's leaving roused King Henry from his grief to arrange the handover of his eldest daughter to the Scots, with regards to any lands. As for his daughter's actual departure, the king left that to his mother, Lady Margaret Beaufort, to organise.

King Henry travelled with his daughter as far as Collyweston, his mother's home in Northamptonshire. It was here at their last moment together that he gave his daughter a gift of a Book of Hours, in which he had written: 'Remember yr Kynde and loving fader in yr good prayers... Pray for your loving fader, that gave you thys booke, and I gyve you at all tymes godd's blessyng and myre. Henry R.'[13]

Margaret left Collyweston on 8 July 1503 with the Earl of Surrey and his wife and 'array of the said Lords, Knights, Ladies and others'.[14] She went through Grantham, Newark, Doncaster and Pontefract to York. Here, she was greeted with crowded streets of well-wishers, who threw flowers. She was also greeted by the fifth Earl of Northumberland, Henry Percy, who had ridden out to meet her with four hundred of his own men. He was dressed in his best attire of crimson velvet from head to foot, so Margaret, not wishing to be underdressed, changed into a robe made from Cloth of Gold.[15]

Her procession had grown so large by now that a separate entrance had to be made at York to fit all the people inside. Once there she was escorted to the cathedral to meet with the Archbishop of York, the Bishop of Durham, the Abbot of St Mary's and other clergymen. She gave thanks for the safe journey so far by leaving an offering at the altar and slept at the Archbishop's Palace. The next day, Mass was heard before she continued on her journey with the Earl of Northumberland through Darlington, Durham and Newcastle. Here was another break, full of celebration. There were games, sports played and songs sung.[16] It was also here that Margaret met Lord Dacre, the warden of the Western Marshes at Newcastle. This would be the first time Margaret meets Lord Dacre, a man who will have an important part to play in Margaret's future life in Scotland.

There was hunting in the park at Alnwick, a chance for Margaret to be herself, away from the prying eyes of the public.[17]

On 30 July 1503, Margaret finally reached the Scottish border at Berwick where she stayed for two days in the company of the Captain of Berwick.[18] On 1 August 1503, the new Queen of Scotland entered the country. With the earls of Surrey and Northumberland by her side, wearing a dress of Cloth of Gold and pearls in her hair, she was every inch a queen as she arrived in Lamberton. There she was greeted by the Archbishop of Glasgow before spending the night at Fast Castle, on the clifftop overlooking the North Sea.

On 3 August, Margaret arrived at Dalkeith Castle, which was owned by the Earl of Morton. There she rested and prepared for her entrance into Edinburgh. Her future husband rode out to greet her, and with that commenced a great celebration of dancing and feasting. This was brought to an abrupt end when a fire broke out at the stables, killing two of Margaret's favourite horses. Margaret was distraught and perhaps in a rare display of tenderness from a rough-and-ready looking Scottish king, James went straight to his future wife to comfort her and made sure that entertainments were laid on to take her mind off her loss,[19] even playing the lute and the clavichord himself.

The next day, Margaret must have felt nervous as she headed into the capital, wearing a gown made from Cloth of Gold, black velvet and ermine trimmings, and a collar of pearls. James once again rode out to meet his future queen, wearing a jacket of Cloth of Gold with purple velvet and black fur to match with his future queen, even with wearing a shirt edged with pearls.[20]

They had one more stop before they entered through the gates of the capital. Just outside the city walls, a play was put on for the couple. The characters were a knight, a fair maiden and an evil robber. A fight began between the knight and the robber, while the fair maiden cried for 'peace'. A deer was let loose to run through the streets of Edinburgh with a greyhound chasing it. The greyhound never caught up with the deer, who made it safely back to the grounds of Holyrood without being harmed.[21] James and Margaret then rode into Edinburgh through a newly erected wooden gate with two towers attached. All the streets were filled with Margaret's new subjects and everyone wished them well as they passed by, and once again flowers were thrown.[22]

Upon reaching the Church of the Holy Cross, they were greeted by the Archbishop of St Andrews, the brother of King James, and the Bishop of Aberdeen, Lord Privy Seal, the Bishops of Orkney, Cauthess, Ross, Dunblane and Dunkeld, with many priests and canons. The Archbishop and the king's brother gave the king a holy relic to kiss, but instead the king passed the relic to his future bride to kiss first. After this, the couple travelled to Holyrood House, which was still under construction at the time, where the couple were introduced to more ladies and lords, before a dance, a feast and then to bed on the eve of the couple's wedding day.[23]

7

...TO A SCOTTISH THISTLE

It was now 8 August 1503, Margaret's wedding day. James had given her a wedding dress cut from the same fabric as his own white damask wedding suit. She wore her hair 'loosely over her shoulders' and a golden crown studded with pearls and other gems, another gift from the king.[1] When we think of white wedding dresses and the royal family, we think of Queen Victoria, for she was the one to have popularised the white wedding dress. However, white wedding dresses was not uncommon before Queen Victoria; Margaret Tudor and Katherine of Aragon wore white and so would Margaret's granddaughter, Mary, Queen of Scots.

Margaret was taken inside Holyrood Abbey by the Archbishop of York and the Earl of Surrey to her future husband who was waiting for her. The king placed his arm around her waist and guided her towards the altar. After the ceremony was completed, a letter from the pope was read out, confirming that he had blessed their union. Then Margaret and James made silent devotions at the high altar.[2] Mass was said and James placed the sceptre of the Scottish state in her hands as she was anointed with holy oil, to become Queen Consort of Scotland.

The next day Margaret wrote to her father

> My most dear Lord and father, in the most humble wise that I can, think I recommend me unto your Grace, be seeching you of your daily blessing and that it will please you to give hardy thanks to all your servants the which by your commandment have given right good attendance on me at this time. And especially to all these ladies and gentlewoman which hath accompanied me hither and to give credence to this good lady the bearer here of, for I have showed her more of my mind than I will write this time … written with the hand of your humble daughter.[3]

Although James was sensitive to how his new wife may be feeling, being only thirteen years old and so far away from home, keeping her mind distracted with jousts and arranging special hunts and ceremonies that involved dancing and music for her, this may not have been completely successful. If we consider Margaret not as a Tudor princess or Queen of Scots but as the thirteen-year-old who had just lost her mother and brother, leaving her father while he was still in mourning and travelling to a different country where she did not understand their customs or the accent, Margaret must have still felt isolated and perhaps even a little bored.

On 29 November, Margaret spent her first birthday as Scotland's new queen at the country's capital. There was dancing and a day-long feast. Her birthday present from her husband was a highly decorated Book of Hours that was meant to have been her wedding present; however, it was late arriving from Flanders. This book is currently at the Austrian National Library in Vienna.[4] After Margaret was widowed, she passed this same book on to her sister Mary, the then Queen of France as a token of friendship, including on page 188 a note: 'Madame I pray your grace/remember on me when ye/loke upon this bok/your lofing syster/Margaret.'[5] This was not the only gift Margaret was to receive from her husband. Weighing an ounce of gold, James gave her a ducat, with sapphire gold rings and two pearl studded crosses.[6] Perhaps with all the gift giving, daily performances, music and dancing, Margaret began to feel more that Scotland was her new home.

However, the fun and laughter was not to last as on 13 January 1504, King James's younger brother and heir, the Duke of Ross, died. James decided after gaining papal dispensation, to allow his eldest but illegitimate son by his mistress Marion Boyd, named Alexander, to receive his brother's title of Duke of Ross. Although Alexander would probably have known Margaret and her brother Henry as children, this elevation might have unsettled Margaret a little, but her husband would always show favour to his illegitimate children and there was not much she could do. At the same time, the death of the heir presumptive must have also put more pressure on Margaret herself to have a child of her own. This, as Queen of Scotland was her duty, and one that was now even more pressing, but understandably Margaret may have felt afraid to do so. As Queen Victoria was purportedly afraid to give birth (extraordinary in the light of the size of her family) because the only reason she was on the throne was that her relation had died in childbirth, so, too, must Margaret have felt, after recently losing her mother in the same circumstances.

In March 1504, Margaret was presented to the Scottish Parliament where a more formal display of her 'morrowing' gift of Kilmarnock was shown. Here, Margaret found out that her father had appointed Sir Ralph Verney as her chamberlain, who would be the head of her household, Edward Bernstede as her treasurer, who would manage her finance and property, and Henry Babington as her almoner, who would deal with distributing money to the poor in Margaret's name.

Sadly, for Margaret, she did not get to be with her new husband for long. James was very proactive about travelling through his realm, often leaving Margaret to disguise himself as a commoner to overhear the lay of his land, as King Henry V is shown to do in William Shakespeare's play of the same name. James would also leave Margaret to visit his mistresses. This then, often-left Margaret understandably bored and she had to find ways to entertain herself. She did this by buying new dresses and jewels, which her husband paid for, and it must have run up quite a bill. When Margaret's father sent the next instalment of Margaret's dowry plus an extra five thousand marks on 9 June 1504, we can imagine it was very welcome indeed.

Christmas of 1504 was spent at Edinburgh and the king and queen were together after the rebellions in the north of Scotland, however this was not to last as in the following year, in which the king had a new mistress, he was not at home that often. This was hardly a wonderful situation for Margaret, but this was certainly not the first mistress the King of Scotland had and no matter what Margaret still had to do her duty and give the king an heir to the throne. However, in the May 1506, Margaret did fall pregnant regardless of the couple still not spending much time together, with the king still travelling across the realm.

On 21 February 1507, seventeen-year-old Margaret gave birth to her first son, named after his father, James. The birth was not an easy one and Margaret surely remembered her own mother passing away while giving birth, as she lay there getting desperately ill. It was a very long labour and there were fears she would not have the strength to complete the task. Her husband therefore actually left Margaret's side so that he could make a pilgrimage to St Ninian's shrine at Whithorn, in Galloway, to pray for the health of Margaret and the unborn child. Meanwhile the doctors at Margaret's bedside tried to help her, but the king 'would not be smothered by any human consolation ... for he had placed all hope in his wife's recovery in God alone.'[7] So convinced was he that a higher spirit would help his situation, that he travelled to St Ninians knowing that it would take him a few days to reach. It was claimed that at the moment he knelt in front of the altar, Margaret recovered.

In honour of this recovery and the birth of a son, a tournament was held. At this tournament King James decided to visit his dressing-up box, and as an unknown knight he took part in the joust. He defeated all of his opponents, allowing him to make a dramatic reveal at the end before the ostensibly shocked crowd.

All too soon, official duties began again and Margaret was rather pushed into making her own pilgrimage to St Ninian's, where she had to give thanks for her survival. On her return, Margaret found herself with child again. This must have terrified Margaret for she had only just got over the horrendous birth of her first child. Then, more pressure was applied to Margaret; in February 1508, while Margaret was still pregnant, her first child passed away. This attached even greater importance to the child she was carrying.

Margaret's father was purportedly highly suspicious of nearly everyone at this point in his reign. This was claimed to be the reason why, when two Scottish noblemen, Sir Patrick Hamilton and his brother, tried to travel to France through England, Henry VII had them arrested. The King of Scotland was furious and to calm the waters, Henry VII sent his ambassador to Scotland to explain. The ambassador would become far more famous in the later years of the Tudor dynasty, for this was a young Thomas Wolsey, the future cardinal who would famously fail to give King Henry VIII his much-wanted annulment from Katherine of Aragon. When Thomas reached the border, he was kept waiting at Berwick, just to highlight how angry the King of Scotland was with England.

However, when Thomas was finally allowed an audience, James claimed he knew nothing of this situation, but after now being told of it, he demanded his nobles to be released; and so began a heated discussion between the King of Scotland and Thomas Wolsey.[8] Although Margaret was there as an ally for her father, no one was listening to her.[9] Instead of Henry VII using his daughter in the talks, it was actually Margaret's husband who exploited her position. James stated that he would be a good son-in-law if Henry VII would be 'loving, kind and like a good father'.[10] The outcome of this high tension spat between the two was that James got his way, Wolsey was sent home and the Scottish noblemen were released.

In July, Margaret took to her chambers at Holyrood to give birth to her next child. This was at a time when, quite handily and thankfully for Margaret, because of this resolved action between the two kings, there was some peace between Scotland and England. This may have helped ease the worries of the expectant mother. Sadly however, once again the labour was hard and the child, a girl, died shortly after her birth.

Distraught and sensing he was not the only one grieving, James took Margaret to Falkland Palace for the next six months to relax, not returning to court life until January 1509. Then, just as Margaret may have begun to feel somewhat at peace with the current events, in April Henry VII died suddenly, purportedly from tuberculosis, leaving Margaret parentless and with a change in title of importance to her Scottish King and lords. Margaret was not the daughter of an English king anymore; she had now gained the lower status of being a sister to a king. This made her position unstable within the Scottish court, as she was deemed less important to the Scottish peace treaty.

However, the new English king, King Henry VIII, seemed at first to cement England and Scotland's relationship by writing to Margaret's husband often: 'Dearest brother and cousin, we have received your loving letters written with your own hand ... of which we are glad considering our tenderness of blood.'[11] So, for now, Margaret may have felt comfortable as her husband and her brother were for the time being friends at a time when Margaret was pregnant again. For fear of another traumatic childbirth, James did the only thing he felt he could do to help, he went on a pilgrimage to St Duthac in Rosshire. The child born in October was named Arthur, in memory of Margaret's own older brother, but by July of the following year Arthur had passed away. In 1511, Margaret made her own pilgrimage to St Duthac to pray for a healthy child. This was at a time when relationships between her husband and her brother were wearing thin.

Sir Andrew Barton, who had been ordered to protect the seas around Scotland, had looted a Portuguese ship. This, he had done before, however this time the Portuguese ship was carrying food for the English and was in the English waters, off the coast of Kent. Henry VIII sent his admirals to confront Barton. When both sides met, a battle ensued in which Barton lost his life. James was enraged and accused Henry of breaking the peace treaty. Henry's response was that '...it did not become a prince to levy the braking of a treaty against another prince for bringing a pirate or thief to justice.'[12] Margaret's husband and brother were now preparing for war, calculating each other's size of ship as a measure of masculinity, while Margaret was now three months pregnant and spent her time visiting shines and chapels. What can this tell us about how Margaret was feeling?

Having previously had no interest in pilgrimages, the Queen of Scotland, after the death of so many children, was trying anything within her power to produce a healthy heir. Although Margaret loved entertainments, over that Christmas she did not join in, choosing instead to watch from afar for fear of harming her unborn child. In her desperation, did she sympathise with her sister-in-law, Katherine of Aragon's plight of the same nature? Though such sympathy would not last, as Katherine as regent eventually brought about the death of her husband at Flodden.

On 10 April 1512, a son was born, again named James. There was no delay before the baptism, James was baptised the next day, Easter Sunday. Prince James's birthplace was Linlithgow Palace, and his early years were spent here. it was a favourite location of both his parents and himself in later life. Linlithgow had been connected with royalty for a long time. In July 1304, Elizabeth of Rhuddlan, the daughter of King Edward I, stayed there before travelling to Knareborough Castle to give birth to her second son, Humphrey de Bohum.[13] Linlithgow was taken over by the Scottish in 1313 by using their own version of a Trojan horse. A known hay seller waited for the gates to open as they normally did, but instead of bringing his wagon inside, he stopped it halfway so the gates could not be closed again, and seven Scottish soldiers jumped out of the wagon and captured the palace of Linlithgow for Robert the Bruce. Robert then sent men to dismantle the castle so that the English could not retake it.[14] James I began rebuilding Linlithgow into a huge royal palace after it was partially destroyed in 1424. He would also rebuild the church of St Michael's, just south of the palace, which had been used as a storeroom.[15] It is believed that James was inspired in his designs by the Palace of Sheen in London, the first nursery of Margaret Tudor.[16] Although James IV loved this castle, spending huge amounts of money and time there, on 31 May 1503 he gave the palace to Margaret.[17]

A little after Prince James was born, Nicholas West, previous chaplain to Henry VII and the Dean of St George's Chapel at Windsor Castle, visited Margaret and her family at Linlithgow. He later described the young prince as '... a right fair child and large of his age'.[18] This James would grow up to adore Linlithgow as much as his parents. He added an outer gateway and an extravagant courtyard fountain.[19] Three oak trees were cut down from Callender Wood and seven from Torwood to provide new kitchen tables and he also improved the ceiling of the chapel by using Azurite, a soft blue copper mineral found in France, and he added stained glass windows.[20] Tennis courts were added to the front garden and an eel trap in the loch.[21] Linlithgow would become famous as the birthplace of James V's only child, Mary, the future Queen of Scots, and the location of Mary's temporary imprisonment by order of her great uncle, Henry VIII.

At first, the young Prince James seemed a sickly child; his parents were unable to find a wet nurse that he would feed from. Three nurses later, one was found. James nevertheless held an honorary dinner for his new son and heir. The feast was spectacular, including boar, oxen, ninety-four pigs, thirty-six lambs, thirty-five sheep and two hundred and thirty birds.[22] King James even bought his wife a brand-new crimson velvet dress for her to wear once she had recovered from giving birth, and English ambassadors arrived with a letter and gifts from King Henry. But with Henry, as always, taking advantage of any situation, he also sent his ambassadors to Margaret to foster friendship with Scotland, now that Henry was on the verge of war with France and wary of the Auld Alliance, the special friendship France had with Scotland.[23]

Margaret seems to have left politics to her husband; she was more concerned with her legacy and getting back what she was owed. Her brother Arthur had bequeathed Margaret the jewels of their grandmother, Lady Margaret Beaufort, and her father had left provisions for Margaret, none of which she had received from Henry VIII. Now with her own son, Margaret wanted more than ever her legacy to be passed on.

She had been expecting the English ambassadors that Henry had sent to be carrying these items and the fact that they weren't was condemned by King James. The importance the King and Queen of Scotland seemed to put on Margaret's legacy appeared to confuse the English ambassadors, as a letter written to the Bishop of Durham by one of them observes that he thought this matter to be of no account.[24] However small a matter it may have been to the English ambassadors, it was very important to Margaret. Margaret may have been exercising foresight, as although the king and queen spent months at Linlithgow with their new son and it had been a happy summer for them all, by the end of the year events would take a turn for the worse. Margaret was pregnant again, this time with a daughter, but in November, Margaret gave birth prematurely and the child did not survive. Margaret's legacy, all she could give her only surviving son, became even more important.

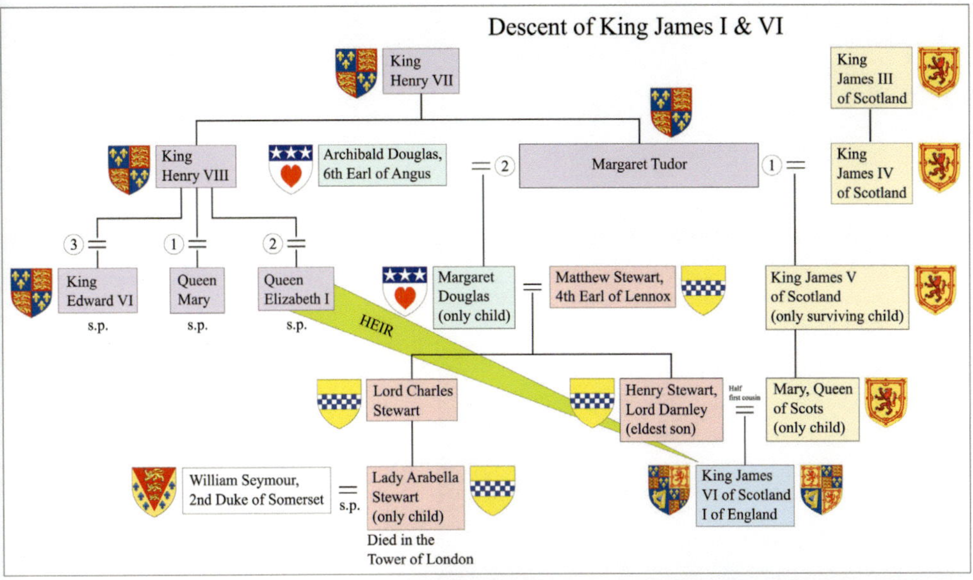

Illustration courtesy Lobsterthermidor under creative commons 3.0.

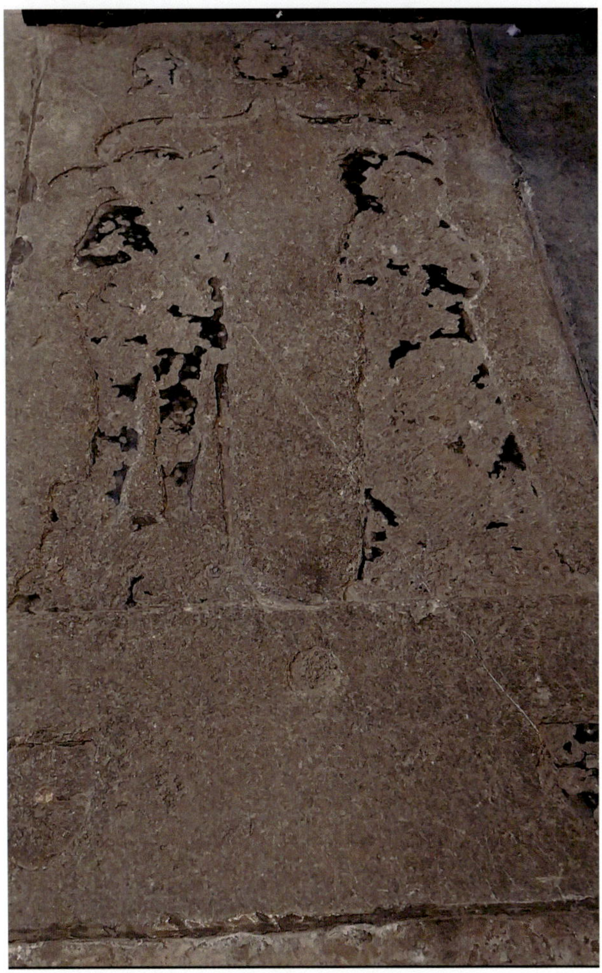

The image of Jacquetta of Luxembourg and her husband, Richard Woodville, grandparents of Elizabeth of York. This is the only memorial of them found to date, on the floor by the High Altar at All Saints Church, Maidstone, Kent. Author's collection.

Micklegate at York, where the head of Richard, Duke of York (father of King Edward IV) was displayed after he was killed by the Lancastrian army at the Battle of Wakefield. Author's collection.

Earl Rivers presenting his book to Edward IV, with Elizabeth Woodville behind the king, by Charles Griginton, undated. Yale Center for British Art.

Three children of Henry VII and Elizabeth of York by G. Vertue 1748: Wellcome Collection.

Winchester Great Hall, showing the round table. Elizabeth of York gave birth to her first child, Prince Arthur, at Winchester. Author's collection.

The funeral procession of Elizabeth of York in 1503, engraving 1784. Wellcome Collection.

Richard III, King of England by G. Vertue *c*.1732. Yale Center for British Art.

Above left: The archway in York that had to be made to allow all of Margaret's entourage to pass as she travelled through York to marry King James IV of Scotland. Author's collection.

Above right: Margaret Tudor, Queen of Scotland. Courtesy the Royal Collection, public domain.

King Henry VIII and Jane Seymour, King Henry VII and his wife, Elizabeth of York. Engraving by G. Vertue after Hans Holbein. Wellcome Collection.

Elizabeth of York. Courtesy the Royal Collection, public domain.

Top left: The plaque in remembrance of Margaret Tudor travelling through York to marry King James IV of Scotland in 1503. Author's collection.

Top right: The black tomb of Elizabeth Tudor, sister of Henry VIII, Westminster Abbey. Author's Collection, with the kind permission of the Abbey.

Right: Winchester Cathedral, where Prince Arthur, brother to King Henry VIII, was christened. Author's collection.

Above: Louis XII and Mary Tudor, from a 16th century manuscript. Courtesy Pierre Gringoire, public domain.

Top left: Mary Queen of France and Charles Brandon, Duke of Suffolk by G. Vertue 1748. Yale Center for British Art.

Left: Butley Priory gatehouse. Creative commons 4.0, eehbagum.

Below left: The last resting place of Mary Tudor, Queen of France, at St Mary's Church in Bury St Edmund's. Author's collection.

Below: Mary's plaque in St Mary's Church. Author's collection.

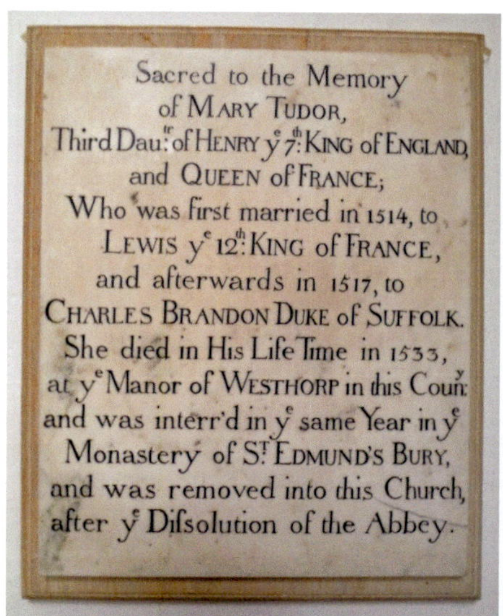

8

FLODDEN AND THE TROUBLING BROTHER

Giving birth to another child prematurely had left Margaret ill. With Margaret so ill, we cannot be sure if she was told at this point that her brother had actually started the war with France. But in the March of 1513 Henry had sent his ambassadors back to Scotland with the news of what he had done, and one of these ambassadors found Margaret praying for her recovery. Over dinner, an ambassador called West told Margaret that war had commenced. Margaret instantly became worried, if England went to war with France, what would happen to Scotland? In England, her brother was also worried but perhaps not over the same thing as his sister was, Henry was more concerned that Scotland would take the opportunity to invade while he was fighting in France. Henry tasked Margaret with keeping the peace, but Margaret had no real say over her husband's actions, as she told West; but this answer was expected, so West had been instructed to use Margaret's much wanted legacy as a lever.[1] The King of Scotland was not happy with his wife being used in this way, telling West: 'The Queen shall lose nothing for my sake! I will pay for her myself.'[2]

This blackmail attempt by Henry VIII infuriated James. Even when his reaction was known, the English ambassadors asked for more. They wanted James to sign a treaty stating he wouldn't invade, and asked to borrow James's flagship, the *Great Michael*, as it was far bigger than Henry's *Mary Rose*. All these requests were, unsurprisingly, turned down. Although James was told by West that Henry did not have plans to attack Scotland himself, the truth was that Henry had already sent troops north, just in case Scotland chose to fight in support of the French and attacked from their side.

On 30 July, Henry sailed to France, leaving his wife Queen Katherine as regent, with the Earl of Surrey as a backup for Henry's troops. Although Henry was forging ahead with his war with France, Scotland was still on his mind. The king's last words to the Earl of Surrey before he left were: 'I trust not the Scots – I pray you, therefore, be not negligent.'[3] This was foresight on the part of Henry VIII, as although Margaret tried her best to stop her husband, James had other ideas, prompted in some way by the chivalric suggestion played on by Queen Anne of Brittany, to challenge England while the king was away. Margaret thought that this was going to end with bloodshed and said 'ye have no reason to assist the French, ye have to keep your promises to England and enjoy peace at home' to her husband.[4] Her words were not enough, so she chose to act, it could be suggested, like a Tudor princess.

She had an old man approach her husband while he was praying inside the church of Linlithgow, dressed like the depiction of St John that was within the church. The old man warned the king that he must not go into battle against England – and he added that the king must not 'commerce with women'.[5] This last statement made James suspicious that this was trickery on the part of his wife. It is intriguing to wonder whether, if the second prohibition had not been voiced, Margaret's plan could have worked, and history would have changed. As it was, King James made a will in which he named Margaret as regent and guardian of their son and heir as long as she stayed a widow, and headed to Dunfermline, where he said goodbye to Margaret for the last time.

Scotland and England met at the Battle of Flodden on 9 September. The battle lasted three hours with the English losing one thousand five hundred men and the Scottish losing ten thousand, one of them being the king. One report has James hit with an arrow that pierced his lower jaw, leaving him helpless, the English almost severing his left hand before slicing his throat.[6] Some other reports state that James was killed by a cannon. The English took no prisoners and the king's body was said to have been left unrecognisable. This led to the myth that the king had actually escaped, but it is generally believed his body was taken by Lord Dacre to Berwick Castle to be embalmed and placed in a lead coffin before it was moved to London.

James's bloodstained coat was sent to Margaret's sister-in-law, Katherine of Aragon, as a trophy, who then sent it on to her husband in France.[7] James's body was said to have been taken to Richmond Palace once it had reached London. Although Queen Katherine first wanted to send James's head to her husband, she had decided against it. James's body being taken to London did pose an unusual problem. What was Henry to do with the body of a king?

James had been ex-communicated by the pope for breaking the Truce of Perpetual Peace and so was not allowed to be buried on consecrated ground. Knowing this, it was reported that Henry VIII still asked to have the Scottish king buried at St Paul's Cathedral as a mark of respect. He did get permission to do this on 29 November 1513 from Pope Leo X, however, something must have gone wrong as this was never done, leaving the body to remain unburied in Richmond's priory[8].

During the reign of the next King of England, Edward VI, John Stow, the historian and author of *The Chronicles of England* and *A Survey of London*, wrote of being shown the body of King James still unburied.[9] Two – or three, if counting Lady Jane Grey – monarchs later, James was apparently still not buried when Lancelot Young, the master glazier of Queen Elizabeth I, 'while smelling sweet spices', found the body of King James. Lancelot decided to cut off the head of the Scottish King and take it home with him to Wood Street in the City of London. After a while, his 'trophy' didn't seem such a prize anymore and he decided to give the head to his local church in Wood Street, St Michael's. This must have been something of a surprising gift for the church; nevertheless, the head was said to have been buried in the vaults under this church.[10]

The church of St Michael's in Wood Street was burned down in the Great Fire of London and over the years the site has been built on several times, including becoming a public house. The name, the King's Head would have been better suited to this public house, but it was actually named the Red Herring before it was knocked down and an office block was built on the site. So potentially, King James IV of Scotland's head now lies at Number 20 Wood Street, City of London.

As for the body, the records seem to stop after the detachment of his head at Richmond. However, in the nineteenth century a skeleton was found at Hume Castle, apparently still wearing the belt James was said to have always worn. Hume Castle being close to the border between England and Scotland would seem to make sense, if we can imagine someone wanting to bring the King of Scotland home. The skeleton has since disappeared without DNA samples being taken. However, there is another twist. It is thought that the skeleton may have found its way back to the Palace of Holyrood, where eight skeletons were discovered in 2002. They were first discovered by gas workers laying pipes from the kitchen of the palace.[11]

We have no record of Margaret asking what happened to her husband, nor does she seem to have ask for his remains. When a messenger finally reached Linlithgow with the news of the king's death, Margaret already seemed to know the outcome of the battle. Knowing that her husband had died on the battlefield, like any Queen Regent, Margaret turned her attention to her son, the heir to Scotland's throne. Her first action was to take herself and her son to Stirling Castle, a much stronger location to protect the both of them if needed. Then she called her nobles to her.

While waiting for her nobles, she quickly despatched letters to her brother Henry to ask for peace for the sake of her son. After the meeting with her nobles, a 'mourning coronation' was held, where the Archbishop of Glasgow held the crown of Scotland over Margaret's seventeen-month-old child's head to establish him as king. By this time Henry had answered her letters with a terse

'If the Scots want peace, they can have it.'[12] A truce was agreed for a year and a day in February 1514; even though Margaret had begged for something more permanent with the English. However, her councillors were only seeing Margaret now as Henry VIII's sister rather than their queen, they were suspicious that Margaret only had her brother's best interests at heart, the man that had caused so many Scottish deaths and deprived them of their king. It didn't help relations with her councillors that because she was eight months pregnant, she had missed the first meeting with her Parliament in March 1514. This allowed members to take the opportunity to discuss further plans for Scotland in her name but without her say so.

Margaret gave birth to her son, Alexander Duke of Ross, at Stirling Castle on 30 April 1514. Alexander was named after Margaret's husband's illegitimate son, who had also died at the Battle of Flodden. When Margaret had recovered from childbirth and went to her council to invite them to the celebration of her son's birth, she was probably aware of the tension from the start. In July that year, dressed in her best gown, she addressed her nobles at Edinburgh Castle. Once again, Margaret's main aim was to ask for peace for the good of her realm. She did seem to have won them over at first, as their response was that they were 'content to stand in one mind and will'.[13] The nobles then sent letters to Margaret's brother, asking for a longer peace settlement as Margaret had always wished.

Thinking all was now well with her Parliament, Margaret decided to visit Perth for the summer, but she had let her guard down too quickly, as this would be where Margaret would make her purportedly biggest mistake. We do not know when precisely Margaret met Archibald Douglas, the sixth Earl of Angus, but soon she had ostensibly fallen head over heels in love with him and had risked all by marrying him secretly.[14] This impulsive action would be repeated by her granddaughter, Mary, Queen of Scots, when she married Henry, Lord Darnley. Margaret had entered Kinnoull Church on 6 August 1514 to marry the earl. The medieval remains of Kinnoull Church, located on the east side of the River Tay in Perth just south of the Queen's Bridge indicate a humble edifice, a surprising place for the wedding of a dowager Queen of Scotland.

Margaret's secret marriage did not stay secret for long. It caused major problems for the bride as her councillors were conflicted, some still being loyal to the queen and others thinking that now she had married again, they did not have to stay loyal. By marrying again, Margaret had given up her right to be regent and guardian to the King of Scotland, her son, according to the strictures of her previous husband's will. Why would Margaret do this?

With hindsight, we know how much Margaret fought for her role and her guardianship over her son for almost the rest of her life. She may not have been fully aware of what she was giving up by marrying Archibald Douglas, and when she did, she might instantly have regretted her decision. However, it is important to note that Archibald Douglas was not a man without power himself, coming from one of the oldest and, in some areas, respected families of Scotland. So, Margaret may have thought she would get the support she needed by placing her faith and her alliances with a family so rooted in the Scottish history. After all, was this not what her father had done, by marrying her mother?

On 26 August 1514, Margaret was called before the council and with yet another echo of what would become of Margaret's granddaughter, Mary Queen of Scots, Margaret was asked to give up her authority. Margaret was now struggling to keep hold of any power she had. Her councillors now wanted the Duke of Albany, the late King of Scotland's cousin, to rule. At this point Henry VIII supported his sister, telling her to hold her ground with the councillors. One may think that this was a sign of brotherly love towards his older sister and that may well be true; but it would also have been beneficial to the English king to have a sister in power in Scotland. It seemed that the Scottish Parliament had already made up their minds, as on 18 September they formally asked the Duke of Albany to return to Scotland as fast as he could.[15] The duke came with his own conditions. He wanted his deceased father to be cleared of all counts of treason and to gain all of his family's rights back.

With support draining from Margaret's side, she was asked to give back the Great Seal that her second husband, Angus, had forcibly taken in anger. In this situation, Margaret turned to the only power she believed she had, she asked her brother to send an army to fight the Scots people who were against her. Again, this action has echoes of what was to come in Margaret's granddaughter's life, when Mary, Queen of Scots would ask Elizabeth I, Margaret's niece, for an army. Mary, much like her grandmother, Margaret, would get the same negative response.

Instead of helping Margaret, Henry turned to his younger sister Mary instead, who had recently become the widow of the French king. Henry wanted to make alliances with the new King of France. To do this, Henry could not attack the Scots to help Margaret as they were allies of the French. Henry's decisions as to whether or not to help his sisters depended on what he could gain. Sensing an opportunity in his sister's desperation, Henry had suggested that if Margaret was to escape to England, *with her sons*, Henry not yet having a male heir, this could make Margaret's son James, King of England, while her other son, Alexander, could have Scotland.

All this could have sounded very promising, but it was not what Margaret had wanted for her son and heir. This strong Tudor rose knew that her eldest child, James, was the natural heir to the throne of Scotland and, like the Tudor mothers before her, her own in Elizabeth of York, and in her grandmothers, both Margaret Beaufort and Elizabeth Woodville, Margaret would do all she could to see her son assume his rightful place in the world. However, through her own Tudor background and her own queenship, Margaret had learned to be tactful with her brother Henry.

She had to reject her brother's idea; this sounds simple enough. But let's not forget who her brother was, a man you did not say no to without risking your own life. Yet, this was what Margaret did, which shows some grit and determination. The way she did it also shows intelligence. She wrote to Henry:

> Yet it comforts mine heart to hear your fraternal desire, but it is impossible to be performed by any manner of fashion that I, my husband or his uncle can devise. Considering what watch and spies there is daily where I am, and I dare disclose my council to none other but God. If I were such a woman that might go with my bairn in mine arm, I trow I should not be long from you, whose presence I desire most of any man.[16]

We can glean from this so much of Margaret's character by what is written, and so much more by what is not. Margaret was able to be diplomatic and queenly in her letters because on the one hand she was writing to her brother, but on the other hand, she was also writing to another monarch. She is not too cold to Henry, she is intimate, 'it comforts mine heart'. She knows her brother's personality and she plays down her queenship, reducing herself to an image of just a 'woman that might go with my bairn in mine arm'. In doing this, she bows down to Henry's authority. She shows us that although they had spent years apart, she still knows her brother very well in ending the letter with flattery, the man 'whose presence I desire most of any man'. Did Margaret learn from childhood that Henry liked to be the centre of attention and that if he was, he reacted better for it? In this political subtlety it can be proposed that Margaret was her father's daughter. It could also be suggested that Margaret knows her brother perhaps better than the male advisors who surrounded him. This may have been because Henry never grew up as the heir to the English throne, so he had spent more of his childhood with his sisters than he would have done otherwise.

That being said, she also probably knew that her letter would not keep her brother at bay for long and it would not have come as a surprise when her brother's response was sent, not to her – just 'a woman that might go with my bairn in mine arm' – but to Lord Dacre at Berwick. Margaret then had to justify herself by sending two men, one named Williamson and the other called Inglis, to explain her position. The choice of these two men was unwise, as Williamson at least seemed to have been on her brother's side: 'Madam, I beseech your grace, at the reverence of God, for your own singular weal and for the promotion of (your) children my native King and Prince, to follow the advice and counsel of your dearest brother, the King of England.'[17]

Margaret believed that if she left Scotland, she would be classed as a rebel in the eyes of the Scottish Council and the chances of her son becoming King of Scotland would be negligible. Everything at this point must have felt like it was slowing down, for Margaret at every turn faced a brick wall. The Scottish Council wasn't making the decision on who should be the next king because they were waiting for the Duke of Albany. Henry VIII was holding him off in France, for his own gain rather than as a favour to his sister. While Margaret still had some power, being the mother to the rightful future king, Henry felt that he himself had some control in Scotland. However, if the duke reached Scotland, the councillors may choose him to be regent instead of Henry's sister, and so Henry would lose any influence he thought he had. The Duke of Albany could not be delayed forever, and with the permission of the King of France to leave and dodging Henry's ships along the way, the duke managed finally to get to Scotland.

Margaret needed the duke to be on her side. She left her rooms at Holyrood Palace, taking up residence in Edinburgh Castle so that the duke could have Holyrood to himself. She also spoke to the duke in French as he could not speak English well. She had hoped the duke was a man to fight for her cause, but on 12 July her hopes were dashed when he was made regent by Parliament. Margaret, now six months pregnant with Angus's child, took her children to Stirling Castle, as she did not want to hand her children over to the care of the Scottish Parliament. Not handing over children makes grim sense when we remember the history of the Princes in the Tower and that those two small boys were Margaret's uncles.

Margaret was on her own, without help from either her brother or her husband. It was time to exercise the Tudor strength that was within her. Margaret wrote to the council expressing her wish to be guardian of her own children as her first husband's will dictated, but she would allow there to be four other guardians in her husband, Lord Holme of Chamberlain, Lord Keith and Sir Robert Lauder. This letter from Margaret seemed to prompt some into helping her as, soon afterwards, Lord Holme and her husband tried to rescue Margaret and her sons, but they were stopped by the Earl of Bothwell. Angus did manage to smuggle himself through a tunnel to speak to Margaret, but he was attacked when leaving and 500 men with him died. Angus was told to stand by the side of the new regent of Scotland as he attacked Stirling, rather than by the side of his wife; but he had chosen to be absent when the Duke of Albany arrived at the castle and his absence was noted.

With the Duke of Albany having over seven thousand men, Margaret had no choice but to surrender. Yet, she would ensure her son was to rule, and here we see a glimpse of her understanding of the power of propaganda that all the Tudors exploited so well; before handing her son over, she dressed him in the finest clothes and even placed a crown upon his head. Once she had handed him over, Margaret asked that she be forgiven with her husband and that she be allowed to visit her children at a later date. The duke's response was favourable as to her and her children, but her husband's non-appearance meant that he was a traitor in the duke's eyes. Margaret was then taken to stay at Edinburgh Castle.

This outcome did not go down well with Henry VIII. He wanted to have Margaret's children under his control, he did not want the Duke of Albany to have the power. In her brother's eyes, Margaret had seemed to give up her position without a fight.

From her point of view, she had been willing to fight, but her brother had not sent an army to help her.

Nevertheless, there now seemed to be secret messages between Margaret and her brother, keeping Henry very much in the loop of all things in Scotland. Although Margaret was basically in the keep of the Duke of Albany at this point, when she wrote to her brother on 20 August, the letter must have seemed so plain that the duke allowed it to reach Henry. But in reality, in the letter Margaret was telling her brother where she was going to be and when, if a rescue attempt was going to take place. 'Brother, I purpose by the grace of God, to take my chamber (give birth) and lie in my palace of Linlithgow within twelve days, for I have not past eight weeks to my time.'[18]

Henry knew that he must divert the duke's attention away from Margaret and her movements, so he ordered Dacre and Lord Holme to attack the borders, while also sending a secret message to Margaret to tell her to divert from Linlithgow and go to the castle at Blackadder. Margaret agreed to the plan but was clever enacting it. She did indeed go to Linlithgow for two days where she was met by her husband, but this was only to keep up appearances, for after those two days she rode at night to Tantallon Castle and then on to Blackadder Castle. This was a daring feat, whether she had been eight months pregnant or not.

At Blackadder Castle she received a letter from the Duke of Albany asking her to return, and if she did, she would finally receive her dowager payments. These had been withheld from her, so this letter must have seemed very tempting, but sensing this, Henry's man Dacre told Margaret that the Duke was in fact assembling troops to attack the castle. The scare worked, and instead she took refuge at the Coldstream Priory.

It seemed that Margaret was fully aware of what leaving Scotland and her children behind could mean, as she tried one last time to communicate with the Duke of Albany before crossing the border. The duke seemed to want to come to a reconciliation as well, as he sent his French ambassador, Du Plains, to meet with her; but again, Henry's man, probably with orders to make sure a truce didn't happen, got involved. Dacre had moved Margaret on to Morpeth Castle, his own residence, before Du Plains could reach her. Feeling the pains of her pregnancy, Margaret was now completely in the hands of this man, someone who had no qualms in moving a heavily pregnant royal once again, to Harbottle Castle. This last move was completely Dacre's own initiative and was not planned with the King of England, as Henry and his wife Katherine had sent essentials for Margaret's confinement to Morpeth Castle instead.

Harbottle Castle was not prepared for any birth, yet alone a royal one. This must have added to the growing fear Margaret had, as she famously hated childbirth and the childbed sickness she always had. Her situation must have seemed very bleak, the child was coming two weeks early, she was without funds, without useful status, she was on the run, in the hands of her brother and had left her other children behind. The fact that the place she was going to give birth in wasn't prepared for her, must have added to the dread. Either on 7 or 8 October 1515,[19] Margaret gave birth to a girl at Harbottle Castle, Northumberland, named after herself and her grandmother, Margaret.

9

A PAWN IN A POLITICAL GAME

Margaret now gives birth to Margaret Douglas, a lady that would go on to have an interesting role in the Tudor period herself, living for some time with her aunt Princess Mary, the future Mary I, suggested as being a lady in waiting to Anne Boleyn and being sent to the Tower of London on many occasions. Margaret Douglas would also go down in history as the mother of Lord Darnley and so she was the great aunt and grandmother of King James VI of Scotland and I of England. This also means, in the complex way these Tudor family trees have tended to grow, that through Margaret Tudor's first marriage and the birth of her son, James V of Scotland, Margaret was the grandmother to Mary, Queen of Scots. Through her second marriage and the birth of Margaret Douglas, she was also the grandmother of Henry, Lord Darnley, who would later marry

Mary, Queen of Scots. So, Mary and Henry's child, the future Stuart king James VI of Scotland and I of England, was the great-grandchild of Margaret Tudor from both his mother *and* father's side of the family.

It is thus through Margaret's side of the Tudor family that the British monarchy continued after the death of Queen Elizabeth I, as the founder of the Tudor monarchy, Henry VII, originally wanted. Margaret, not Arthur or Henry VIII, was perhaps the real 'Tudor rose' her parents had wanted to make from their union of the Houses of York and Lancaster. Margaret's importance to the history, and even how we see the British monarchy today, has perhaps been obscured by louder, more extravagant characters in her family.

After the birth of Margaret Douglas, Margaret Tudor suffered from pains that suggest her sciatic nerve was the cause, as she was unable to move without screaming. It was Henry's man, Dacre, who takes over yet again in Margaret's life. Margaret was writing many letters, one to the Duke of Albany in which she explains why she left Scotland, 'for fear and danger of [her] life' and asking yet again if she could be the 'tutrix of the young king and prince, my tender children, to have the whole rule and governance, as well of them as of the said realm of Scotland, according to the last will and testament of my late spouse and husband, the late King of Scotland'.[1] The reply to which was a flat no: 'We cannot consent that you have the tutory of the King's grace and his brother, nor the governance of the realm.'[2] She also wrote to the pope, the King of France and Venetian ambassadors, but with her being in so much pain after giving birth, we can't be sure who was wielding the pen.

With no help, Margaret was completely in the hands of her brother. Was she questioning whether she could truly trust her own brother? For how could anyone fully trust Henry VIII? How would Margaret have felt if she had known that he was writing to the King of France, warning him to stay away from 'the affairs of Scotland', as his involvement in helping Margaret might 'injure our friendship'?[3]

At the end of November 1515, Margaret was well enough to travel in a litter to Cartington, two miles from Rothbury in Northumberland. This would later become a major Royalist centre during the Civil War. She stayed for two days, then she was moved to Brinkburn Priory, then Morpeth. One of Henry's men, Sir Christopher Garney, was sent to keep an eye on her and report that 'it would pity any man's heart to hear the shrieks and cries of her grace giveth when she is moved or turned.'[4] Margaret was so ill, that the council was reluctant to tell her that her son Alexander had died. She wasn't told until March of the next year.

During a temporary truce between England and Scotland, the Scots were judging Margaret's actions, but without knowing the role Henry VIII had played in them. Margaret had sided 'against the independence of that country of which her son was sovereign, whilst Albany, with much earnestness and sincerity, offered a complete restoration to all those right and revenues, as queen-dowager, which she has forfeited by her marriage.'[5] Margaret had listened to her brother, a family member, when she was vulnerable, being pregnant first and then ill. She had been lied to and manipulated into believing there was a risk to her life from the Duke of Albany and the Scottish councillors. Margaret did not know who to trust. She was without her husband, she did not know that he had made his own peace with Scotland and even gained a mistress, the lady he was once betrothed to, Lady Jane Steward of Traquaire. Margaret was also, no doubt, missing one son and grieving for the other.

To make matters worse, during this truce, Scottish envoys would visit Margaret's brother in England to discuss Margaret's situation without her. Dacre, Henry's man, took charge yet again and wrote to the Duke of Albany with complaints to which Margaret signed her name. Under the sway of Dacre, she moved south again in April to Newcastle, Durham and back towards York. By May, Margaret was staying at the home of Sir Thomas Lovell, the Lord Treasurer, in Enfield. Sir Thomas was an old family friend and astute in financial matters.

In 1485, Sir Thomas Lovell was created Chancellor of the Exchequer and Esquire of the Body to Henry VII. He would later become treasurer of the King's and Queen's chambers.[6] He was elected speaker of the Commons, and he headed the meeting concerning Henry's marriage to Elizabeth of York. He even gave five hundred pounds of his own money to the security of her plate. He showed his loyalty to Margaret's parents during the Lambert Simnel affair. Sir Thomas fought with his brothers at the Battle of Stoke Field in 1487. He was at the tournament to celebrate Prince Henry's new title of Duke of York, and he accompanied the prince to Calais in 1500. When Prince Henry became king, Sir Thomas was given the role of Treasurer of the Household and was made a Knight of the Garter. He was also for a time the Constable of the Tower. He was the man Katherine of Aragon chose to help rally the men in the Midlands to fight the Scots.

So, when Margaret stayed with him at Elsyng Palace, known later as Enfield House, she would have taken the opportunity to discuss her situation and what she could do to get some financial backing for her cause. Elsyng was eventually owned by Henry VIII.[7] At the time of writing, there are plans to add to the Tudor finds on this site.[8] The main aim for the archaeological team is to find the Tudor gate house.[9]

Margaret then moved to William Compton's house in Tottenham, where she finally came face to face with her brother. They had not seen each other for thirteen years. Margaret was wearing a royal purple velvet dress trimmed with the Cloth of Gold. Although she was the one asking for help, she was making the point that her status was still on par with her brother's. The purple velvet was the material Henry had sent her, another signal. Henry, too, was dressed in his finest, wearing green and yellow velvet and a flat velvet cap, which set off his auburn hair. After the private moment between the siblings, they arrived together at Baynard's Castle, where rooms were already made up for Margaret. After the pain that Margaret had suffered, the comfort of Baynard's Castle must have been a blessed relief.

Henry delayed sorting the situation out by using his well-known tactic of having a celebration to distract. This time the celebration was in honour of Margaret's return to London. Margaret travelled to Greenwich Palace and was reunited with her sister, Mary. The two women who probably knew Henry better than any of his advisors – or indeed better than the king knew himself – were together again. They had grown up with him and shared the triumphs and tragedies of Henry's early life, experiences that helped form the man and the monarch.

So much had changed since the three surviving children of Elizabeth of York and King Henry VII had been together in the same room. They had all become monarchs of different countries, all had children of their own. At this point Henry had lost at least three children, a daughter in 1510, a son in 1511 and another son in 1513.[10] Mary had two daughters from her second marriage,

Anne Brandon, the Baroness Grey of Powys and Mary Brandon, the Baroness Monteagle. Margaret had given birth to James Stewart, Duke of Rothesay, a daughter and Arthur Stewart, also titled Duke of Rothesay who died, the future James V, then a daughter who passed away in 1512, Alexander Stewart, Duke of Ross and finally Margaret Douglas.

Henry ordered a two-day joust for Margaret. Someone was missing from this family reunion however, Margaret's second husband, Angus. Henry had given Angus permission to travel with his wife to England, but Angus had chosen to stay in his estates in Scotland to defend himself against any attacks from Albany. This was tantamount to refusing an invitation from Henry, who remarked that Angus's absence was 'done like a Scot'.[11] The next day, the celebrations continued in Queen Katherine's rooms, but then came the long-awaited meeting with her brother to discuss Margaret's situation.

Staying true to form, Henry believed a compromise with Albany was out of the question and the only solution was for Albany to give up his regency of Scotland and return to France. Henry repeated this to the Scottish ambassadors as well as giving them a long list of complaints, apparently from Margaret. The message was sent back to Scotland. Henry, ever the gracious king, would allow Albany to travel through England to get to France, if he chose to leave Scotland as Henry suggested. It was probably true that Albany wished to return to France to be with his wife, but the Scottish councillors would not allow Albany to leave. Henry's attempt to influence matters in Scotland was once more blocked. Margaret must have felt like a pawn in the political game as she waited at Baynard's Castle while negotiations continued between her brother and the land in which she was queen.

While all this was happening, news reached England that little James V was ill. It is interesting how Margaret and Henry reacted. Margaret, as we would expect, was in fear for her child, after losing others in the recent past she did not want to go through the grief of saying goodbye to another. The fact that James was Scotland's heir may have played a secondary role in Margaret's feelings. Henry acted as a king first rather than the child's uncle, as even though he had lost children and heirs himself, Henry chose to not express anxiety, like his sister, but instead show anger. He suspected that Albany was trying to snatch control of Scotland by poisoning the child in his care. This wasn't unheard of; in Henry's lifetime, Ludovico Il Moro, Duke of Milan had almost certainly poisoned his nephew Gian Galeazzo Sforza, while under his care, in 1494.[12] Henry wrote to Albany and told him that if the young king died, he would be held responsible for it.

Even though the news of the illness may have caused a setback in the negotiations, some headway was still being made, as the Scottish council did agree to send Margaret her clothes, jewellery and furniture. She had not had her own items to sell or use for such a long time, so this was a step forward. The uplift in her spirits must have been short-lived when the expected sum of fourteen thousand three hundred and thirty-four pounds turned out to be one hundred and fourteen pounds instead, due to other people, mainly her husband Angus, taking her money while she had been away.

Margaret spent the Christmas of 1516 at her brother's English court, at his expense, without money to buy New Year's gifts. However, Margaret being a Tudor, was proud and the lack of funds had embarrassed her. She asked for a loan. The man she asked is often described as her brother's right-hand man, known by some as the 'Alter Rex'. If we take a moment to look closer at this man, perhaps we might find that he was more than a politician or functionary, even considered on occasion as a family member, a father figure. Cardinal Thomas Wolsey had helped the young King Henry get his way on many points, he advised the king not to execute his own sister, Mary, Dowager Queen of France after her treasonable marriage without Henry's permission. Wolsey had instead convinced the king to embrace his sister. Wolsey oversaw the building plans for the tombs of Henry's father and mother at Westminster Abbey, not to mention organising the tomb for Henry VIII himself for when the time came. Here was a man who genuinely cared for the members of the Tudor family and it is this person Margaret turned to in her time of need. She writes to him, asking for a loan of two hundred pounds: 'I beseech you heartily that I may have it tomorrow night at the farthest for else I will be disappointed.'[13] Wolsey did not disappoint, he helped Margaret as he had helped all the other children of King Henry VII and Elizabeth of York. At Christmas 1516, watching her younger brother sparing no expense over his extravagant Christmas festivities while she had to borrow to buy gifts, did she feel that she had outstayed her welcome?

Although the negotiations between England and Scotland were progressing, the Scottish council stayed firm on one point, Margaret was the king's mother and as such would be 'heartily welcomed' back in Scotland, but she would not have any authority.[14] On 17 April 1517 Margaret received a formal letter from her son stating that it was 'lawful to our dearest mother to come into this, our realm, freely and peaceably with her train'.[15] Although Margaret suspected she would not be allowed to see her son as he was being moved to Edinburgh Castle to be closely guarded, Margaret did leave London to start her long journey north again. She said goodbye to her brother and his wife at Windsor, insisting that she wanted to be the mediator between England and Scotland, she did not want to put herself into the hands of anyone else anymore. Remarkably, her brother agreed to it.[16] As well as giving Margaret hope that she could control her own life, he also gave her a horse with trapping, cloth, jewels, plate and two fine gold cups to take back to Scotland.[17]

Margaret left Windsor on 16 May 1517. By the time she reached Doncaster she was feeling unwell, and she did not arrive at York until June. There she learned that the Duke of Albany was leaving Scotland for France and had left a council of people such as the Archbishops of St Andrews and Glasgow, the Earls of Angus, Arran, Hentley, Argyle and his friend and deputy Sieur de la Baste to form the regency in his place. Margaret wrote to her brother, keeping him in the loop.

Once Margaret was over the border, she made her way to David's Tower to see her son but was denied entry. The governor of the tower, Sir Patrick Crichton, had received no word from the council allowing her in. Margaret gave up and retired to her apartments at Holyrood. It would not be until August that she was finally able to see her son. The meeting was short and only happened as the boy king was moved to Craigmillar, where the governor was more sympathetic.[18]

Margaret moved to Newark Castle, on the south side of the River Clyde as she considered her situation. This castle would have been a relatively new building when Margaret stayed there, being built in 1478 by George Maxwell when he gained the Barony of Finlanstone.[19] It was a castle that Margaret may have known with her first husband, King James IV, who stayed there in 1495 before setting sail for the Hebrides.[20] Although it was later updated, the tall tower and the gatehouse remain from Margaret's day.

The person who had helped her leave Scotland, Lord Holme, had been executed, and with no other friend or supporter, Margaret only had her husband on the council to help her cause. It may have seemed all was lost for her, however with the murder of Albany's deputy, Sieur de la Baste, his head impaled on a spike at Duns, Margaret saw an opportunity to regain the regency. Margaret wrote to her brother for help; however, the response was not what Margaret wanted to hear. She would get help from her brother, but only after she had taken back the regency herself. This would not have been easy in any circumstances, yet alone having no help from her husband and a lack of money. She did the only thing she could, she wrote to her brother again: 'I stand no sore case, and I get not the King's grace my brother's help and my lord cardinal's: for such jewels as his grace gave me at my departing from him, I am so constrained that I must put it away for money.'[21]

Lack of money and allies were not the only problems for Margaret. At Christmas 1517, Margaret was at Tantallon Castle in East Lothian. This castle, which looked out over the Firth of Forth, was the last curtain-walled castle to be built in Scotland[22] and was her husband's family's stronghold. Here, she learned the truth about her husband. Not only had he been taking the rents from her lands, but he had also forced himself into the property at Newark and was openly living with his mistress and their child. This was arguably the lowest point for Margaret. However, like her parents before her, Margaret shows her Tudor grit and does not give up.

10

A PAWN NO LONGER

Margaret turns to her husband's enemy, the new deputy governor, the Earl of Arran at this point. Her husband was ordered to leave Newark, but he would not. She did, however, receive two thousand of the nine thousand pounds owed to her, but Angus was still demanding any money Margaret had, being legally her husband. Angus, angrily, now wanted to be free of his bond that meant other people could collect Margaret's rents, making sure Margaret would at least get some of the money. Angus wanted to go back to collecting the rents himself. Even with his poor treatment of his wife, the Tudor Princess and Dowager Queen of Scotland, Angus was backed by his powerful clan and in the stronger position.

Margaret was not prepared to make any changes to the bond, why would she? This was her only real financial income, she was poor, and her husband had already taken enough from her. Once again, Margaret wrote to her brother. In October 1518, Margaret writes possibly her longest letter to her brother. She describes her situation as 'evil' and tells him that she had been resisting selling the jewels Henry had given her, but now her situation was so bad that she may have to do it. Calling Henry, her 'dearest brother' she writes, 'I have no other to help me but you'. What may have worried Henry more than his sister's plight was Margaret's description of how powerful her husband was and perhaps an off the cuff statement his sister makes: '...wherefore I beseech your grace, when it comes to that point, as I trust it shall to be a king prince and brother to me, for I shall never marry but where you will bid me.'[1]

For Margaret to marry again meant divorce. Henry, ironically, was not happy with the whole idea of divorce. Henry didn't legally divorce any of his six wives, regardless of the well-known nursery rhyme. Katherine of Aragon's marriage was annulled by the Church of England, Anne Boleyn's marriage was annulled two days before her execution, Jane Seymour's marriage ended with her death, Anne of Cleves's marriage was annulled, Catherine Howard's marriage was annulled before her execution and Katherine Parr's marriage ended with the death of the king. Knowing the efforts Henry made to not legally divorce, we can understand Henry's reaction to Margaret's statement. After speaking to Katherine, Henry sends Katherine's Friar, Bonaventure Langley, to Margaret to effect a reconciliation between Margaret and her husband.

This must have confused Margaret, she wanted her brother's support but instead of money to raise an army, she got a priest, who was telling her to go back to a husband that mistreated her, took her money, took a mistress and had a child with her, offering her no support. Although Margaret received letter after letter from her brother, Katherine of Aragon and even Cardinal Wolsey, Margaret graciously thanked them for sending her a priest but she had no intention of going back to her husband.

In February 1519, Margaret worked her magic with the Scottish council and although she was to lose the lands of Ettrick, she was to gain the yearly sum of two thousand marks, a fact that made her husband furious, but he was unable to do anything about it, which must have given Margaret pleasure. While Margaret was slowly finding her feet and was able to discuss with the councillors a better solution to her own situation, her brother tries one more time, sending another priest to Margaret with the same mission. This friar, Henry Chadworth, spent eight weeks with her and although we do not know what was actually said between them, he won out and Margaret returned to her husband. We need to keep in mind that her husband was a part of a powerful clan and maybe Margaret thought she might be able to use some of that power to gain her son and heir back. So perhaps the friar had nothing to do with her apparent reconciliation. Returning to her husband meant that she now had the Archbishop of St Andrews, the Bishops of Duffield, Aberdeen and Murray as well as the Earls of Hentley, Argyll, Ruthin, Morton, Glencairn and Marshall, and the Lords of Glamis, Hay and Grey behind her.[2] She went after her son, but her plans were delayed when she contracted smallpox in the winter of 1519.

Her husband was beginning to gain too much power for the Scottish Council, so much so that the council asked Margaret to write to King Francis I of France to ask for the return of the Duke of Albany. Margaret jumped at the chance and also asked the duke to help her finally get the divorce she wanted. This was against Henry VIII's wishes, for Henry it was better if Angus, Margaret's husband, ran Scotland, not the Duke of Albany so Henry ordered Dacre to make Margaret retract her letter. Luckily for Henry, the French King, at this point, thought well of Henry and instead of returning Albany to Scotland and upsetting Henry so soon after the Field of Cloth of Gold, he instead sent Albany to Rome.

Henry may have first thought that he had won, that at least Albany was not in Scotland to take power, but with Albany being in Rome he was able to promote the idea of Margaret's divorce by using his own family connections with the pope, meanwhile Margaret was told by her brother to remember of 'what family you are'.[3] Margaret was indeed born a Tudor princess but she now had a son and heir to the Scottish throne and like her mother before her, who was born a Yorkist but became a Tudor through motherhood, Margaret was choosing the family she had married into rather than the family she had come from, to support her child.

In early 1521, Albany's friend Gonzolles returned to Scotland, asking for the council to increase Margaret's income, even going so far as to finance her from his own purse until the council gave her money themselves. With Henry's ability to forward think and twist people of the court to do his own bidding, he should have been able to see what Margaret was trying to do here by siding with Albany. Albany had always been the one to have given Margaret everything and here we see him doing the same. It would have been natural in the Tudor world for Margaret to use a member of court to help her situation, it was something her brother would have done if he had been in his sister's position. And yet, Henry doesn't seem to see this, he, could not believe after all the 'help' and advice he and his councillors had given his sister that she had chosen to go against her own brother and blood to side with Albany. Dacre wrote to Margaret threatening her that if she did not desist, she would not get any more 'help' from her brother. Margaret's reply to Henry shows her standing strong, her Tudor fiery blood up. She did not want to be her younger brother's pawn anymore or wait anxiously for some action on her behalf. Margaret now seemed sick of her brother telling her what to do. She writes: 'As to my Lord Angus, if he desired my company or my love, he would have shown me more kindly than he hath done.' She then lists all the mistreatment she had suffered from her husband and makes the point that she 'had no help of the King's grace, my brother'.[4] If Margaret thought that by showing the Tudor strength that both siblings shared that she would receive some sympathy from her brother, she would be mistaken. There was no sympathy from the English court for this Tudor rose.

When Albany arrived in Scotland on 18 November 1521, Margaret rushed to meet him at Stirling. They travelled together to Linlithgow and then to Edinburgh to finally meet with Margaret's son, James. As a show of trust, at Edinburgh Albany was given the keys to the castle, but he passed them straight to Margaret. Finally, it seemed that Margaret had really the only thing she had ever wanted, the only thing she had asked her brother to help her get, access to her son. It was not her brother, her Tudor kin, who had gained her access, it was the Duke of Albany. The support she gave the duke in return was so firm that it set rumours circulating at the English court, mainly from Wolsey and Dacre, that Albany may try to marry Margaret after he gained her a dispensation to divorce from the pope. Albany was married at this time, but nothing was made of the fact.

The rumours even went so far as to suggest that after Albany married Margaret, he would usurp James, Margaret's son, and take the crown for himself. The English rumours were not believed by the Scottish Council and Albany was still welcomed into Scotland.

The only people who were not welcoming towards Albany were the Clan Douglas, her husband's clan, so Albany had to do something quickly to shut the Douglas clan down. The first action he took was to remove members of the clan from office. He went so far as to accuse Gavin Douglas, Bishop of Dunkeld, and Margaret's husband Angus, of high treason. They both went into hiding; Gavin made his way to the English court, hoping for Henry's backing, and Angus was probably helped into hiding by Dacre.

After everything her husband had done to her, Margaret still had enough compassion to ask Albany, if her husband was caught, that he be exiled rather than executed. Albany agreed to her wishes and continued to petition Rome for her divorce. For the first time in a very long while, Margaret had some security to rest a little. However, she still had Henry's man, Dacre, to worry about. He had at one time supported her, but now Dacre had turned against her. She must have imagined her brother had done the same.

Margaret wasn't going to hide away and let Albany fight all her battles for her. She wrote to Dacre herself: 'My lord, I write sharply and plainly to you; for I have good cause, both for the King, my son's sake and mine own; for ye have fortified my lord of Angus against me and counselled him to trouble me, in the contrary of the band that ye caused me to take of him, which ye would break again, which ye should not have done to your master's sister.'[5] Dacre did not respond in a helpful manner and instantly Margaret complained to her brother over the behaviour of his men. As would become Henry's fallback position when there was an awkward situation, Henry stayed out of the way, allowing others to do the work.[6]

Although Henry was hearing all sorts of rumours about his sister, Margaret still believed her brother would see through these rumours and that he would agree to the peace Margaret wanted for both countries. However, when on 1 February 1522 Thomas Benett arrived in Edinburgh with a handful of letters from Henry, Margaret was surprised to learn how angry he was over her actions. Her brother was listening to the rumours, something Henry would often do, when it suited him, later in his reign. She told Thomas that it was obvious her brother was listening to 'seditious and ill reports made and contrived against her by very false persons'.[7] She wrote to her brother to justify her actions and to state: 'It does me a great displeasure in my heart of your unkindness' to believe in these rumours.[8] It was not only Margaret who received hard words from the King of England, the Duke of Albany also received a letter accusing him of 'dishonest love' for his sister, threatening a battle with him if he continued.[9]

All starts to become clearer when his King at Arms tells the Scottish Council of Henry's displeasure, stating its origin, and that because of this displeasure, Albany should be sent back to France. The council stood by Albany, also stating that little James was being well looked after by his mother, which was exactly what Margaret had wanted in the first place. The council wrote as a last note; 'This country desires peace with England, if it can be had with honour, but will not consent to Albany's removal.'[10] In Henry's eyes, regardless of what his sister wanted, Angus was still her husband and he should be living with her, which is why Henry continued to support and shelter him. Eventually, Albany's men caught up with Angus and it was he, not Albany, who was exiled to France.

With Angus being exiled to France and with Scotland asking for peace with England, all might have seemed set for Margaret to begin the rest of her life with everything she wanted. However, this was when the Treaty of Rouen between Scotland and France, which included provision for the future marriage of James V and a daughter of Francis, happened. Originally negotiated in 1517, this confirmation of the Auld Alliance meant that France could demand Scotland to go to war with England, due to Henry going back on his word at the Field of the Cloth of Gold and signing a new treaty with Charles V, the Holy Roman Emperor, to fight the French. Albany reluctantly gathered eighty thousand men to travel to the Scottish border. This must have reminded Margaret of the Battle of Flodden, where she lost her husband, the battle that was the catalyst for all the hardships she had faced and had only just recovered from. Margaret instantly asked the Scottish council to move her son from Edinburgh to Stirling for protection, she then asked, yet again, for peace, even without the letter she had received from Dacre asking for the same thing, when he had realised his troops were outnumbered.[11] Margaret was the Tudor rose who had always wanted peace. It is suggested that Margaret herself rode out to secure the peace treaty signed by Albany and Dacre. With that action of Margaret's, both men then agreed to a month's truce and war was averted.

Henry was not happy with Margaret's peacekeeping. Neither was the King of France happy with Albany, who had then been sent to France to explain his actions. This ultimately meant, in a convoluted way, that Henry had his wish and had removed Albany. Now, Henry turned his sights on his sister. With Albany out of the way, Henry tried to charm his sister once again. Margaret received many letters from Dacre, Wolsey and from her brother, praising her efforts for keeping the peace. Pulling out all the stops, Henry allowed the truce with Scotland to be extended to sixteen years if Scotland did not allow Albany back, and even went so far as to offer the hand of Henry's daughter Mary to James V.

Albany, on the other hand, had sent Margaret and the councillors one thousand French coins as payment for their loyalty. So, Margaret had to play the courts of Scotland, England and France well at this point. She had to keep her brother happy, even though it was he who had made so much trouble for her. Slowly and without Albany by her side, Margaret began to restore her faith in her brother. The timing was good, as her son James V wanted freedom from Albany's rule, too. This he expressed in a letter to Parliament and when Margaret read it out, the response was divided. Although the lords did not wish to upset James V as he was coming of age, they wanted to wait for Albany's return first.

Margaret was not happy with this decision and planned to kidnap her son while he was out hunting and have him appear in person before the council to plead his own case. Margaret believed she could do this if she had the help of her brother.[12] Henry chose to help his sister this time, by telling Surrey to attack Jedburgh to focus the Scottish attentions there rather than on Margaret. But Margaret's plans came to nothing and the Scottish town that Henry's men attacked was burned consequently. Margaret had lost her chance of snatching her son back, as

Albany had now returned with four thousand French troops. Margaret was now in fear of what Albany would do after she had once again sided with her brother; she may have hoped to continue to have her brother's support, but as she could no longer bolster English influence in Scotland, Margaret was not a lady worth paying court to for Henry anymore.

At first it seemed Margaret's fears were unfounded, as Albany visited the young James and Margaret. reassuring them of his continued support; however, Albany had one thing and one thing only on his mind and that was to invade England. In November 1523, he laid siege to Wark Castle in Northumberland while Margaret took her son to Stirling for safekeeping until they received news of who was on the winning side. With lack of support at the borders, Albany had to retreat to Edinburgh and called another Parliament meeting. He turned his attentions on Margaret, ordering her to quit Stirling, leaving her son behind, but she refused.

In the spring of 1524, a truce between England and Scotland was made until midsummer. Margaret was unhappy that she was not consulted as she had been before. There was also a lack of correspondence from her brother too. Margaret then heard a rumour that her husband Angus had been invited to England by her brother. This news must have hurt Margaret's feelings and Albany used this opportunity to gain Margaret's trust again. He did this by organising a place for her to stay in France, should Angus arrive in Scotland, and by holding firm on James marrying a French princess to confirm the Auld Alliance. Once more, Margaret was the Tudor rose entwining France, Scotland and England together, but she was there with no real support from any side. Her situation was to change again when Albany was allowed by the Scottish Parliament to return to France, believing that he would be back in Scotland in three months. This allowed Margaret to return to her original plan of taking her son away from his guardians so that he could start to take control. To do this, Margaret began building bridges with almost everyone around her.

On 26 July 1524, the twelve-year-old King of Scots rode out from Stirling Castle with his mother and with the backing of the English and the Scottish people to escape his French guardians. Margaret's son was now no longer under the regency of the Duke of Albany. Mother and son rode on to Edinburgh Castle to a happy welcome from the Scottish people. This moment was what Margaret had been fighting for ever since she had lost her husband and her title at the Battle of Flodden. Her son was on the throne of Scotland with his mother by his side and having the backing of his uncle in England.

One wonders if this was what Henry VII envisioned and wanted when he sent his eldest daughter to Scotland all those years ago. Henry VIII sent Margaret's son letters of congratulation and a jewelled sword while making him a member of the Order of the Garter. In this moment, Margaret had achieved her goal and the goal of the Tudor bloodline, perhaps even more successfully than her brother had done at this point. However, the happiness Margaret must have felt would soon disappear when her brother returned to a familiar demand. Still not able to allow his own sister to follow her own wishes in life, Henry pushed once again for Margaret to return to her husband, the Earl of Angus. For this, Henry allowed Angus to travel as far north as Newcastle. From there he bombarded Margaret with letters, but she sent them all back unopened. Her husband was not prepared to walk away, so, he decided with a band of four hundred men, including the Earls of Lennox and Buccleuch, to cross the border without anyone's permission, head into Edinburgh and scale the walls of the castle. Margaret ordered the cannons to fire at her husband and four men were killed.

Shocked with how much hatred Margaret had for her husband, she was asked to make amends with him yet again. Her straightforward reply to this was for them to 'go home and not meddle with Scottish affairs'.[13] Margaret now blamed her brother for allowing her husband to travel so far north and by doing so, risking not only her life but the life of her precious son.[14] This tiger mother had the Tudor and York strength of her parents within her. In addition, she was able to portray the pain and distress her brother's actions had caused in a way that her brother could understand. This was no mean feat, but Margaret knew her brother, knew how to work him, perhaps better than other women or indeed men that surrounded him. She forced her brother to listen to her and he acquiesced; from then on Angus would no longer be supported by Henry.

This was still a worrying time for Margaret politically. Although she may have wanted her brother to drop his guard on the subject of her husband, they both knew that this might open the door to the French, who may think if they offered Margaret help with her husband, they could poach her away from her brother. The French shortly afterwards sent Margaret a 'gift' of thirty thousand crowns. Now Margaret had to play both sides, she needed Albany to obtain her divorce from her husband and she needed her brother for his army to protect her and her son, neither of which was forthcoming. All the while, her husband Angus was gaining in popularity. Margaret tried to take the situation into her own hands and offered her husband ten thousand marks if he would agree to a divorce, but he did not respond. She then offered him entry into Edinburgh and an invitation to attend the next Parliamentary meeting. This, Angus did accept, and he took every opportunity to show off, with all his men and support behind him. The opening of Parliament was a display of unity, James entered with his mother, Angus followed behind carrying the crown. It was decided that Margaret would stay with her son at Holyrood, while another peace treaty with England was being negotiated by a new regency council. With no support from her brother and news that Francis I had been captured, the chances of a divorce were low, so Margaret turned back to her husband at Whitsuntide, while still believing something would stop this unwanted reconciliation, as she had already begun an affair with Henry Stewart, who was married and seeking his own divorce.

By having this affair, Margaret had once again upset her brother, as he believed this made him look bad in the European courts, something that did not seem to exercise him much in later years when his own actions did the same. At this point Margaret makes another political mistake in missing the Parliamentary meeting in July, which allowed the councillors to take the one main power Margaret had away from her, her son. James's care would now be delegated to certain men on a rota basis. When it was time for Angus to hand back the king, he did not and arrogated to himself full power over the King of Scotland. Angus had gone too far and luckily for Margaret; people began to turn away from him and switch their allegiance to her.

11

THE SON'S RULE

Margaret planned to get her son back, yet again. The Scottish Parliament meanwhile, knowing that Margaret now had support behind her from the people and most of the council, tried to help, by declaring in June that at the age of fourteen James V was old enough to rule. However, no one could actually get to the boy. Angus had forced him to announce that he was perfectly happy with his stepfather. Nevertheless, the boy had his mother's ingenuity, for he was able to get a few letters out to her explaining his real feelings. Two attempts were made to rescue James, both failed, one ending in the death of the Earl of Lennox.

Margaret was forced to comply with Angus's wishes, if she wished to see her son. Rather than lay low with her lover until events calm down, instead Margaret has her lover, Henry Stewart, the Master of the Scottish Artillery, by her side, even at the

Scottish court ruled by her son under the control of her husband. Here again was family history repeating itself. We have described how Jacquetta of Luxembourg, Margaret's great-grandmother, fell in love with Richard Woodville, a soldier, like Henry Stewart, and not quite of Jacquetta's status, as again Henry Stewart was to Margaret. Jacquetta was not meant to have married without the king's permission, but she knew what she wanted and went for it, nevertheless. Margaret was doing the same here. She was angry at her son's rejection of Henry Stewart and the fiery Tudor temper was raised. From Margaret's perhaps misguided view, she had been through so much, she had done so much for her son while going without herself, that having a man by her side who seemed to love her and was not using her was Margaret's ultimate prize, but she was being denied this.

In this heated row with her son, Margaret left him with Angus and stayed at Stirling Castle. Again, perhaps not the wisest thing to do, as being away from court meant that Margaret did not find out until December 1527 that her divorce had been granted in February that year. Nearly a whole year had passed when technically Margaret was a free woman, and she had not known it. It must have seemed beyond irony to Margaret when, after all those years of her brother pushing her to stay with her husband and not divorce, she finds out that she is finally free of her husband at the same time her brother wants out of his marriage to his first wife.

Margaret's third marriage, to Henry Stewart, was on 3 March 1528. Henry, Lord Methven, was the son of Andrew Stewart, Lord Avondale and his wife Margaret Kennedy. Being a relation to Murdoch Stewart, second Duke of Albany, Henry was actually a relation of Margaret's first husband, James IV of Scotland, they were fourth cousins twice removed. Once again, no matter what

Henry VIII was doing himself, by remarrying Margaret was in his bad books. He writes: '(for) the weal of your soul, avoid eternal damnation. Relinquish the adulterous company of him that is not, nor may not be, of right your husband.'[1] Her son wasn't happy with her either, and it would seem James took more direct action than writing a letter, for on 'his' orders Stirling Castle, where Margaret was, was attacked. Although who actually ordered the attack in James's name is debatable. Angus may have used the king's name to make the attack himself, frustrated that he no longer had access to Margaret's money.

James was still looking for any chance to escape from his stepfather, and one came soon after the attack on Stirling. This could suggest that if James ordered the attack, he did so to make Angus drop his guard for the escape. James was put under the guard of James Douglas at Falkland. With him, the king lied about going to bed early for the next day's hunting and waited until the palace was quiet when he entered the stables, mounted a horse and rode straight to Stirling to be with his mother. This could imply he had not been the one to order the attack on her, however, in escaping the control of Angus, James had nowhere else to go but to his mother.

Not only had Margaret got her son back, but all the nobles of the land were being hostile to Angus. Once the king's flight was discovered, an attempt was made to follow him to Sterling, but with a band of loyal men now behind him, James was able to prevent Angus's men from coming near his person. Margaret and her son rode triumphantly into Edinburgh with all their nobles by their side. In September 1528, Angus was formally accused of treason and of keeping the king against his will, and a bounty of one hundred marks was put on his head.

Both Margaret and her son, now working together and on the same lines as each other, suspected that 'dear uncle Henry' might defend Angus, as he had before. James wrote to Henry to ask if 'Angus or his adherents seek help in England it may be refused'.[2]

There have been many words to describe the famous Tudor king, but, predictable, is usually not one of them, however, this was exactly what he had become to Margaret and the Scottish King. Henry did indeed defend Angus yet again, pressing James to pardon him, but this was refused. James would never forgive his stepfather, but Margaret was, perhaps surprisingly, more tolerant. As long as Angus stayed away from her, her son and Edinburgh, she would be content. As much as Margaret never seemed to be diverted from what she wanted, she also never seemed to change what she wanted, or ask for more. Margaret's son was on the Scottish throne, her new husband was made Lord Methven, meaning he now had lands of his own, Margaret herself was secure in both title and money. Margaret may have felt she could afford to be at least neutral concerning her ex-husband. Though a stronger argument for her behaviour may have been because Angus had taken his and Margaret's daughter, Margaret Douglas, into his care, against Margaret's wishes, so she had to keep him somewhat on side.

Meanwhile, Margaret threw herself into the role of the king's mother and travelled with her son on his summer progress to the Highlands, while also planning the entertainments for the English embassy in 1531. It is possible, after so much trouble, that in these moments of peace, Margaret allowed her guard to be dropped and didn't truly realise what her brother was doing, but her son certainly did. James had managed to find out that his uncle was paying Angus one thousand pounds a year to keep him on side with the English, allowing Angus to travel over the border to raid Scotland. Although these were the underlying issues between uncle and nephew, it is interesting that Margaret still chose to send gentle letters to her brother, even though in Henry's responses he described Margaret, quite openly, as 'the mother of our enemy'.[3] However, when Henry needed Margaret to arrange a meeting with her son after Henry had married his second wife, Anne Boleyn, he was quick to write to her to use her position once again.

From Margaret's point of view, she was just happy to have been asked to be involved in political issues, but her son was less happy with his uncle's request, with many of his council thinking it was a bad idea, especially with Henry's recent break from Rome. Margaret was thinking more of her family. Mary Tudor, Margaret and Henry's sibling, had died in 1533, now Henry and Margaret were the last of King Henry VII and Elizabeth of York's children. Margaret wanted peace for her family, what was left of it. She had chosen to step away from the council meetings, allowing her son to rule, but she still had some sway with her son and by 1536 James had agreed to meet his uncle. Henry suggested they meet in York, while James wanted to meet in Newcastle. James also wanted to know the reason for this meeting and told his uncle he would not be discussing Angus or his uncle's recent title as Supreme Head of the Church of England. His mother had spent twenty thousand pounds on clothing for the occasion. However, James felt pushed into a corner, which caused him eventually to turn on his mother and refuse the meeting at the final moment. Margaret was beginning to realise she had no more control over her son's actions and that might have prompted her statement that she was 'weary of Scotland'.[4]

Margaret turned to her brother to ask for a visit to England and even asked for the money she had spent on the meeting between her son and her brother to be repaid to her. This was rather a bold move considering the situation between her son and Henry, even the situation between her daughter and Henry. For her son had just embarrassed the King of England by not turning up for a meeting that he had promised to attend, and Margaret's daughter, Margaret Douglas had also embarrassed the king. Henry had spent a lot of money on Margaret, so that his niece looked the part at the English court, knowing perhaps that her mother was not in a position to do this for her. However, Margaret Douglas had attached herself to Anne Boleyn's uncle, with Anne Boleyn at this point being executed. aligning herself with any member of Anne's family infuriated Henry, so much so that Henry had Margaret Douglas taken to the Tower of London. One would think that this might not have been the right time for the mother of these two children to have asked for a visit, let alone ask to get her money back for the clothes that she had bought.[5]

Margaret has been accused of abandoning her daughter in favour of her son and heir, but as soon as she had heard that her daughter was in the tower, she wrote to her brother pleading for her daughter's life. Her letter starts strongly, explaining she cannot believe Henry would send his own niece to the tower; however, she warms by the end of the letter, perhaps realising Henry meets force with force, so she then begs for a pardon.[6] Margaret also asked for her daughter to be sent to her. Henry wasn't going to allow that to happen, but as her daughter's health deteriorated inside the tower, Margaret became more and more desperate, writing to Thomas Cromwell, taking a classic

Tudor line by describing her daughter as a valuable item, as she had been written into succession now by Henry and she hadn't consummated her marriage to Thomas Howard. This may sound callous, but Margaret was writing to Cromwell and her brother, and she may have changed tack to suit the way of thinking of her correspondent. To some extent this worked, as Henry did release Margaret Douglas from the tower, however, she was to spend a year with the nuns at Syon Abbey.

Meanwhile, James, King of Scotland had fathered five illegitimate children so far and had not yet married. Margaret wanted to change this and pressed for her son to marry her brother's daughter, Princess Mary. Margaret was not the only one pressing for a marriage for the Scottish King, the Duke of Albany, while in France, suggested that James should marry Catherine de Medici, while James actually wanted to marry his mistress. All three options were dismissed when the King of France proposed three other options, Marie of Guise, Marie of Bourbon and Isabelle of Navarre. At the beginning it was thought that James would marry Marie of Bourbon, so he set sail for France, leaving his mother in a role that she might never have thought she would be in again, Queen Regent of Scotland. In January 1537, Margaret must have felt history was repeating itself, not only had she become Queen Regent again but she had also found out that her husband, Henry Stewart, had been stealing rents from her properties and had housed his mistress in one of them, as Archibald Douglas had done.

The speed with which Margaret asks for another divorce indicates not only the pain she must have felt at another betrayal, but also the strength she still had. Her husband had a mistress and was stealing from her, her brother wasn't replying to her letters, her son was still in France, she felt the council wasn't listening to her and she was without protection and money. Everyone seemed to have moved on, her son was finding a wife, her brother had found a wife that he seemed to like in Jane Seymour and was looking forward to the son he was now bound to have. Was Margaret just a thing of the past?

When Henry eventually took some interest in what was happening over the border, he sent one of his men, Ralph Sadler, to find out more information, giving him just two hundred pounds to give to his sister, in hopes this would be enough to tie her over.[7] When Sadler returned explaining that Margaret was indeed in great difficulty, instead of helping her, Henry sent his man to France to speak to Margaret's son, in hopes that he would be able to help his mother out, rather than Henry having to do it. However, the situation with Margaret's son had changed while he had been in France, he had not in fact married Marie of Bourbon as planned.

On 1 January 1537, James had married King Francis's daughter, Madeleine of Valois in the Notre Dame Cathedral in Paris. This wasn't the King of France's first choice for a match, but finally he had relented, and the newlyweds spent the first few months of their marriage at the French court. This was when Sadler appears in France to tell James of his mother's situation. He did not want to leave France but wrote to his own council for them to sort out her affairs. Meanwhile, Henry had sent a secret envoy to Margaret, and she informed them that she believed her best course of action was to divorce her husband and that she had hoped to spend the rest of her days in England, if her brother would allow it, after she had discussed this with her son.

Her son arrived back in Scotland on 19 May and the country rejoiced at having a new queen. Margaret, now Queen Dowager, had matters to discuss with her son but her needs were put off because of the new Queen of Scotland's health. Madeleine took to her bed at Holyrood Palace and James called for her French doctor. Possibly suffering from tuberculosis, she never recovered and passed away on 7 July. Perhaps, it was the wrong time to ask and for fear that Margaret may return to her previous husband, Angus, but her son refused to grant his mother a divorce. Mother and son argued over this for a long time until Margaret decided, possibly in her rage, to head over the border once again, but did not manage to get much further before her son's men caught up with her and took her back to Stirling Castle. We do know how unhappy Margaret was at this time as she writes to Thomas Cromwell: 'The King, my son is more unkind to me daily and I had rather be dead than treated as I am.'[8]

James was more concerned about fighting against Angus and the Douglas family, being unable to forgive him for the mistreatment he endured from Angus in his youth. James ordered the execution of Angus's sister Janet, after she had been accused of witchcraft, even though there was no evidence against her. Her servants were tortured to lay false charges. James made this death a public burning at Edinburgh Castle, on 17 July 1537, making her young son watch, a sign of how deep his hatred for his stepfather went.

With now both Kings of England and Scotland being widowers, they were both looking for new wives and both sought the hand of Marie of Guise. It was Francis I's choice to make Marie a bride of the Scots rather than a bride of England, but Marie herself was quoted as stating, after she found out that Henry was interested in her and because of her height: 'I may be big in person, but my neck is small.'[9]

A proxy marriage was held at Notre Dame on 18 May 1538. James's representative was Lord Marshall and after this wedding, Marie said her goodbyes to her son Francis by her first husband, knowing in all likelihood she would not see him again. Marie arrived in Scotland on 10 June and James rode out to meet her to take her to St Andrews. After the marriage was blessed, Marie was treated to a tour of James's palaces.

Margaret had made amends with her husband and her son at this point and while enjoying the company of her new daughter-in-law, Margaret became calmer and more pious, something her namesake, Margaret Beaufort, would no doubt have liked. Margaret Tudor seemed to have found some peace but the same could not be said for Margaret's brother, by attempting to annul his marriage to Anne of Cleves and marry Catherine Howard.

In 1540 and 1541 Margaret became a grandmother with the births of James, Duke of Rothesay and Robert, Duke of Albany however both boys passed away within days of each other in April 1541.[10] Margaret wrote to her brother: 'Here hath been great displeasure for the death of the Prince and his brother, both with the King, my dearest son and the queen his wife; wherefore I have done great diligence to put them in comfort'.[11]

In September 1541, it looked as if Margaret would finally see her son and brother meet at York, but once again, at the last minute, Margaret's son changed his mind, and this made Henry very angry. Margaret would never get her wish for peace in the lands she knew. Perhaps, this last trouble with her brother and son also affected Margaret's health, as a month later she took to her bed at Methven Castle, after what would seem to have been a stroke. At first it looked as if she would recover, so she made no will and refused her priests; but her condition worsened and her son was called for. James did not make it in time and Margaret passed away on 18 October 1541.

James arranged a grand funeral for his mother to be held at the Carthusian Abbey of St John in Perth. A woman that saw no lasting peace in her life did not find peace in death, either. During the Scottish Protestant Revolution of 1559, the abbey was ransacked and her tomb destroyed, her remains were burnt and the ashes were scattered on the grounds.

After wanting peace in England and Scotland for most of her life, wanting to complete her father's Henry VII's designs for her, although she would not see it for herself, it would be through her bloodline, through her great grandson King James VI of Scotland, that these two countries would finally unite. For James VI of Scotland also became King James I of England too.

12

FROM CRADLE TO CASTILE – MARY TUDOR

Now we turn to the other Tudor Rose in Henry VIII's early life and who Henry looked more favourably to, compared to the Tudor Rose we have just been discussing. Henry VIII's younger sister Mary Tudor's date of birth was recorded inside Elizabeth of York's Book of Psalms, within the Psalter Volume,[1] and in Margaret Beaufort's Book of Hours, where she wrote: 'Today was born Mary, the third daughter of Henry VII' beside the date of 18 March.[2] With these two rather personal documents stating the same date, we can fairly asssume that Mary Tudor was indeed born on 18 March 1495.[3] However, it is worth also noting the Tudor (Julian) Calendar, which is different from the Gregorian Calendar that we use today, would have made the Tudors class her birth year as 1496.

She was the fifth child and third daughter of King Henry VII and Elizabeth of York.[4] At the time of Mary's birth, her father had been king for eleven years. Elizabeth of York would have given birth without the help of her mother, Elizabeth Woodville this time around, who had been with her daughter for the first three pregnancies but who had passed away in 1492, before Mary was born. So instead, Elizabeth had the midwife, Alice Massey with her, who had helped Elizabeth of York with other births.[5]

It is possible Mary was named after the Virgin Mary, as she was born close to 25 March, the Feast of the Annunciation of the Blessed Virgin. Although there is no record to date of Mary's christening, it's probable that her christening followed the strict rules set out by Mary's grandmother, Margaret Beaufort, rules followed in the previous royal christenings.

She was assigned a wet nurse and moved into the royal nursery at Eltham Palace, where the close relationship she would been known to have later on in her life with her older brother Henry, began.[6] Mary would spend her first seven years at Eltham, under the care and guidance of Elizabeth Denton.[7]

At just two years old, Princess Mary received three pairs of hosen and eight pairs of single-soled shoes.[8] As the princess grew so did her wardrobe and the five-year-old Mary had gained a 'gown of green velvet, edged in purple tinsel and lined with black buck ram; a gown of black velvet edged with crimson; kirtles of tawny damask and black satin edged with black velvet and two pairs of knitted hosen'.[9] This would have been when Mary was given her own household staff, which included teachers, a wardrobe keeper, ladies in waiting, and her own doctor. The latter called frequently as Mary seemed to have a fragile immune system at a young age. The royal apothecary Richard Babbam appeared in the records as receiving payments for giving medicine to Mary from 1504-1509, and Doctor Robert Yaxley was paid thirteen pounds, six shillings, eight pence for his services to Mary over ten weeks in autumn 1513.[10] Sadly, the records do not record what Mary was being treated for, it may have been one of the common childhood illnesses, but we do know that Mary's health was a cause for concern in her later life, which may suggest something different. We can compare Mary's early health issues with the child, that would take Mary's name, Henry VIII's daughter, and Henry's other daughter Elizabeth, both of whom suffered from ill health when young. Perhaps health issues ran in the family, but it may suggest something more than that. When his daughters were ill, Henry may well have been quicker to call the physician than most, for he would have seen and remembered what health problems would had done to his beloved younger sister, Mary. This possibility may give us a unique view of Henry VIII and how his relationships with his three main Tudor Roses of his childhood, that of Elizabeth of York, Margaret of Scotland and Mary of France, could have impacted on Henry's thoughts or indeed actions in later life.

Mary's part of Eltham was decorated in the finery befitting a Tudor princess, with carpets, wall hangings, furniture, blankets, cushions and luxurious bedding. These were signed off by her father Henry VII himself, as he did not skimp on the upbringing of any of his children.[11] At the age of just four, Mary met Desiderius Erasmus at her nursery. He did write of his visit, but he was more interested in Mary's brother, Henry and instead only writes briefly of Mary herself.

This was also when Mary gets her first marriage proposal, to Massimiliano, Count of Pavia, Italy, the son of the well-known Duke Ludovico Sforza, a man who had employed none other than

Leonardo Da Vinci to build aqueducts and who would later appear in paintings depicting Leonardo showing the duke plans of one of his great masterpieces, *The Last Supper*. There is an interesting myth that surrounded the Duke Ludovico with a link to the Tudors. When he was young, he was said to have had a 'commoner' playmate by the name of Cesarino della Gnona. One day they decided to change places and this is said to have formed the basis for the book, *The Prince and the Pauper* by Mark Twain, however in that story the author changes the main characters to be Edward VI, Henry VIII's son, and Tom Canty, a London pauper.[12]

In asking for a marriage between his son and Mary Tudor, the duke was of course hoping for an alliance with England as the duke was against France at this point[13]. However, at this time England and France were at peace, and although the duke had a wealthy Italian state, it was possible Mary's father wanted more for his daughter. Ever the diplomat, Henry VII may have used the excuse that Mary was too young to marry her to the duke's son.

As we have mentioned, Henry VII saw in his daughters the opportunity to help cement his dynasty, as they would become future players on the international marriage stage. For Mary, this would not be any different than it was for Margaret, and Mary's education was of the highest quality. She learned French and Latin with a number of tutors including John Palsgrave.[14] John would later travel with Mary when she was to marry the King of France in 1514, and would then become a tutor to King Henry VIII's illegitimate son, Henry Fitzroy.[15] Mary would also be taught, like her mother, her grandmother and indeed her great grandmother before her, the art of dancing, singing, playing cards, embroidery and playing a musical instrument.[16] Mary could also play the lute and the clavichord, like her mother and older brother Henry.

When Mary turned six, she would have seen political issues played out in front of her during a visit of Juana of Castile, the sister to Katherine of Aragon, and Juana's husband, Prince Philip, to England. Mary showed off her dancing skills and presented herself as a polite young princess to the other nobles, something she would continue to do for the rest of her life.[17]

In 1499, Mary's brother, called Edmund, was born, but he would only survive for fifteen months. In 1500, there was another match proposed for Mary, to Philip, Duke of Burgundy's son Charles, who was just four months old. Mary's brother received a marriage proposal to the duke's eldest daughter Eleanor at the same time, these tow marriage proposals were to be a part of a friendship treaty with hopes that Henry VII would be able strengthen England's power in Europe with it.[18] However, the Burgundian alliance did not last long and the duke would seek a French bride for his son instead of Mary Tudor. Within five years however, the Tudor family would be returning to this treaty and Mary's hopes of marrying Charles, the future Holy Roman Emperor.

The following years, Mary would have to have coped with changes within her family. For example, Mary would gain a sister-in-law, in the Spanish Princess Katherine of Aragon. Their friendship would continue into Mary's adult life. Mary would have first seen Katherine when she made her formal entry into London on 12 October 1501. On the 14th, Mary attended the wedding of her eldest brother Arthur to Katherine at St Paul's Cathedral. On 24 October 1502, her eldest sister Margaret married King James IV of Scotland. Two months later, on 2 April 1502, Prince Arthur died.

Although there is no record of Mary attending her brother's funeral in Elizabeth of York's accounts, like their mother, the daughters wore black for the rest of the year.[19] As the family grieved for Arthur, Elizabeth gave birth again on Candlemas Day, 2 February 1503, but as mentioned previously, both mother and child did not survive for long.

So much had happened to Mary in such a small space of time. Mary was too young to understand everything at seven years old, but she was old enough to understand the impact of Arthur's death, which must have changed her father's outlook. Perhaps, Mary saw a physical difference in her father. The stress of keeping his throne secure may have taken a toll. In her mother, Elizabeth of York, in mourning black, the change was more noticeable, following the stress of carrying her last child. With these changes in her parents and the fact that her oldest sister was leaving soon to go to Scotland, it may well have been natural for Mary to cling on to her eldest brother, Henry. This helps to explain the singular relationship Mary was to have with one of England's most notorious monarchs.

Three years after the death of Elizabeth of York, marriage for Mary was once again on the agenda. On 16 January 1506, Philip, once Duke of Burgundy but now King of Castile after his marriage to Katherine of Aragon's sister, was sailing to Spain when the wind blew his ship off course and on to the English shores. Henry VII used this piece of good fortune to his advantage and welcomed his royal guests with open arms. The royal couple would be in England for three months while their ship was being repaired, and Henry used the time to renew their previous friendship treaty, and this of course also reintroduced the possible marriage for Mary.[20]

On Sunday 1 February 1506, at Windsor Castle Mary was presented to her now future father-in-law. It was Mary's chance to show off her skills, knowledge and beauty to her new family and by all accounts, she made a good impression.[21] The Treaty of Windsor was signed on 9 February 1506 and Philip and Joanna left England on 23 April 1506. Philip died in the same year and his wife was then claimed to be unfit to rule. Still, Henry VII pushed for the treaty to be upheld and for Charles to marry his daughter.[22] To remind everyone that Mary was meant to marry Charles, there was a jousting celebration in the May and June of 1507, ostensibly in memory of Philip and Joanna's visit to England the previous year. Sixteen-year-old Prince Henry was allowed to organise the jousts. The event points to an affection on his part for his sister, as it was held at Henry's own manor at Kennington and he made sure Mary was the star of the event.[23]

Mary played the role of Dawn Summer Lady May, dressed in a gown of green embroidered with spring flowers, and was surrounded by her ladies, also in green. As the Lady May, the eleven-year-old Mary addressed the whole assembly:

> Most highe and excellent Princess under your patient support by which I am called the Ladye Mave in all monethes of the yeare to lustye hearts most pleasant certifie your Highness have under signe and scale fully authorized by the hand of my Ladye and Sovraigne Dame Somer; I have free licence during the tyme of my short Raine to passe my tyme and a ffortnight in the month of my sister June as shal be to my comfort and most solace. Wherefore I have sailed in the soaring seas I have cast out myne anchor under the support of your … licence to rest me and my said servants which have long been travailed in the stormy seas sons of March and April for I see in mynde that noble courageous hearts are determined to have my Ladye Somer in exercise of Chivalric.[24]

A chivalrous address. The jousts were held between two o'clock and six o'clock, the period defined by the church bells, and while the courtiers would charge at each other to break their opponents' lances, Mary sat surrounded by flowers, the emblem of the Tudors and the Tudor colours of green and white, in the pavilion overlooking the action.[25]

Henry and Mary's relationship here seem close. The public had lost Prince Arthur, Elizabeth of York and Princess Margaret to Scotland now, but in Mary and Henry they saw the Tudor future. Conceivably, this made Henry VII yesterday's man. How did Mary feel? She had just lost her mother and her father seemed distant. However, here, at this event, her brother Henry was showing he cared for her. Was Henry making Mary feel important and special? Did this make her latch on to her brother far more than any other woman did? Did Henry like this feeling, or at the very least, enjoy being her knight in shining armour? Did this form a trust, a bond, so that when later Mary went against her brother's wishes, it shocked him all the more?

On 21 December 1507, Henry VII signed a treaty with the Holy Roman Emperor Maximilian.[26] One part of this treaty focused on Mary's upcoming marriage to Charles, in which the families on both sides haggled over the cost, who was going to pay for what and when.[27] At this point, Henry VII was continuing the plans he and his wife had formulated for their children. Margaret was being married to Scotland, Henry was in the process of being married to Katherine of Aragon through negotiations, and Mary would be married to Charles V; England seemed to be gaining more and more strength in Europe.

A year later, on 17 December 1508 at Richmond Palace, her father's favourite home, Mary was married by proxy to Charles.

For this occasion, the Great Hall of Richmond was covered in silk and every chance was taken to exhibit Henry VII's wealth. Mary arrived with her sister-in-law, Katherine of Aragon, and her ladies.[28] Sieur de Bergues stood in for the young Charles and they exchanged vows before the Archbishop of Canterbury. Afterwards, the royal party attended high Mass at the Chapel Royal, with a feast and wine flowing.[29] There was another joust in which Mary, now the Princess of Castile, sat next to her sister-in-law, another Princess of Spain.[30] While the royal family celebrated, so did the rest of the capital with bonfires being lit and people dancing in the streets, music playing late into the night.[31] Henry VII made his son-in-law a Knight of the Garter, and the day after the proxy marriage Charles wrote in French to Mary: 'My dear companion, with good grace and as cordially as I can, I recommend myself to you. I have charged my Lord of Bergues and my other ambassadors, orders to your country to inform you of the good tidings, which is the thing I most desire, as knows the blessed Son of God, whom I pray, my good mate, to give you by his grace your heart's desires.'[32] All seemed to be going well, from England's side of things anyway, but from the groom's own family, it seemed less so.

King Ferdinand of Aragon, the father of Katherine of Aragon and grandfather of Charles V, was not happy that no plans had been made for his daughter Katherine to marry into the English royal family, even though Katherine was still living in England, yet Mary Tudor was being married into his royal family.[33] He felt that the friendship between England and Spain was now bypassing him and his daughter in favour of his grandson and Henry VII's daughter. So unhappy was King Ferdinand that in April 1509 he wrote a letter to Henry VII accusing him of acting in a high-handed manner because Katherine remained in England and so was under his control. King Ferdinand had had enough of Henry VII demanding more and more from Spain, and it was clear that this Spanish king was beginning to withdraw from the friendship treaty between the two countries. He was now asking for something in return, he wanted his daughter, Katherine, to be married to the future King Henry VIII first, and then he would consider a marriage between Charles and Mary. If Henry VII did not agree to this, Katherine was to return to Spain.[34] However, regardless of how King Ferdinand felt about the marriage and the fact that Charles had entered the marriage as a minor, which could suggest he had no say in it, and that he was too young to have consummated the marriage, a 'proxy' marriage had already taken place, which meant that Mary was the Princess of Castile, even without seeing her husband Charles.

By 19 March 1509, Henry VII had drawn up his will and paid the forty shillings to do so.[35] His heir was in a position to take over, his daughter Margaret was Queen of Scotland and he believed he had secured Mary's position as Queen of Spain. In his will he states that once Charles reached the age of maturity, the marriage could be consummated, and he set aside fifty thousand pounds for Mary's dowry that would be paid by him or by his heirs.[36] It is interesting to note that Henry states in his will that should the marriage end through Charles's death, Mary's dowry should stay with her to her next marriage; this would suggest that he certainly saw his daughter as very important to the future security of the realm and his legacy.

13

FROM A TUDOR ROSE TO A FRENCH LILY

King Henry VII died on 21 April 1509, at his favourite palace of Richmond. His passing was kept from the public for two days before it was announced after supper on St George's Day.[1] In the funeral procession Mary wore new clothes[2] and rode a horse covered in black velvet. Her father was buried in the Lady Chapel at Westminster Abbey, next to his wife Elizabeth of York. We can imagine Mary was grief stricken, even if she did not know her father that well. But with every royal passing there was a shift in the dynamics of the family unit, with titles and roles changing, and Mary had to learn very quickly she was now the king's sister and must obey her brother's rule.

Mary watched her brother's coronation procession from a window in a room that her grandmother, Margaret Beaufort, had rented for the day in Cheapside, at the cost of two shillings and ten pence.[3] She must have been proud to see the brother she had doted on throughout her childhood becoming the King of England. Perhaps, this made Mary think ahead to her own marriage, when she would become a queen. Her brother was crowned with his new Queen Consort, Katherine of Aragon, on 24 June 1509 at Westminster Abbey. The celebrations were cut short however, as just five days later Margaret Beaufort died. The death of their grandmother may have hit Henry and his sisters hard; Margaret had been a constant presence for the siblings, but now the past was gone. Henry VIII and his sisters were the future of the Tudor dynasty.

Mary may well have felt isolated at this point when we consider that her parents had died, her influential grandmother had died, her older sister was now Queen of Scotland with her own family, and now her older brother had become King of England and was a married man. However, Mary was not forgotten. Henry VIII wanted his favourite sister at court, and when she wasn't there, he would send her gifts.[4] Back at court, Mary spent a lot of time with her brother and his wife, enjoying regular court entertainments.[5]

In October 1509, the wardrobe records tell us that Henry sent gowns to his sister,[6] and again on 5 November the following year. Buying clothes for his favourite sister became a habit that continued into late 1513, when a new treaty was signed between Henry VIII and Margaret of Austria, Mary's future husband's aunt. In this treaty, a location and date was set for Mary's wedding day with Charles V, Calais in 1514.[7]

During this time, Charles was writing to Mary, telling her of his health and asking after hers[8] and Mary must have felt well cared for by her brother also, for he was going out of his way to make sure the final steps toward her marriage was being taken. He was providing her with attire worthy of a Tudor rose, but also for the role of the Princess of Castile that she would become. Henry paid for a gold coronet for her to wear on her wedding day and ensured her rooms were well appointed, with gold plate, china, tapestries, cushions, chests, carpets and damask curtains. Mary also had two gentlewomen who slept with her and about a hundred people to serve her.[9]

There was a stark difference in Henry's behaviour towards the sister he saw on a constant basis compared to the sister in Scotland. Can this tell us something of Henry VIII's general behaviour, that when a person was face to face with Henry, he could be polite, courteous and often generous, but the moment a person left his presence, Henry's attention span was limited, and he felt he had the freedom to be as cold or as cruel as he wished? This might explain his constant need to be entertained by the circle of courtiers around him, why they knew they had to keep Henry interested in them, for if the king tired of them, they would drop from his 'gravitational' pull, running the risk of attack. Did he do this with his sister, Margaret, and are the fates of Thomas More, Thomas Wolsey, Thomas Cromwell, or even Anne Boleyn, examples of this behavioural trait?

Mary seemed to have everything, but six years into her role as Princess of Castile, her future grandfather-in-law, Maximilian I, started to make some abstruse excuses as to why his grandson Charles could not marry Mary. They included Charles catching a fever from the moon.[10] This was also around the time that the Holy League was formed. The Holy League was an alliance of the Holy Roman Empire, the Papal States, Spain and England against France, after the invasion of Italy by the French King

Charles VIII.[11] Maximilian kept claiming his empire was poor and needed funds from Henry so that they could go to war together.[12] This frustrated Henry and, in addition, he felt betrayed by his father-in-law, King Ferdinand, as he didn't hold up his end of the agreement to provide England with support from Spain in the war against France. Then King Ferdinand signed a one-year truce with France, this was not hardly what Henry wanted his father-in-law to do.[13] Henry was growing more and more angry, so the delay of Mary's marriage could not have come at a worse time. Henry began to look away from the Roman Empire and towards making his own treaty with France instead. King Louis XII of France, Charles VIII's successor, was eager for Henry VIII to do this, and for this alliance to go ahead Mary would play an important, but to her, unexpected role. Mary would marry the French King, becoming Queen Consort of France.[14]

Louis XII of France was an interesting choice of husband for Henry VIII's favourite sister. Louis was born on 27 June 1462 in the Château de Blouis in Tourane, to Charles, Duke of Orléans and Maries of Cleves.[15] Louis was only three years old when his father died, making him the Duke of Orléans in 1465.[16] At the age of fourteen Louis was pushed into marrying the French King Louis XI's daughter, Joan. It was believed that Joan had a disability, similar to Richard III but perhaps more pronounced, as she was said to have walked with a limp and had a hump on her back, suggesting a curvature of the spine.[17] It was thought that this disability would mean that Joan would not be able to have children, and by marrying Louis off to her, the King of France had hoped to cancel out the Orléans part of his royal house of Valois.[18] However, when Louis XI passed away and his son, Charles VIII, who had previously helped Henry VII when he left Brittany to make his claim to the English throne, passed away also without an heir, Charles's cousin Louis was the closest relative to the French throne and so he became Louis XII in 1498. One year later, Louis asked for a papal dispensation to annul his marriage to Joan and immediately married Anne of Brittany, the previous French King's widow. She had been previously promised in marriage to Edward V, one of the Princes in the Tower, Mary's uncle.[19] By marrying Anne, Louis had held on to the peace between Brittany and the rest of France. They married on 7 January 1499, with her second coronation as Queen of France on 18 November 1504, at St Denis Basilica.[20] When ten years later Anne died without giving her husband a male heir but two daughters, Louis cemented his power, as Henry VII did with his daughters, Margaret and Mary. Louis married his daughter Claude to Francis, son of Charles, Count of Angoulême and married Renée to Ercole II, Duke of Ferrara.[21] However, without a son to be his heir, Louis was keen to marry again.

Louis was always considered to be sickly and fragile ever since he had come to the throne aged thirty-eight, and when he married Mary, Louis was fifty-two and suffering from gout.[22] Mary's dowry was set at fifty thousand crowns, and on 30 July 1514 Mary formally renounced her marriage to Prince Charles of Spain. Mary married Louis by proxy on 13 August 1514 at the Great Hall at Greenwich Palace. Mary wore a 'petticoat of ash-coloured satin and a gown of purple satin and cloth of gold in chequers; she wore a cap of cloth of gold and chains and jewels like the Queen.'[23] The wedding was presided over by William Warham, Archbishop of Canterbury and when the ceremony was over, Mary had to go through the ritual of allowing the Duke of Longueville, who was standing in for King Louis in the proxy wedding, to touch

Mary with his naked leg, symbolising the consummation of the marriage.[24] Mary then attended high Mass with her brother and his wife, after which was a banquet, where Henry and the Duke of Buckingham danced for two hours.[25] Mary had been focused on marrying Charles of Spain, having been titled Princess of Castile for six years. Now, at the command of her brother, she was to be made Queen Consort of France instead. Did she feel anger towards her brother for changing her life so much? Did she feel that she was a pawn in a political game?

She started receiving gifts from her new husband of plate, seals and of jewellery. One piece of jewellery was a very large diamond with a pear-shaped pearl in the centre, known as the 'Mirror of Naples'. Louis also sent an artist named Jean Perreal to paint a portrait of Mary.[26] As a queen she would have had ladies to command within her own household and be highly respected, so of course there were positives to being the Queen of France. She was a subject of the King of England whether the king was her brother or not and as such had to do his bidding. There really was no choice for Mary, regardless of how she personally felt.

Within two months of her proxy marriage, Mary would be Queen Consort of France, there would be no waiting for years to meet her husband this time. Mary was considered to be very beautiful. Before Louis had seen Mary, he was already describing her as a 'nymph from heaven' because of all he had heard and read from other people who had met her.[27] Beauty was something famed in Mary's family, Elizabeth of York and Elizabeth Woodville were well known for their looks and according to the descriptions of Mary, she seems to have inherited them, as well as her height, like her brother, from her grandfather, Edward IV. As was the norm, now that her marriage to King Louis was formalised Mary begins to write letters to her husband: 'I now most desire and wish to hear good news of your health and good prosperity. By the hand of your very humble companion, Mary.'[28]

Henry once again showed his love for his sister, as he made sure her wardrobe was fit for a queen to travel with to her new country, spending a huge amount, reported by some to have been over £40,000.[29] As well as clothing, hangings and tapestries from Brussels travelled with her, some portraying scenes from the story of Hercules. She would also travel with an array of jewellery, including gold chains and bejewelled rings, brooches and bracelets.[30] With all this, Mary would look every inch a queen when Henry 'gave' her to the French. One could imagine Henry wanted his sister to look her best, but was there also an element of letting the people of France know how important Mary was to Henry personally? They were close, they had each other when both parents had died and now Henry VIII was perhaps feeling like a proud father, handing her over to become Queen of France. Another item that travelled with Mary, an indication of Mary's main role in becoming Queen Consort of France, was a cradle 'covered with scarlet without a frame'.[31]

Mary would also have had a number of ladies travelling with her to France, as Henry had sent the word out to all his nobles to find ladies of good reputation that could speak French. Two were the daughters of Thomas and Elizabeth Boleyn, Mary and Anne.[32] John Palsgrave, Mary's old schoolmaster, now turned secretary, also accompanied her, along with Thomas Howard, Duke of Norfolk, the Marquess of Dorset, the Bishop of Durham and the Earl of Surrey.[33] There was another person, central to Mary's future life, travelling with her; Charles Brandon, the Duke of Suffolk.[34]

Charles's place with the Tudor dynasty was set from the moment his father, Sir William Brandon, died at the Battle of Bosworth, standing beside the future Henry VII as his standard-bearer. As reward for the bravery his father had shown Henry, his son was brought up in the new royal court of Henry VII, and was able to get to know and become the future Henry VIII's closest friend. He was rewarded by the Tudor court, becoming Master of the Horse in 1513 and he would gain much land. In that same year he became Viscount Lisle,[35] as he had entered into a marriage contract with his ward, Elizabeth Grey, who was only eight years old at the time. As the daughter of John Grey, Second Viscount Lisle she inherited his and Lady Muriel Howard's considerable fortune on John's death in 1504.[36]. Being a constant at the Tudor court did not just mean Charles was within Henry VIII's orbit, the other children of Henry VII and Elizabeth of York would have known of Charles Brandon, too, including Mary Tudor.

Mary would leave London on 23 September 1514. However, at Dover, a terrible storm rolled in, leaving Mary, her ensemble and her brother unable to travel until the storm had passed. It was apparently at this moment that Mary makes a bold move for which she would go down in history. Mary asks her brother if her husband should die before her, 'She would be free to choose her next husband herself'. With hindsight, this can sound like pure fantasy. However, in a later letter Mary does write to her brother describing this scene at Dover, very much reminding her brother of it, so there is evidence for her words.[37]

Such prescience shows Mary had strength, perhaps we could suggest her certain Tudor or Woodville strength. There was intelligence in the timing. Henry needed her to become Queen

Consort of France, he could not go back on this now without making himself and his country look incredibly bad in political terms, so he could not really say no to his sister. In Mary's boldness and intellect, did Henry VIII recognise his beloved mother, Elizabeth of York, in his younger sister? This may be another reason for their greater intimacy compared to Henry's relationship with his other sister, Margaret.

There could be another comparison made here. She was challenging Henry. Does this, ironically considering these two women were inimical in later life, remind us of Anne Boleyn? Mary was implying, in 1514, that should her husband die, should a *king* die, she would like to choose her next husband. This is echoed in what Anne Boleyn was meant to have said in 1536 to the Tudor courtier, Henry Norris: 'You look for dead men's shoes. For if aught came to the King but good, you would look to have me.'[38] There was of course one major difference in these statements: the timing. Mary's foresight in seeing a king's death was expressed before the Treason Act of 1534 and Anne Boleyn's imagining a king's death happened after it. The act made it treasonable to deny the Act of Supremacy. The act also made Henry VIII 'the Head of the Church on Earth so far as the law of God allows', and to deny this, would be punishable by death. However, it introduced a sort of blanket interdiction so that anyone who refused to accept Henry and Thomas Cromwell's policies could face death. If anyone maliciously wishes, desires in words or writing, imagines, invents or attempts to do bodily harm to the king, queen or the heirs apparent, they are acting treasonably. In 1534, the queen in question was Anne Boleyn and the heir was her daughter Elizabeth.

So, an act that had been passed to protect Anne Boleyn, was also ultimately the tool used against her. This was because Anne's purported words could have been seen as the play of courtly love and this may well have been Anne's intention, but on the other hand these words could be taken as if she had imagined the king's death and because of which, she would eventually be accused of adultery, incest and treason. The first two would not be reasons for the death sentence, the last, as we have discussed, was. Wishing or imagining a king's death, even in a few wrongly chosen words, was treason. 'You look for dead men's shoes' was a simple line, possibly said in jest, but was ammunition that helped to bring about Anne Boleyn's downfall. Mary Tudor, twenty-two years before, had been free to hint at the same thing.

On 2 October 1514, the storm had passed and Mary was able to travel and by 4 October had arrived in France, where she was greeted by the Cardinal d' Ambroise and the Duke of Vendôme.[39] Over the next few days, Mary travelled slowly through France, through towns such as Montreuil, Abbeville and Etaples, where Mary was welcomed.[40] Mary was entertained with many pageants, stories of Apollo and Diana, of Andromeda and Perseus and Solomon and the Queen of Sheba.[41]

Then came a piece of royal theatre. Louis wanted to meet his new bride; however, it was tradition that a French king should not see his bride before the wedding. They could however, meet accidently, so the king 'innocently' went hawking near to where Mary was based. Knowing the part, she had to play in this, Mary faked surprise at seeing the king, even though she happened to be wearing the same colours as he was. The king then wrapped his arms around Mary and kissed her.[42] After this, the king left Mary to continue her journey as planned.

The wedding was held on 9 October 1514.[43] Mary wore a French gown made from gold brocade, trimmed with ermine and many jewels.[44] Louis was wearing an outfit that matched Mary's in style and colour. Once the ceremony was over, Mary curtseyed to her new husband and the couple shared a kiss.[45] Mary was finally a married woman; she had been transformed from her brother's Tudor rose into a French lily. Now her status in the world equalled that of her siblings.

14

QUEEN AND DUCHESS

As soon as Mary and Louis XII were married, Mary's new husband wanted to send her English ladies-in-waiting back home, believing they might be spying for Henry VIII. Mary had only been married for three days and to lose all the faces she had known must have hit her hard. Mary wrote many letters, to her brother and to Thomas Wolsey, in the hope they could change her husband's mind. To try to make up for his decision, Louis gave Mary even more jewellery.[1] Eventually, the king did allow some of Mary's ladies to stay with her, including 'Madamoyselle Boleyne'.[2] This is interesting, as we know later that Mary voiced her critical opinion of Anne Boleyn. Perhaps her dislike of Anne had begun when she knew her at a young age.

Charles Brandon was still with Mary's ensemble at this point, ostensibly as a participant in the jousts in celebration of Mary's future coronation, but he was also there to convince Louis to work with England against Ferdinand of Aragon after Henry was betrayed by him. Henry also had bad feelings towards Ferdinand because Henry had also thought that with the death of Isabella of Castile, Castile would be divided equally between Isabella's daughters, one of which happened to be Henry's wife, Katherine of Aragon.[3] Charles Brandon wrote to Henry explaining that when he met with the king, who was still ill, he was lying in his bed. He also mentions that Mary was sitting beside her husband during this meeting. Charles mentions that the king was very pleased with Mary, calling her 'the greatest jewel'. Charles's real reason for being there was not mentioned in the letter, when there could have been a chance of someone else reading it. Any information about his assignment would have been given to Henry in person. What this letter does reveal however, is that Mary was acting as a dutiful and caring wife. Perhaps Mary wanted to make her brother proud of her performance in the first role he had given her.

The couple's journey to Paris was a slow one due to Louis's ill health and Mary would continue to be the caring wife, sitting by his side, singing and playing the lute for him.[4] It was noted that the king could not bear to be without Mary.[5] The English ambassadors wrote to Henry, mentioning how well Mary was being received and he in turn, wrote to Louis expressing his happiness that the king liked his sister, adding, 'We gave her advice and counsel, before her departure from us.'[6] It's a characteristic Henrician interpretation; the truth was probably that Mary's behaviour was born of her education, tutors, mother and grandmother's teaching, rather than anything her brother may have said to her before she left England.

Mary's coronation had to take place in the Cathedral of St Denis, as it was a French custom that no uncrowned queen should enter Paris. She was crowned on Sunday 5 November 1514. Mary was led through the cathedral by Francis d' Angoulême to a cushion in front of the high altar. Cardinal de Brie anointed her with oil before placing the Royal Sceptre in her right hand and the Rod of Justice in her left. The Cardinal then placed a ring on Mary's finger and the Matrimonial Crown of France upon her head.[7] All three of Henry's roses were queens, his mother had been Queen Consort of England, his sister Margaret had been made Queen Consort of Scotland and now his sister Mary was Queen Consort of France. Henry VII and Elizabeth of York's mission was complete.

Although this coronation was a fairly low-key event, Mary's entrance into Paris certainly made up for it. She arrived at nine o'clock in an open carriage covered in Cloth of Gold wearing a gown of gold brocade with many jewels.[8] Tapestries were hung in the streets of Paris and the whole town was covered in images of English roses and French lilies; the people came out to see their new queen. As Mary travelled through the city, she was greeted with many pageants and choirs. A pageant of Solomon and the Queen of Sheba represented the wisdom of Mary's husband, the four virtues represented in different forms. The gods and goddesses of Phoebus, Minerva, Stella Maris, Concord and Diana were also represented, all entwined with the symbolism of the English rose and the French lily. Mary's procession ended at the Notre Dame, where she met with doctors, lawyers and members of the church before she entered the cathedral. When she entered, the bells started to ring, and she was formally welcomed into the city by the archbishop.

By six o'clock in the evening, Mary had returned to the Palace Royale.[9] Now it was time to feast. Inside the palace in the very large Grande Salle a banquet was held, which included a mechanical phoenix that beat its wings until it ignited while the dishes were being served. Louis had retired earlier in the evening, but even Mary had fallen asleep. She had to be carried to her rooms.[10] Mary soon wrote to her brother, telling him that her husband seemed loving and kind to her. She ends the letter by addressing herself as Henry's 'loving sister' rather than the Queen of France.[11] She is playing to Henry's ego here, she had learned how to deal with her brother.

Louis was still very ill and by the end of December, Mary probably knew time with her new husband was going to be short. She still did her duty, keeping the king entertained with her wit, conversation, singing and playing the lute. Louis died on 1 January 1515.[12] Events moved very quickly after this and when Mary was told of her husband's death, she apparently fainted. She had only been married for eighty-two days, now she was the Dowager Queen of France, who must retire from royal French court life and, as a widow of France, wear white. As was tradition, Mary shut herself away from public view for forty days at the Hôtel de Cluny in the Rue des Mathurins St Jacques, to reveal whether she was pregnant.[13] Mary was in a foreign country, alone, with no man to support her. Mary writes to her brother and Thomas Wolsey suggesting that to save face she might have to marry someone of lower rank than her. This was pertinent when we know who Mary was to marry next. However, instead of mentioning who she had in mind, she was presenting herself as a weak woman who needed a strong man to guide her through this lonely time, and that was the only reason she would consider marrying again and marrying someone of lower rank. Mary was preparing the ground before she took the step she knew would infuriate her brother.

Thomas Wolsey's response was that she was not alone, Henry would not forsake her and that she was not to do anything in a hurry; and he particularly mentions that she must refuse any offers of marriage unless she had spoken with her brother.[14] Wolsey was perhaps sensing something was afoot. Over the years of working within the Tudor court, he did get to know the children of Henry VII and Elizabeth of York very well. Perhaps he had known of the conversation Mary had with her brother in Dover, or even of the relationship Mary had with a childhood friend, Charles Brandon.

Although Wolsey was writing to Mary with good intentions, he may have forgotten that he was writing to another Tudor, for although her response was polite, the tone was sharp. Mary's point of view was that she had done nothing but her brother's wishes and that alone deserved her brother's love, no matter what she did from now on: 'You will not reckon in me such childhood.' She signed the letter, 'By your loving friend, Mary Queen of France'.[15] From Mary's forceful response, it looks as if she had already made up her mind, she had played Henry's puppet for long enough, now this Tudor rose would have her own life. Henry possibly misjudged his sister at this time, seeing her as the little sister that she was when he last saw her, not believing she would take matters into her own hands.

Henry meanwhile wrote to the new King of France, Francis I, letting him know that he was sending men to bring Mary home.[16] The men that were chosen to collect Mary were Nicholas West, Sir Richard Wingfield and Charles Brandon, Duke of Suffolk.[17] What makes Henry's choice of Charles Brandon interesting is the suggestion that Henry had apparently warned Charles before he left to not do anything foolish – marrying Mary in France – if he wanted to, he must wait until back on English soil.[18] It has often been thought that the marriage of Mary Tudor and Charles Brandon came as a surprise to everyone and caught Henry VIII on the back foot, but from this warning and other evidence this is probably untrue. Two friars from England were sent to Mary before Charles got there to try and change Mary's mind about Brandon. They told her the King's Council would never consent to such a marriage. Charles wrote to Wolsey, stating he believed the friars must surely have been coached to say that to Mary by the Duke of Norfolk, starting a rivalry between the two men.[19]

In addition, we have the fact that even in Mary's period of recent widowhood, she writes to her brother to remind him of his promises and she mentions it early on in the letter:

> Sir, I beseech your grace that you will keep all the promises that you promised me when I took my leave of you by the waterside. Sir, your grace knoweth well that I did marry for your pleasure at this time, and now I trust that you will suffer me to marry as me liketh for to do.

The letter continues in a similar vein.[20] With all this taken into consideration, that Henry VIII had no idea of what may happen between Mary and Charles seems almost impossible, so the fact that Henry still sends Charles to collect Mary is intriguing.

When Charles arrived in Paris on 31 January 1515, he was faced with two problems. The first was the fact that Henry also sent Charles to collect Mary's plate and jewellery. However, if the jewellery was given to Mary as queen, rather than being personal gifts, it was the property of France rather than Mary's. Secondly, once Charles arrived, he found Francis I did not want to give up

Mary Tudor. He could use her for his own political ends; as a beautiful, eighteen-year-old widow, Mary was a valuable asset.

It seems that sometime soon after Charles arrived in Paris, Mary and Charles did in fact marry without the consent of Henry. The facts surrounding this clandestine wedding day are of course sparse. However, we do know they married at the Chapel in Cluny, between 31 January when Charles arrived in Paris and 3 February 1515, as this is the date Charles writes to Wolsey, telling him that the King of France now knows of their marriage.[21]

Charles seems to have been quite frantic over the action he and Mary had taken and writes to Henry explaining his actions and pleading with him for forgiveness.[22] As for Mary, she had put a stop to either Francis or Henry using her in their political games. Mary had played her brother well here. In a letter to her brother, after she knew that Henry knew of her marriage, she puts the blame at the King of France's door. She had only married Charles to stop Francis from marrying her off to one of his nobles. The thought of Francis doing this to his own sister and probably even worse, gaining the upper hand, would have alarmed him, and if looked at in this way, in marrying Charles Brandon Mary was still being a loyal sister. Once again, like Margaret, it is the king's sister who understands his thinking better than most. Mary plays up to the fact that she was being pushed and pulled in all directions, that she was just a helpless female and by marrying Charles Brandon she was, in the long run, protecting England and her brother. Mary hoped that by showing how important Henry still was to her, she could calm any anger her actions may have evoked. We have no letter from Henry in response, but we do have a letter from Wolsey that explained what the king wanted before allowing the couple to return to England. In return for

Henry allowing the couple to remain married and return, Henry demanded all of Mary's money, plate and jewellery.[23]

As the days went on and with no word from Henry himself, the couple were getting desperate. Mary offered her 'Mirror of Naples' diamond to her brother hoping to get a response. However, as this was the diamond given to Mary by the previous King of France, Francis argued that it wasn't Mary's to give, it belonged to France.[24] Francis stating that the King of England could not have the precious item did evoke a response in Henry and he began to fight for his sister, or her diamond at any rate.[25]

It is hard to know Henry's true feelings about his sister's actions, as he was a great showman. The actions of the couple were treasonable and Charles Brandon had broken a promise to the king.[26] But more importantly, Henry had to display his control, so he had to punish them. Henry 'won' against his sister by taking all her money and jewels, but once everything was more settled Mary's tone in her letters to her brother had changed. Once she had signed them as a 'loving sister', now she was 'Mary, Queen of France'. From this point on, Mary could see herself as on a par with her older brother.

While still in France, the couple had another wedding day that was less secret, on 31 March 1515.[27] The marriage left the couple in limbo, Francis had no use for Mary and the couple could not return home without her brother's permission. Mary once again took matters into her own hands by choosing to leave Paris on 16 April and head for the English owned Calais. The couple then waited at Calais for consent to travel to England.[28] Finally, Henry gave his permission, Mary was after all, now on English soil. On 2 May 1515, Mary Tudor arrived at Dover with a new husband and new titles, Mary Dowager Queen Consort of France and Duchess of Suffolk.

15

FROM CLOTH OF GOLD TO CASTLE GREEN

Mary Tudor and Charles Brandon met up with Henry VIII near Birling Manor[1] and the royal ensemble travelled together towards London, where Mary and Charles were to have yet another wedding day, their third, on 13 May 1515 at Greenwich Palace and this time it was in the presence of Henry and Katherine of Aragon.[2] Mary and Charles had to sacrifice a lot for this to happen. Not only did Mary have to hand back her entire dowry, the couple had to pay a twenty-four thousand pound fine and Charles had to give up his wardship of Lady de Lisle, which meant losing all his rights to her property.

The Duchess of Suffolk was the lady of the manor at Suffolk Place in London, a large mansion along what is now Borough High Street in Southwark. If it still existed, it would be close to the famous Borough Market and the Victorian Marshalsea prison, known for once housing the parents of Charles Dickens, and opposite St George the Martyr Church. Mary's home had turrets and cupolas and it was much grander and larger than the other two-storey buildings along the same street. It was handily placed on the road from London to Dover, making it ideal for hosting a royal foreign visit, as it did in 1521 for Charles V, the Holy Roman Emperor and Mary's previous fiancé, or arguably her first husband.

Suffolk Place looked every inch a modern Tudor palace, with turrets we might recognise from the White Tower of the Tower of London and the overall look of the red bricked Hampton Court Palace. It had a similar Great Hall, inner courtyard and large kitchens and tower with vistas across the whole capital.[3] Although Mary and Charles would live in splendour and make a show of things to the outside world, in the first years of their marriage they were constantly scratching around for money. Mary's only source of income was the four thousand pounds a year from her dowry payments paid to her by Francis I, and during this time England was at war with France, so these payments were irregular. Charles, having lost his wardship of Lady Elizabeth Lisle and therefore no longer able to draw income from her lands was forced to borrow from the crown.[4] They did try to keep a low profile at court to save money but, with both of them being high-status members of Henry's court, there was only so much time away from court that they would be allowed to have.

Mary and Charles attended the banquet held at York Place to celebrate Thomas Wolsey becoming a cardinal on 15 November 1515. Regardless of Mary's financial position, Mary was still the second highest ranking woman in England and as such was allowed to sit at the head table with her brother and his wife.[5]

It is suggested that Mary spent more time at court from then onwards, as when on 18 February 1516, Queen Katherine gave birth to a girl, it has been suggested that the child was named Mary after her. At this time, Mary was pregnant herself, giving birth on 11 March 1516. On this date, she was at Cardinal Wolsey's Bath Place when she gave birth to a healthy baby boy, between ten and eleven o'clock at night.[6] The location and timing suggests Mary's labour had started unexpectedly. Henry was godfather and the child was named after him, being christened at Suffolk Place.[7]

Less than two months later, Margaret Tudor arrived in London. Mary had not seen her sister since Margaret had left London to become Queen of Scotland in 1503 and in the thirteen years that had passed, much had changed between them. They must surely have spent some time getting to know each other again, exchanging their own stories of hardship, queenship, and having their own children. After this meeting with her sister, Mary and Charles took some time away from court to visit Butley Priory.[8] Mary would visit the priory several times in her life, on her last visit she would spend two months there in 1530.[9]

Towards the end of 1516, Mary became unwell. Charles describes his wife's conditions as 'ague', a fever sometimes connected to malaria.[10] It is interesting how Henry reacts to the news that his sister was unwell, for Henry sends his doctors to her and even visited her himself as she lay in her sick bed.[11] This might not seem odd from a loving and worried brother but could be seen as very curious behaviour for Henry VIII, as he often ran away from illness; for example, when his 'beloved' Anne Boleyn caught the Sweating Sickness, he sent her away from court to Hever Castle, where she was treated by the king's junior doctors, always keeping the best doctors for himself, just in case.[12] Yet, in one of Charles Brandon's letters to Wolsey, he mentions the king had visited his ill sister. This can be viewed as another example of how close Henry VIII felt to his younger sister, even after all that had happened. Mary was able to recover in time to see her sister Margaret return to Scotland.

Mary became pregnant once again, and once again her labour seemed unexpected, as she was obliged to give birth at Hatfield House while visiting, the famous future nursery of Anne Boleyn's daughter and where that daughter would be told that she was to be Queen Elizabeth of England. Mary gave birth on 16 July 1517 to a girl. It could be suggested that as she was born on St Francis Day, she was named Frances. Or it may have been a nod to Francis I of France and the special friendship Mary once had with him as the Queen of France. Frances had two godmothers, Queen Katherine and Princess Mary. Both were unable to attend the hurried christening, so Lady Elizabeth Boleyn, the mother of Mary, George and Anne, stepped in for the queen, and Lady Elizabeth Grey for Princess Mary.[13]

After this birth, Mary spent some time at her country home of Westhorpe Hall in East Anglia. In 1518 Mary became ill again. We know this because Charles writes to Wolsey, excusing himself from court to look after his wife. The letter implies that Mary was in a lot of pain, but it gives no reason.[14] Mary did seem to improve but only for a short time and Charles and Mary wrote separately to say that a visit from Mary's brother may help her to recover.[15]

Some good news was on its way for Mary, however, as on 2 October 1518, the Treaty of Universal Peace was signed between England and France at St Paul's.[16] For Mary, this meant the remainder of her dowry was settled and regular payments would start to be paid.[17] Mary's appearances at court decreased and by the end of 1518 there seems to be no record of her at court at all. This may have been due to ill health or the fact that she was meant to have had another child, named Eleanor, between 1518 and 1521, although there is no record of the time of this birth or the time of the christening. Mary does appear in the records for the famous Field of the Cloth of Gold meeting between Mary's brother, King Henry VIII and Mary's friend, Francis I, in 1520. We know of this because Charles Brandon answers Wolsey's questions as to how many horses and people Mary would be taking with her.[18] We can tell from this that plans were made to include Mary at this event, but the list of those who went with her sadly no longer survives.

Henry was hedging his bets and did not wish to rely upon a peace treaty with France. So, before the spectacular Field of the Cloth of Gold meeting, Henry sent an invitation to Charles V, the Holy Roman Emperor and King of Spain, to visit England.[19] Charles V arrived at Dover on 26 May 1520, where he stayed at Dover Castle. Henry rode out to meet him and they headed for Canterbury. At the cathedral they were blessed by the archbishop and afterwards the royal party moved into the archbishop's lodgings, where Charles was greeted by his aunt, Queen Katherine. All staying the night there, they had breakfast and then to Mass, which Mary attended. Mary sat with Queen Katherine, in the second enclosure, away from her brother and the man to whom she was once engaged.[20] Mary and Charles V had never actually met. Still, they had exchanged letters of some meaning between them and Mary's life would have turned out to be very different if their marriage had gone ahead. Perhaps Mary mused upon this when she later dined with her brother, Queen Katherine and Charles V. After dining, there was dancing, which Mary had always loved. She apparently asked Charles V to dance with her, but he declined. One can imagine the awkwardness of this scene, especially if Charles V felt he had lost a great beauty or prize when he looked at her, considering he was still an eligible bachelor.[21] Afterwards, Henry and the royal party said goodbye to Charles V before the party travelled on to France to the Field of the Cloth of Gold.

On 31 May 1520, Henry and his court, including Mary and Charles Brandon, sailed from Dover, landing in Calais and arriving in Guisnes by 5 June.[22] Upon the field of this long-awaited event, were many tents decorated in red cloths, with Tudor roses, Fleur-de-lis, greyhounds, lions and dragons, all trimmed in gold and Mary had her own accommodation within these tents.[23] Mary's role at this event can often be overlooked, compared to the actions of the two great Renaissance princes. but Mary was a Princess of England and the Dowager Queen of France. As such, she would have known the customs of the English and the French. Her importance was highlighted when she travelled to the tiltyard in a litter decorated with lilies and the monograms of 'L' and 'M', in remembrance of her marriage to Louis XII.[24] She was given her own table to dine, showing the respect given to her for her earlier role as Queen of France.[25]

Sadly, there is no record to date of Mary after this event before 1522. Time was presumably spent away from court, perhaps another attempt to save money, especially after an event where Mary may have had to spent largely to look the part. We next catch a glimpse of Mary at what some see as an important moment within the Tudor, or at the very least, Boleyn chronicles, the pageant called Château Vert, or the Green Castle, held on the evening of Shrove Tuesday in 1522 at Cardinal Wolsey's York Place. The stage was set with a makeshift wooden castle at one end of the hall. In the towers of this play castle were eight beautiful ladies, each dressed in white satin with their 'quality' written on a yellow satin slash. Their 'qualities' were beauty, honour, perseverance, kindness, bounty, pity, mercy and constancy. The reason this is sometimes considered a key moment is that Henry VIII was in attendance when a certain Anne Boleyn made her debut at the English Court as 'perseverance'. Though at this time, Henry's eyes probably weren't on Anne but on her sister, Mary Boleyn, who played 'kindness' in this event.[26]

Mary Tudor also played a role in this event, that of 'beauty', as she had been famous for this quality all her life.[27] Set against these women were eight men, representing danger, disdain, unkindness, scorn, sharp tongue, offhandness and jealousy. These eight women of good virtues needed rescuing from the eight people of bad virtues and there were eight soldiers willing to do this, headed by Henry VIII himself, Henry choosing to save, of all the ladies, his sister Mary.[28]

This could have been another sign of brother and sister affection, however could there be something else hinted at here, perhaps unconsciously? That of all the virtues Henry VIII personally saves, he saves 'beauty'. This may suggest to us what Henry VIII thought was important in a wife, but perhaps we could take this one step further, as beauty was one of the well-known qualities of his mother, Elizabeth of York. Could Henry be choosing to 'save' his beloved and dearly missed mother here, by saving the one sister that may have reminded him of his mother? It is an interesting concept to think about, whether it was consciously or unconsciously made by Henry.

In the same year of this event, Mary's young son died. There is no record of the date or the reason why, but taking into consideration his age of just five or six, it could have been a childhood illness or even an accident. How Mary may have coped with this, we do not know, but she was pregnant at the time and would soon have another boy, who the couple also named Henry.[29] There are to date no records of this birth date or christening.

For this son, Mary and Charles Brandon sought a good marriage, as this young Henry Brandon was the only legitimate male heir to the English throne, so an only wife of high status would do. In 1528, the first step was taken by Charles Brandon by gaining the wardship of Katherine Willoughby. She was the heiress of the later Lord Willoughby de Eresby, Katherine had been given a large inheritance calculated to the exact amount of two thousand, two hundred and sixty-six pounds, thirteen shillings and four pence.[30] This would make any future husband of Katherine's a rich man.

The Tudor world changes very quickly and by 1523, all thoughts of a peace treaty between England and France, following the Field of the Cloth of Gold, had disappeared, with England now declaring war on France.[31] This once again halted the much-needed dowager payments to Mary.[32] At this time, Charles V visited England again, Mary and Charles wined and dined him at Suffolk Place. The evening must have gone well, as Charles Brandon managed to secure a small imperial pension from Charles.[33]

While Charles Brandon went off to war, Mary stayed in England, perhaps looking after the children at their country home of Westhorpe. However, the conflict did not go to plan as Henry VIII and Charles V had different aims. Henry wanted to attack

Paris and Charles V wanted to focus on the Pyrenean frontier and war with Italy. Then the winter brought heavy rain, so that many of Charles Brandon's men died of the cold or the plague, making Charles give up and come home in the new year.[34]

However, there was soon another chance to go to war with France, when the French king was captured and was Charles V's prisoner.[35] In this, Henry saw another chance to attack the French, weaker without their king. Mary may have been critical of her brother's actions but was clever enough not to openly mention her feelings. With the French King captured, it seemed Mary's pension from France had dried up. The people of England were not happy with being taxed for another war, however, and when actions did not seem to go Henry's way, he eventually blamed the war – and the taxes – on Thomas Wolsey.[36] This meant the plan to invade France was eventually dropped, but so was Charles Brandon's war pension, making money, once again, in short supply for the family. In 1525, Mary writes to Wolsey asking for help to try and get her pension from the French,[37] while Charles Brandon was forced to borrow from the crown again.[38] In aspects other than financial, 1525 started well for the Brandons. On 18 June 1525, Mary and Charles's son, Henry, was made the Earl of Lincoln in a royal ceremony shared with Henry Fitzroy, Henry VIII's illegitimate son with Bessie Blount, at Bridgewell Palace.[39]

On 30 August, the Treaty of More, between England and France was signed, which meant Mary's pension payments were not only reinstated but also backdated.[40] In 1526, Francis I was released by Charles V and so Mary wrote to the French king that she was happy to hear of his release, that he always had her love and care and if she could have done anything to help him, she would have done.[41]

Mary was now thirty years old. The next six years of Mary's life seemed to be a little obscure. We know Mary was against the annulment between her brother and Queen Katherine. This may have been for religious reasons as Mary, like all of her siblings, including her brother, was raised as a Catholic. This may have also increased Mary's dislike for Anne Boleyn, as Anne could have been seen as being a part of the Reformation that was sweeping across Europe. However, perhaps Mary's dislike of the annulment was on a more personal level. Mary had a long and affectionate friendship with Katherine. They had known each other for over twenty years at this point and the records tell us that they were often together at royal events. They may have bonded in grief over the deaths of their children and of Prince Arthur; they even may have bonded over their shared love for Henry VIII. There may well have been times when Mary, being the younger of the two, looked up to Katherine as a sister but also as a queen. Perhaps Mary saw Katherine as the rightful Queen of England, which meant Anne Boleyn never could be.

Mary still harboured a dislike for Anne Boleyn and her brother's marriage in 1532, a year before Anne's coronation. This we know as Mary was strong-willed enough to voice her feelings publicly, knowing that if it got back to Henry VIII himself, it could put her in a dangerous position. Mary's dislike for Anne did not go unnoticed, it even resulted in a quarrel between Charles Brandon's men and the Duke of Norfolk's men, the Duke of Norfolk being Anne Boleyn's uncle.[42]

Within this time period, Katherine Willoughby, Charles's new ward and possible wife for Mary and Charles's son, had been sent to live with the Brandons. Mary would have then spent some time on Katherine's welfare and education, for her to become a suitable future wife for her son. Katherine would have spent this time learning from Mary, as to the running of a household and how to conduct herself at court. Katherine would follow in Mary's footsteps and become a frequent letter writer.

One of the last actions Mary was to take was to organise the marriage of her daughter, Frances Brandon, to Henry Grey, the heir to Thomas Grey's fortune and titles. With this marriage, the Tudor roses twist and entwine themselves around the same family tree yet again, with Henry Grey being the grandson to Elizabeth of York's half-brother, Thomas Grey. The wedding took place in May 1533 at Suffolk Place. This would be the last time Mary was seen in public.[43] She would not be at the coronation of Anne Boleyn in May 1533. It has been suggested that her absence could be explained by her dislike for the new Queen Consort of England, however Mary had once again been ill for some time and was perhaps unfit to attend.

Mary, one time Princess of Castile, Dowager Queen of France, a mother, a wife and Henry VIII's Tudor rose, died on 25 June 1533, between seven and eight o'clock in the morning.[44] Mary passed away at the age of thirty-seven, the same age as her mother, Elizabeth of York was when she died. The cause of death is unknown to date, but there had been suggestions of angina, a bad kidney infection or even grief over her brother's annulment and the rise of Anne Boleyn.[45]

Her coffin was draped in deep blue velvet and she lay in state at her country home of Westhorpe Hall for three weeks before her funeral was held on 21 July 1533. Mary was buried at Bury St Edmund, with her daughter, Frances, being the chief mourner. On top of her coffin was an effigy of Mary, wearing her robes of state with a golden crown and sceptre to symbolise her role as Queen Consort of France.[46] In the abbey of Bury St Edmunds, Mary lay until 1784, when her body was moved to the church of St Mary's, her last resting place being marked by a slab on the floor.[47]

It may seem strange that neither Henry VIII nor Charles Brandon was at Mary's funeral, however this was customary at the time. As Mary had been a Princess of England and Dowager Queen of France, a court funeral without her body was planned, where Henry and Charles could attend. This was held on 10 and 11 July 1533 at Westminster Abbey.[48]

Sadly, even in death, Mary was not left alone as on 6 September 1784, Mary's body was moved to St Mary's.[49] It was recorded then, that Mary just seemed to fit inside the coffin, suggesting she was close to being six foot tall. Her brother was known to have been six foot two inches, their height probably inherited from their grandfather, King Edward IV. Hauntingly, it was reported that Mary's eyes had been removed, although the teeth were intact. Her hair, even after over two hundred years, was golden in colour and still visible and souvenirs of locks of her hair were taken.[50]

There are no official records to date to give us an idea of what Mary's death meant to the men that surrounded her before she died. Charles Brandon's next marriage three months after the death of Mary, on 7 September 1533 to his ward, Katherine Willoughby can seem heartless, especially as Katherine was meant to marry Charles and Mary's son. Katherine came with money and money was the thing Charles Brandon needed in 1533. This could make us question if Charles ever had any genuine feelings for Mary at all. However, it is worth remembering that Charles did face the wrath of Henry VIII and of being charged with treason simply because of his choice to marry Mary Tudor, a mortal risk he did not have to take.

Charles Brandon died on 22 August 1545, on the sixtieth anniversary of his own father's death at the Battle of Bosworth. Despite wanting to be buried without any ceremony at Tattershall, Charles was in fact buried at great expense to Henry VIII at St George's Chapel at Windsor Castle, the burial place of Henry and Mary Tudor's grandparents, Edward IV and Elizabeth Woodville. From this, we could suggest that Henry wanted his brother-in-law and best friend to be well remembered. However, did Henry do the same for his sister, Mary?

A famous suggestion of how Henry VIII remembered his sister is in the naming of his flagship, the *Mary Rose*. However, Mary (despite the title of this book) was never referred to as Mary Rose in her lifetime, plus, when Henry ordered the *Mary Rose* to be built, he also ordered another ship named *Peter Pomegranate*, to be made. The *Mary Rose* ship was not meant to have been a flagship on its own, it was meant to have been one of a pair. With Peter being the saint and the pomegranate being the symbol of Katherine of Aragon, the *Mary Rose* might therefore have been named after the Virgin Mary and the rose as the symbol of the King of England himself, as a counterpart to the pomegranate.

However, there is one arrangement Henry made concerning the succession after Mary had died that could define how much his Tudor rose meant to him. It could be suggested that Henry had spent his whole reign working for the continuation of his dynasty, changing his country to do so. With that in mind, it is obvious that his succession was very important to him, so his actions pertinent to it give us a good perspective on the man and how he felt. In his will, Henry wanted, if his children had no heirs, the succession to pass to 'the heirs of the body of Lady Frances, eldest daughter of his later sister the French Queen. In default, to those of Lady Elyanore, the second daughter of the said French Queen'.[51] No mention was made of Henry's other sister Margaret, or her heirs.

For his final moments and years spent upon this earth, the mighty Henry VIII chooses his sister Mary over his sister Margaret to carry on his legacy. Although he ultimately doesn't get his wish, as it would be Margaret's heirs who would eventually succeed to the English throne, this was the final act of remembrance for his younger sister Mary, the 'beauty' Henry had once saved at the pageant of Château Vert, who had so dearly reminded him of his mother, Elizabeth of York, Henry VIII's first Tudor rose.

NOTES

'Letters and Papers, Foreign and Domestic' refers to *Letters and Papers, Foreign and Domestic, of the Reign of Henry VIII: preserved in the Public Record Office, the British Museum and elsewhere in England*, a multi-volume edition of documents from the reign of Henry VIII. The series was edited by J.S. Brewer, James Gairdner and R.H. Brodie, and originally published between 1862 and 1932.

Introduction

1. Du Chesne, André: Histoire généalogique de la maison royale de Dreux et de quelques autres familles Illustres qui en sont descendues par femmes. S. Cramoisy. 1631.
2. Dodd, Gwilym and Biggs, Douglas: The Reign of Henry IV: Rebellion and Survival 1403-1413. York Medieval Press. p36. 2008.

3. Barker, J: Conquest: The English Kingdom of France 1417-1450. Harvard University Press. 2012.

1 *Learning from the Shadows – Jacquetta of Luxembourg*

1. Monstrelet, La Chronique d'Enguerian de: En Deux Livres Avec Pieces Justificatives 1400–1444, six volumes, Pans 1857–62 Vols PP55-56.
2. Monstrelet, La Chronique d'Enguerian de Monstrelet: En Deux Livres Avec Pieces Justificatives 1400–1444, six volumes, Pans 1857–62.
3. Neillands, Robin: The Hundred Years War. Routledge 2001.
4. Tuetey, Alexandre: Journal d'un bourgeois de Paris, 1405–1449. Public Manuscripts of Rome and Paris. Champion P289–230. 1881.
5. Weir, Alison: The Wars of the Roses: Lancaster and York. Reprint P.84. Ballantine Books. 2009.
6. Grummitt, D: The Calais Garrison, War and Military Service in England 1436-1558. The Boydell Press. 2008.
7. Williams, E. Carleton: My Lord Bedford 1389-1435, Being a Life of John of Lancaster, First Duke of Bedford, brother of Henry V and Regent of France. P228. Longman's, Green and Co Ltd. 1963.
8. Williams, E. Carleton: My Lord Bedford 1389-1435, Being a Life of John of Lancaster, first Duke of Bedford, brother of Henry V and Regent of France. P247. Longman's, Green and Co Ltd. 1963.
9. Purse, Amanda Harvey: from the forthcoming book, The Staffords: In the Shadows of the Tudor Throne. Amberley Publishing 2026.

10. Proceedings and Ordinances of the Privy Council. (POPC) 163-4.
11. Gairdner, J: The Paston Letter: III. London. 1904.
12. Wolffe, B. P: Henry VI. Yale Monarchs. Yale University Press. P315. London. 2001.
13. Gairdner, J: The Paston Letters: I. 506.
14. Haigh, P: From Wakefield to Towton. P31. Pen and Sword Military. 2014.
15. Sadler, John: Towton: The Battle of Palm Sunday Field 1461. P78. Pen and Sword Military. 2011.
16. Squires, Anthony: The Greys: A Long and Noble Line. P15. Silk Press Books. 2002.
17. In 1469, Jacquetta was accused of witchcraft by Richard, Earl of Warwick – Calendar of Patent Rolls 1467-1477. P.190
18. The records included Richard Woodville wanting to be interred at St James's Abbey, Northampton. Chapman, Andy and Morris, Steve: 'The Medieval Abbey of St James (Part 1)'. The Former Express Lift Site, Northampton. Northamptonshire Archaeology. 1999
19. Chapman, Andy and Morris, Steve: 'The Medieval Abbey of St James (Part 1)'. The Former Express Lift Site, Northampton. Northamptonshire Archaeology. 1999.
20. Borman, Tracy: The Private Lives of the Tudors. Hodder. 2017. Stride, P. and Lopes, Floro K: 'Henry VIII, McLeod syndrome and Jacquetta's curse': The Journal of the Royal College of Physicians of Edinburgh. 43(4). PP353-60. 2013.
21. Stride, P. and Lopes, Floro K: 'Henry VIII, McLeod syndrome and Jacquetta's curse': The Journal of the Royal College of Physicians of Edinburgh. 43(4). PP353-60. 2013.

2 *Learning from the Queen of England – Elizabeth Woodville*

1. Ashdown-Hill, John: Elizabeth Widville, Lady Grey. Pen and Sword History. 2019.
2. Cokayne, George Edward: The Complete Peerage. Vol IV. P418-419. London. St Catherine Press. 1916.
3. Horrox, Rosemary: Grey Sir Richard. Oxford Dictionary of National Biography. Oxford University Press. 2004
4. Ibid
5. Ibid
6. Vergil, Polydore: Edited by Sir Henry Ellis: Three books of Polydore Vergil's English History, comprising the reigns of Henry VI, Edward IV and Richard III. Volume 29. 1844.
7. Hight, Julian: Britain's Tree Story. P.44. National Trust. London.
8. Ibid
9. Ibid
10. Clark, David: Barnet 1471: Death of a Kingmaker. P94. Pen and Sword. 2007.
11. Crawford, A: Howard Household Books. P229. Volume I. Stroud. 1992.
12. Ashdown Hill, John: Eleanor Talbot: The Secret Queen. Stroud. 2016.
13. More, Thomas: The History of King Richard III. PP61-62. University Press. 1924.
14. Fitzroy, Charles and Harry, Keith: Grafton Regis: The History of a Northamptonshire Village. PP19-20. Merton Priory Press. 2000.
15. Ashdown Hill, John: The Private of Edward IV. Stroud. 2016.
16. Fitzroy, Charles and Harry, Keith: Grafton Regis: The History of a Northamptonshire Village. P29. Merton Priory Press. 2000.

17. History of Mote Park: Moteparkfellowship.org.uk
18. This suggestion comes from a poem written by Antonio Cornazzano. Fahy, Conor: The Marriage of Edward IV and Elizabeth Woodville: A new Italian Source. English Historical Review. Vol 76. PP660-672. 1960.
19. Smith, G: The Coronation of Elizabeth Wydeville. London. 1935.
20. Ibid
21. Ibid
22. Ibid
23. Searle, W. G: The History of the Queens College of St Margaret and St Bernard in the University of Cambridge. 1446-1560. P69.Cambridge University Press. 1867.
24. Calendar of Patent Rolls. Edward IV. 1461-1467: 196.
25. Calendar of Patent Rolls. Edward IV. 1461-1467: 446.
26. Okerlund, Arlene: Elizabeth Wydville: The Slandered Queen. P81. Tempus Publishing. 2005.
27. Fabian: The New Chronicles of England and France. P665. Ed. Ellis, Henry. Rivington. London. 1811.

3 Daughter to a King – Elizabeth of York

1. Fabyan, Robert: The New Chronicles of England and France. Ed. Henry Ellis. P654. London. 1811.
2. Ed. Harris, Mary Dormer: The Coventry Leet Book or Mayor's Register. P346. Eary English Text Society. 1907.
3. Stone, John: The Chronicle of John Stone: Monk of Christ Church 1415-1471. P113. Cambridge: Antiquarian Society. 1902.
4. Rosser, Gervase: Medieval Westminster 1200-1540. PP68-74. Oxford Clarendon Press. 1989.

5. Kingsford, Charles Lethbridge: English Historical Literature in the Fifteen Century. P387. Oxford. 1913.
6. Garrett MS. 168. Manuscripts Division. Department of Rare Books and Special Collections. Princeton University Library.
7. BL Add. MS 5001. British Library. London.
8. Harthan, John: The Book of Hours: With a Historical Survey and Commentary by John Harthan. Crowell. New York. 1977.
9. Scott, Kathleen L: Later Gothic Manuscripts 1390-1490: Survey of Manuscripts Illuminated in the British Isles. Volume II. NO55. London. 1996.
10. Purse, Amanda Harvey: *In the forthcoming book* The Staffords: In the Shadows of the Tudor throne. Amberley Publishing. 2026.
11. BL Royal MS 14 EIII. British Library. London.
12. Middleton, Roger: Manuscript of the Lancelot-Grail Cycle in England and Wales: Some books and their owners in a companion to the Lancelot-Grail cycle. Ed. Carol Dover. Woodbridge. 2003.
13. BL Royal MS 16 FII.
14. Backhouse, Janet: 'Illuminated Manuscripts Associated with Henry VII and Members of his Immediate Family' in the Reign of Henry VII: Proceedings of the 1993 Harlaxton Symposium. Stamford. 1995.
15. Ed. Myers, A. R: The Household of Edward IV: The Black Book and the Ordinance of 1478. P131-132. Manchester University Press. 1959.
16. Ed. Nicolas, Nicholas Harris: Privy Purse Expenses of Elizabeth of York: Wardrobe Accounts of Edward IV. PP29-41. London. 1830.

17. Ed. Nicholas, Nicholas Harris: Privy Purse Expenses of Elizabeth of York: Wardrobe Accounts of Edward IV. London. 1830.
18. Acts of Sovereigns and other Supreme Authorities, Louis XI, King. London. 1483. Held at the British Library. London.
19. Scofield, Cora: The Life and Reign of Edward the Fourth. P142. London. 1923.
20. Commies, Philippe de: The memoirs of Philip de Commies, Lord of Argenton. Books. London. 1855.
21. Sutton and Vischer-Fuchs: The Reburial of Richard, Duke of York 21-30 July 1476. 19. Richard III Society. 1996.
22. Anstis, John: The Register of the Most Noble Order of the Garter, from its Cover in Black Velvet usually called the Black Book. P197. London. 1724.
23. Ed. Henry, William: Illustrations of ancient state and chivalry. From Manuscripts preserved in the Ashmolean Museum. P30. London. 1840.
24. Shepherd, Robert: Westminster: A Biography From the Earliest Times to the Present. P285. A&C Black. 2012.
25. Ed. Henry, William: Illustrations of ancient state and chivalry. From Manuscripts preserved in the Ashmolean Museum. P33. London. 1840.
26. Purse, Amanda Harvey: In the forthcoming book The Staffords: In the Shadows of the Tudor throne. Amberley Publishing. 2026.
27. Ed. Henry, William: Illustrations of ancient state and chivalry. From Manuscripts preserved in the Ashmolean Museum. P33. London. 1840.
28. Scofield, Cora: The Life and Reign of Edward the Fourth. P242. London. 1923.

29. Salmon, Marylynn: Medieval Syphilis and Treponemal Disease. Amsterdam University Press. 2022.
30. Brewer, Clifford: The Death of Kings: A medical History of the Kings and Queens of England. P97. Gutenberg Press. 2000.
31. Ed. Pronay, Nicholas and Cox, John: The Crowland Chronicle Continuations: 1459-1486. P150-151. London. 1986.
32. Davis, R: Extracts from the Municipal Records of the City of York. P142-143. London. 1843.
33. Hill, John Ashdown: The Private Life of Edward IV. P210. Amberley Publishing. 2016.
34. Lyell, L. and Watney, F.D: Acta of Court of the Mercers' Company 1453-1527. P146. Cambridge. 1936.
35. Sutton A. F and Visser-Fuchs, Livia, with Griffiths, R. A: The Royal Funerals of the House of York at Windsor. Richard III Society. London. 2005

4 *Sister and Niece to a King*

1. Ed. DuBoulay, F. R. H: Registrum Thomas Bourchier Cantuariensis Archbishop AD 1454-1486. P378-379. Lambeth Palace Library.
2. Commies, Philippe de: The Memoirs of Philip de Commines, Lord of Argenton. Ed. Andrew Riscoble. Book 5. Ch 20. London. 1855.
3. Kendall, Paul Murray: Richard the Third. P257-258. W. W Norton and Company. 2002.
4. Ed. Pronay, Nicholas and Cox, John: The Crowland Chronicle Continuations 1459-1486. P161. London.1986.
5. Ed. Pronay, Nicolas and Cox, John: The Crowland Chronicle Continuations 1459-1486. PP154-155. London. 1986.

6. Mancini, Dominic: The Usurpation of Richard III. Ed. By C. A. J. Armstrong. P106. Sutton Publishing Ltd. 1984.
7. Ed. Pronay, Nicholas and Cox, John: The Crowland Chronicle Continuations 1459-1486. PP154-155. London. 1986.
8. Edwards, Rhoda: The Itinerary of King Richard III. P2. Richard III Society. 1983.
9. The National Archives: SC 1/45/236.
10. Kendall, Paul Murray: Richard the Third. P182. Norton. 2013.
11. Edwards, Rhoda: The Itinerary of King Richard II. P2. Richard III Society. 1983.
12. Hammond, P. W. and Sutton, A. F.: Richard III: The Road to Bosworth. P99. London. 1985.
13. Ed. Pronay, Nicolas and Cox John: The Crowland Chronicle Continuations 1459-1486. PP158-159. London. 1986.
14. Mancini, Dominic: The Usurpation of Richard III. Ed. By C. A. J. Armstrong. PP62-63. Sutton Publishing Ltd. 1984.
15. Ed. Pronay, Nicolas and Cox, John: The Crowland Chronicle Continuations 1459-1486. PP158-159. London. 1986.
16. Calendar of Patient Rolls 1476-1485. Numbers 1036, 1037 and 1038. British History Online.
17. More, Thomas: The History of Richard III. Within the Note on the Text part of the book. First published in 1557.
18. More, Thomas: The History of Richard III. P3. First published in 1557. Hesperus Press Limited. 2005.
19. More, Thomas: The History of Richard III. P82. First published in 1557. Hesperus Press Limited. 2005.
20. More, Thomas: The History of Richard III. P82. First published in 1557. Hesperus Press Limited. 2005.

21. More, Thomas: The History of Richard III. P83. First published in 1557. Hesperus Press Limited. 2005.
22. 126 Folios belonging to Christopher Barker. Manuscript MS 2M6. College of Arms. Queen Victoria Street. London.
23. McKisack, May: The Fourteenth Century: 1307-1399. P494-495. Oxford University Press. 1959.
24. Tout, T: 'Mortimer, Edmund de Earl of March and Ulster'. Dictionary of National Biography. Vol 39. P 123-5. Smith, Elder and CO. London.
25. Tait, James: 'Plantagenet, Edward'. Dictionary of National Biography. P401-4. Vol 45. Smith, Elder and Co. London.
26. Pugh, T. B: Henry V and the Southampton Plot of 1415. P79. Alan Sutton. 1988.
27. Pugh, T. B: Henry V and the Southampton Plot of 1415. P78. Alan Sutton. 1988.
28. Tout, T: 'Mortimer, Edmund de Earl of March and Ulster'. Dictionary of National Biography. Vol 39. PP123-5. Smith, Elder and CO. London.
29. Baldwin, D: The Lost Prince: The Survival of Richard of York. Stoud 2007.
30. Williamson, James A: The Tudor Age. P25. D. McKay Co. 1961.
31. Mervin, Barbara: Enquiring History: Tudor Rebellions 1485-1603. P22. Hodder Education. 2014.
32. Weir, Alison: Princes in the Tower. P234. Vintage. 2008.
33. www.revealingrichardiii.com.
34. Chrimes, Stanley Bertram: Henry VII. P73. Yale University Press. 1999.
35. Wroe, Ann: Perkin. PP148-151. Vintage. 2004.

36. Hepburn, William: The Household and Court of James IV of Scotland. P67. Boydell. 2023.
37. Accounts of the Treasurer of Scotland. Volume I. PP257, 262-264. Edinburgh. 1877.
38. Accounts of the Treasurer of Scotland. Volume I. PP299-300. Edinburgh. 1877.
39. Weir, Alison: Princes in the Tower. P238-240. Vintage. 2008.
40. Ed. Thomas, A. H and Thornley, I. D: The Great Chronicle of London, held at Guildhall Library. 1938.
41. www.revealingrichardiii.com.
42. www.revealingrichardiii.com.
43. Amin, Nathen: Henry VII and the Tudor Pretenders: Simnel, Warbeck and Warwick. P279. Amberley Publishing 2020.
44. Calendar of State Papers: Spain. P167-180. 'July 1498'.
45. Mancini, Dominic: The Usurpation of Richard III. Ed. By C. A. J. Armstrong. P93. Sutton Publishing Ltd. 1984
46. Ed. Pronay, Nicolas and Cox, John: The Crowland Chronicle Continuations 1459-1486. P163. London. 1986.
47. Ed. Pronay, Nicolas and Cox, John: The Crowland Chronicle Continuations 1459-1486. P163. London. 1986.
48. Vergil, Polydore: Three Books of Polydore Vergil's English History: Comprising the Reigns of Henry VII, Edward IV and Richard III. Ed. Henry Ellis. P196. London. 1844.
49. Clarke, Peter D: 'English Royal Marriage and the Papal Penitentiary in the Fifteenth Century'. English Historical Review 120. P488. 2005.
50. Ed. Pronay, Nicolas and Cox, John: The Crowland Chronicle Continuations 1459-1486. P171. London. 1986.
51. Ellis, Henry: Original Letters, Illustrative of English History. Second Series. 4:149-150. AMS Press. New York. 1970.

52. Ed. Pronay, Nicolas and Cox, John: The Crowland Chronicle Continuations 1459-1486. P175. London. 1986.
53. Ed. Pronay, Nicolas and Cox, John: The Crowland Chronicle Continuations 1459-1486. P175. London. 1986.
54. Vergil, Polydore: The Anglica Historia of Polydore Vergil AD 1485-1537. Ed. Denys Hay. P3. Royal Historical Society. London. 1950.
55. Buck, George: The History of Richard the Third. 1619. Ed. Arthur Noel Kincaud. P191. Alan Sutton. Gloucester. 1979.
56. Hanham, Alison: 'Sir George Buck and Princess Elizabeth's letter: A problem in Detection'. Ricardian. 7 June 1987. P399.

5 *Wife and Mother to a King*

1. Bennett, Michael: Lambert Simnel and the Battle of Stoke. P31. St Martin's Press. New York. 1987.
2. Ed. Campbell, William. Materials for a History of the Reign of Henry VII, from Original Documents Preserved in the Public Record Office. 1:6. Longman and Turbner. London. 1873.
3. Sutton, Anne F and Hammond, P. W.: The Coronation of Richard III: The Extant Documents. PP204-27. Alan Sutton. Gloucester. 1983.
4. Legg, L. G. W: English Coronation Records. PP198-212. London. 1901
5. Purse, Amanda Harvey: The Boleyns: From the Tudors to the Windsors. Amberley Publishing. 2022.
6. Ed. Campbell, William: Materials for the History of the Reign of Henry VII. From original documents preserved in the Public Record Office. 2:3-29. Longman and Turbner. London. 1873.
7. Rotuli Parliamentorium. 6:288. London. 1832.

8. Ed. Campbell, William: Materials for the History of the Reign of Henry VII. From original documents preserved in the Public Record Office. 1: 122-23. Longman and Turbner. London. 1873.
9. Ed. Campbell, William: Materials for the History of the Reign of Henry VII. From original documents preserved in the Public Record Office. 1:264. Longman and Turbner. London. 1873.
10. Calendar of Papal Letters: 14:14. Held at Her Majesty's Stationary Office. London. 1960.
11. Shakespeare, William: 1 Henry VI. Act 2. Scene 4.
12. Anglo, Sydney: 'The British History in Early Tudor Propaganda'. Bulletin of the John Ryland's Library 44. P28-29. 1960-61.
13. Ed. Grose, Francis and Astle, Thomas. The Antiquarian Repertory: A Miscellaneous Assemblage of Topography, History, Biography, Customs and Manners. 1: 355. London. 1807.
14. Madden, F: Genealogical and Historical Notes in Ancient Calendars, collected Topographical et Genealogical I. P277-79. 1834.
15. Leland, John: De Rebus Brittanicus Collectanea. Ed. T. Hearne. 4:204. London. 1774.
16. Leland, John: De Rebus Brittanicus Collectanea. Ed. T. Hearne. 4: 180. 240-7. London. 1774.
17. Leland, John: De Rebus Brittanicus Collectanea. Ed. T. Hearne. 4: 206. London. 1774.
18. Leland, John: De Rebus Brittanicus Collectanea. Ed. T. Hearne. 4: 207. London. 1774.
19. Leland, John: De Rebus Brittanicus Collectanea. Ed. T. Hearne. 4: 207. London. 1774.

20. Ed. Cambell, William. Materials for a History of the Reign of Henry VII. From Original Documents preserved in the Public Record Office 2:349. Longman and Turbner. London. 1873.
21. Ed. Cambell, William. Materials for a History of the Reign of Henry VII. From Original Documents preserved in the Public Record Office 2:349-459. Longman and Turbner. London. 1873.
22. Vergil, Polydore: The Anglica Historia of Polydore Vergil AD 1485-1537. Ed. Denys Hay. P18-19. Royal Historical Society. London. 1950.
23. Ed. Cambell, William. Materials for a History of the Reign of Henry VII. From Original Documents preserved in the Public Record Office 2:221. Longman and Turbner. London. 1873.
24. Ed. Cambell, William. Materials for a History of the Reign of Henry VII. From Original Documents preserved in the Public Record Office 2:142. Longman and Turbner. London. 1873.
25. Kendall, Paul Murry: Richard the Third. PP349-50. W. W. Norton. New York. 1956.
26. Kendall, Paul Murry: Richard the Third. P379-78. W. W. Norton. New York. 1956.
27. Leland, John: De Rebus Brittanicus Collectanea. Ed. T. Hearne. 4: 207. London. 1774.
28. Vergil, Polydore: The Anglica Historia of Polydore Vergil AD 1485-1537. Ed. Denys Hay. P3. Royal Historical Society. London. 1950.
29. Leland, John: De Rebus Brittanicus Collectanea. Ed. T. Hearne. 4: 218. London. 1774.
30. Ed. Gairdner, James: Three Fifteen Century Chronicles. P.106-13. Camden Society. 1880.
31. Leland, John: De Rebus Brittanicus Collectanea. Ed. T. Hearne. 4: 219-20. London. 1774.

32. Leland, John: De Rebus Brittanicus Collectanea. Ed. T. Hearne. 4: 227-28. London. 1774.
33. Calendar of the Close Rolls Henry VII 1485-1500. 68. Preserved in the Public Record Office. London.
34. Gunn, Steven and Monckton, Linda: Arthur Tudor, Prince of Wales: Life, Death and Commemoration. P10. Woodbridge. 2009.
35. Leland, John: De Rebus Brittanicus Collectanea. Ed. T. Hearne. 4: 254. London. 1774.
36. Ed. Grose, F: Antiquarian Repertory. Four Volumes. P51-2. London. 1807-9.
37. Scarisbrick, J. J: Henry VIII. P3. Yale University Press. 1997.
38. Lysons, Daniel: The Environs of London: Being an Historical Account of Towns, Villages and Hamlets, within twelve miles of that capital. Gale Print Editions. 2010. Stebbing, Samuel: A Genealogical History of the Kings and Queens of England and Monarchs of Great Britain. From Conquest Anno 1066 to the Year 1707. Gale Print Editions. 2018.
39. Starkey, David: Henry: The Prince who would turn Tyrant. P59. Harper Press. 2009.
40. E 404/81/1. 31 December 1491 and 20 July 1492. Held at the National Archives, London.
41. Ed. Nicolas, N. H: The Privy Purse Expense of Elizabeth of York: Wardrobe Accounts of Edward Fourth PIXXXV.
42. Calendar of Patent Rolls. Henry VII. 1485-1494. P434, 489, 441, 453.
43. E 404/81/3. Warrants dated 17 September 1493 and 13 March 1494. Held at the National Archives. London. Ed. Gairdner, J: Letters and Papers Illustrative of the Reigns of Richard III and Henry VII. Two Volumes. (Rolls Series 1861-1863) 391. 393.

44. E 404/82. Warrant dated 26 October 1495. Held at the National Archives.
45. Kingsford, Charles Lethbridge: Vitellus Axvi in the Chronicles of London. P213. Clarendon Press. Oxford. 1905.
46. Bentley, Samuel: Excerpa Historica or Illustrations of English History III. 94. London. 1831.
47. Stevens, John: Music and Poetry in the Early Tudor Court. P382. Methien and co. London. 1961.
48. Bentley, Samuel: Excerpa Historica or Illustrations of English History III. 124. London. 1831.
49. Ed. Brewer, J. S: Letters and Papers: Foreign and Domestic – Henry VIII. I:409. London. 1920.
50. Ed. Kipling, Gordon: The Receyt of the Lady Kateryne. 12 -15. Oxford University Press. 1990.
51. Ed. Kipling, Gordon: The Receyt of the Lady Kateryne. 31. Oxford University Press. 1990.
52. Ed. Kipling, Gordon: The Receyt of the Lady Kateryne. 37. Oxford University Press. 1990.
53. Ed. Thomas, A. H and Thornley, I. D: The Great Chronicle of London. P311. George Jones. 1938.
54. Ed. Kipling, Gordon: The Receyt of the Lady Kateryne. 44. Oxford University Press. 1990.
55. Ed. Kipling, Gordon: The Receyt of the Lady Kateryne. 58. Oxford University Press. 1990.
56. Leland, John: De Rebus Brittanicus Collectanea. Ed. T. Hearne. 5:373-4. London. 1774.
57. Leland, John: De Rebus Brittanicus Collectanea. Ed. T. Hearne. 5:373-4. London. 1774.
58. Ed. Nicolas, Nicholas Harris: Privy Purse Expenses of Elizabeth of York: Wardrobe Accounts. 10.103. 1830.

59. Ed. Nicolas, Nicholas Harris: Privy Purse Expenses of Elizabeth of York: Wardrobe Accounts. 14.54. 1830.
60. Ed. Nicolas, Nicholas Harris: Privy Purse Expenses of Elizabeth of York: Wardrobe Accounts. 22,29, 88-89.93. 1830.
61. Ed. Nicolas, Nicholas Harris: Privy Purse Expenses of Elizabeth of York: Wardrobe Accounts. 62.69. 1830.
62. Laynesmith, J. L: The Last Medieval Queens: English Queenship. 1445-1503. Oxford University Press. 2005.
63. Ed. Thomas, A. H. and Thornley, I. D: The Great Chronicle of London. P321. London. 1938.
64. Ed. Nicolas, Nicholas Harris: Privy Purse Expenses of Elizabeth of York: Wardrobe Accounts. 97. 1830.
65. Ed. Grose, F: Antiquarian Repertory. Four Volumes. 4:655. London. 1807-9.
66. Ed. Grose, F: Antiquarian Repertory. Four Volumes. 4:656. London. 1807-9.

6 From an English Rose … – Margaret Tudor…

1. Marshall, Rosalind Kay: Scottish Queens: 1034-1714. P85. Tuckwell Press Ltd. 2003
2. Leland, John: De Rebus Brittanicus Collectanea. Ed. T. Hearne. 4:253-255. London. 1774.
3. Watkins, Sarah Beth: Margaret Tudor: Queen of Scots: The Life of Henry VIII's Sister. P3. Chronos Books. 2017.
4. Green, Mary Anne Everett: Lives of the Princesses of England from the Norman Conquest. Volume Four. P54. London. 1857.
5. Westminster Abbey Archives: www.westminster-abbey.org.
6. Information from the staff at Westminster Abbey.
7. Westminster Abbey Archives: www.westminster-abbey.org.

8. Stickland, Agnes: Lives of the Tudor Princesses. Longmans, Green and Co. London. 1868.
9. Green, Mary Anne Everett: Lives of the Princesses of England from the Norman Conquest. Volume Four. London. 1857.
10. Green, Mary Anne Everett: Lives of the Princesses of England from the Norman Conquest. Volume Four. London. 1857.
11. Green, Mary Anne Everett: Lives of the Princesses of England from the Norman Conquest. Volume Four. London. 1857.
12. Leland, John: De Rebus Brittanicus Collectanea. Ed. T. Hearne. London. 1774.
13. Stickland, Agnes: Lives of the Tudor Princesses. Longmans, Green and Co. London. 1868.
14. Leland, John: De Rebus Brittanicus Collectanea. Ed. T. Hearne. London. 1774.
15. Leland, John: De Rebus Brittanicus Collectanea. Ed. T. Hearne. London. 1774.
16. Young, John: The Fyancells of Margaret, Eldest Daughter of Henry VII as quoted in Leland: Collectenea. Volume four. Ed. Thomas Hearne. Oxford 1710-1712.
17. Young, John: The Fyancells of Margaret, Eldest Daughter of Henry VII as quoted in Leland: Collectenea. Volume four. Ed. Thomas Hearne. Oxford 1710-1712.
18. Young, John: The Fyancells of Margaret, Eldest Daughter of Henry VII as quoted in Leland: Collectenea. Volume four. Ed. Thomas Hearne. Oxford 1710-1712.
19. Young, John: The Fyancells of Margaret, Eldest Daughter of Henry VII as quoted in Leland: Collectenea. Volume four. Ed. Thomas Hearne. Oxford 1710-1712.
20. Leland, John: De Rebus Brittanicus Collectanea. Ed. T. Hearne. London. 1774.

21. Green, Mary Anne Everett: Lives of the Princesses of England from the Norman Conquest. Volume Four. London. 1857.
22. Leland, John: De Rebus Brittanicus Collectanea. Ed. T. Hearne. London. 1774.
23. Leland, John: De Rebus Brittanicus Collectanea. Ed. T. Hearne. London. 1774.

7 ... *To a Scottish Thistle*

1. Green, Mary Anne Everett: Lives of the Princesses of England from the Norman Conquest. Volume Four. London. 1857.
2. Green, Mary Anne Everett: Lives of the Princesses of England from the Norman Conquest. Volume Four. London. 1857.
3. Green, Mary Anne Everett: Lives of the Princesses of England from the Norman Conquest. Volume Four. London. 1857.
4. Morrison, Elizabeth: Luminating the Renaissance: The Triumph of Flemish Manuscript Painting in Europe. P373. Getty Museum. 2003.
5. Morrison, Elizabeth: Luminating the Renaissance: The Triumph of Flemish Manuscript Painting in Europe. PP373-374. Getty Museum. 2003.
6. Green, Mary Anne Everett: Lives of the Princesses of England from the Norman Conquest. Volume Four. London. 1857.
7. Leslie, Bishop John: The History of Scotland: From the Death of King James I in the Year M. CCCC.XXXVI, to the year M.D.LXI. Bannatyne Club. 1830.
8. Buchanan, Patricia: Margaret Tudor: Queen of Scots. Scottish Academic Press Ltd. Edinburgh. 1985.
9. Goodwin, George: Fatal Rivalry: Flodden 1513. London 2013.
10. Buchanan, Patricia: Margaret Tudor: Queen of Scots. Scottish Academic Press Ltd. Edinburgh. 1985.

11. Harvey, Nancy Lenz: The Rose and the Thorn. Macmillan New York. 1975.
12. Hall, Edward: Hall's Chronicle, containing the History of England. Ed. H. Ellis. London. 1889.
13 Woolgar, Christopher: The Great Household in Late Medieval England. Yale. 1999.
14. Scott, Ronald McNair: Robert the Bruce, King of the Scots. Edinburgh. 1982.
15. UndiscoveredScotland.co.uk: St Michael's Church.
16. Dunbar, John G: Scottish Royal Palaces. East Linton. 1999.
17. Bain, Joesph: Calendar of Document Relating to Scotland 1357-1509. Volume Four. Edinburgh. 1888.
18. Ellis, Henry: Original Letters. Volume One. Harding, Triphook and Lepard. London. 1824.
19. Dunbar John G: Scottish Royal Palaces. East Linton. 1999.
20. Paton, Henry: Accounts of the Masters of Work Volume One. Edinburgh. 1957.
21. Fleming, David Hay and Bevendge, James: Register of the Privy Seal 1542-1548. Volume Three. Edinburgh. 1936.
22. Green, Mary Anne Everett: Lives of the Princesses of England from the Norman Conquest. Volume Four. London. 1857.
23. Ed. Brewer, J. S: Letters and Papers: Foreign and Domestic – Henry VIII. London. 1920.
24. Taylor, Ida A: The Life of James IV. Wentworth Press. London. 1913.

8 Flodden and the Troubling Brother

1. Chapman, Hester: The Sisters of Henry VIII. Jonathan Cape Ltd. Bath. 1969.

2. Buchanan, Patricia: Margaret Tudor: Queen of Scots. Scottish Academic Press Ltd. Edinburgh. 1985.
3. Chapman, Hester: The Sisters of Henry VIII. Jonathan Cape Ltd. Bath. 1969.
4. Drummond, W: History of Scotland. London. 1745.
5. Buchanan, Patricia: Margaret Tudor: Queen of Scots. Scottish Academic Press Ltd. Edinburgh. 1985.
6. Goodwin, George: Fatal Rivalry: Henry VIII, James IV and the Battle for Renaissance Britain. Weidenfeld and Nicolson. 2013.
7. Ed. Brewer, J. S: Letters and Papers: Foreign and Domestic – Henry VIII. London. 1920.
8. Goodwin, George: Fatal Rivalry: Henry VIII, James IV and the Battle for Renaissance Britain. Weidenfeld and Nicolson. 2013.
9. Goodwin, George: Fatal Rivalry: Henry VIII, James IV and the Battle for Renaissance Britain. Weidenfeld and Nicolson. 2013.
10. Stow, John: Survey of London: Cripplegate Ward. 1598.
11. Sheerin, Jude: 'Medieval Skeltons are found at palace', Independent. Thursday 26 September 2002.
12. Ed. Brewer, J. S: Letters and Papers: Foreign and Domestic – Henry VIII. London. 1920.
13. Stickland, Agnes: Lives of the Tudor Princesses. Longmans, Green and Co. London. 1868.
14. ScottishChurches.org.uk. 6 August 1514.
15. Buchanan, Patricia: Margaret Tudor: Queen of Scots. Scottish Academic Press Ltd. Edinburgh. 1985.
16. Green, Mary Anne Everett: Letters of Royal Illustrious Ladies of Great Britain. H. Colburn. London. 1846.

17. Green, Mary Anne Everett: Lives of the Princesses of England from the Norman Conquest. Volume Four. London. 1857.
18. Green, Mary Anne Everett: Letters of Royal Illustrious Ladies of Great Britain. H. Colburn. London. 1846.
19. Date within the Encyclopaedia Britannica and the archives at Westminster Abbey state 8 October 1515, however some modern historians have believed this to be 7 October 1515.

9 A Pawn in a Political Game

1. Green, Mary Anne Everett: Letters of Royal Illustrious Ladies of Great Britain. H. Colburn. London. 1846.
2. Green, Mary Anne Everett: Lives of the Princesses of England from the Norman Conquest. Volume Four. London. 1857.
3. Chapman, Hester: The Sisters of Henry VIII. Jonathan Cape Ltd. Bath. 1969.
4. Buchanan, Patricia: Margaret Tudor: Queen of Scots. Scottish Academic Press Ltd. Edinburgh. 1985.
5. Harvey, Nancy Lenz: The Rose and the Thorn. Macmillan New York. 1975.
6. Jobson, Archbold William Arthur: 'Lovell, Thomas'. Dictionary of National Biography. Volume Thirty-Four. London. 1893.
7. 'Enfield, Manors': A History of the County of Middlesex. Volume Five.
8. The history for this came from the author's own family, whose family members had taken part in the event.
9. WWW.enfarchsoc.org. Enfield Archaeological Society.
10. Henry VIII: September 1513. 21-30. British History Online.
11. Perry, Maria: Sisters to the King. Andre Deutsch Ltd. London. 1998.

12. Guicciardini, Francesco: History of Italy. Originally 1561. Princeton University. 1984.
13. Ed. Brewer, J. S: Letters and Papers: Foreign and Domestic – Henry VIII. London. 1920.
14. Chapman, Hester: The Sisters of Henry VIII. Jonathan Cape Ltd. Bath. 1969.
15. Buchanan, Patricia: Margaret Tudor: Queen of Scots. Scottish Academic Press Ltd. Edinburgh. 1985.
16. Green, Mary Anne Everett: Lives of the Princesses of England from the Norman Conquest. Volume Four. London. 1857.
17. Buchanan, Patricia: Margaret Tudor: Queen of Scots. Scottish Academic Press Ltd. Edinburgh. 1985.
18. Hannay, R. K: Acts of the Lords of Council in Public Affairs, 1501-1544. P91. Edinburgh. 1932.
19. Register of the Privy Council of Scotland. Volume Five. Edinburgh. 1882.
20. www.historicenvironment.scot
21. Green, Mary Anne Everett: Lives of the Princesses of England from the Norman Conquest. Volume Four. London. 1857.
22. Lindsay, Maurice: The Castles of Scotland. Constable. London. 1986.

10 A Pawn No Longer

1. Green, Mary Anne Everett: Letters of Royal Illustrious Ladies of Great Britain. H. Colburn. London. 1846.
2. Ed. Brewer, J. S: Letters and Papers: Foreign and Domestic – Henry VIII. London. 1920.
3. Green, Mary Anne Everett: Lives of the Princesses of England from the Norman Conquest. Volume Four. London. 1857.

4. Green, Mary Anne Everett: Letters of Royal Illustrious Ladies of Great Britain. H. Colburn. London. 1846.
5. Green, Mary Anne Everett: Letters of Royal Illustrious Ladies of Great Britain. H. Colburn. London. 1846.
6. Green, Mary Anne Everett: Letters of Royal Illustrious Ladies of Great Britain. H. Colburn. London. 1846.
7. Perry, Maria: Sisters to the King. Andre Deutsch Ltd. London. 1998.
8. Green, Mary Anne Everett: Lives of the Princesses of England from the Norman Conquest. Volume Four. London. 1857.
9. Leslie, Bishop John: The History of Scotland: From the Death of King James I in the Year M. CCCC.XXXVI, to the year M.D.LXI. Bannatyne Club. 1830.
10. Ed. Brewer, J. S: Letters and Papers: Foreign and Domestic – Henry VIII. London. 1920.
11. Buchanan, Patricia: Margaret Tudor: Queen of Scots. Scottish Academic Press Ltd. Edinburgh. 1985.
12. Green, Mary Anne Everett: Lives of the Princesses of England from the Norman Conquest. Volume Four. London. 1857.
13. Perry, Maria: Sisters to the King. Andre Deutsch Ltd. London. 1998.
14. Green, Mary Anne Everett: Lives of the Princesses of England from the Norman Conquest. Volume Four. London. 1857.

11 The Son's Rule

1. Chapman, Hester: The Sisters of Henry VIII. Jonathan Cape Ltd. Bath. 1969.
2. Buchanan, Patricia: Margaret Tudor: Queen of Scots. Scottish Academic Press Ltd. Edinburgh. 1985.

3. Green, Mary Anne Everett: Lives of the Princesses of England from the Norman Conquest. Volume Four. London. 1857.
4. Chapman, Hester: The Sisters of Henry VIII. Jonathan Cape Ltd. Bath. 1969.
5. Perry, Maria: Sisters to the King. Andre Deutsch Ltd. London. 1998.
6. Green, Mary Anne Everett: Letters of Royal Illustrious Ladies of Great Britain. H. Colburn. London. 1846.
7. Ed. Gairdner, James. Letters and Papers: Foreign and Domestic – Henry VIII. London. 1920
8. Chapman, Hester: The Sisters of Henry VIII. Jonathan Cape Ltd. Bath. 1969.
9. Marshall, Rosalind Kay: Mary of Guise. Harper Collins. London. 1977.
10. Bain, Joseph: Hamilton Papers. Volume One. Edinburgh. 1890.
11. Green, Mary Anne Everett: Letters of Royal Illustrious Ladies of Great Britain. H. Colburn. London. 1846.

12 *From Cradle to Castile – Mary Tudor*

1. Laynesmith, J. L: The Fifteenth Century XV: Writing Records and Rhetoric. Boydell Press. 2017.
2. Meyer, C. J: The Tudors: The Complete Story of England's Most Notorious Dynasty. P6. New York. 2016.
3. Green, Mary Anne Everett: Lives of the Princesses of England. Volume 5. London. 1854.
4. Loades, David: Mary Rose Tudor Princess, Queen of France, the extraordinary life of Henry VIII's sister. P26. Amberley Publishing. 2012.
5. Breverton, Terry: Jasper Tudor Dynasty Maker. P17. Amberley Publishing. 2014.

6. As mentioned in BBC Scotland: Medieval Lives: Birth, Marriage and Death. 2013.
7. Brown, Mary Croom: Mary Tudor, Queen of France. P8. London. 1911.
8. Brown, Mary Croom: Mary Tudor, Queen of France. P9. London. 1911.
9. Green, Mary Anne Everett: Lives of the Princesses of England. P4. Volume 5. London. 1854.
10. Green, Mary Anne Everett: Lives of the Princesses of England. P4. Volume 5. London. 1854.
11. Richardson, Walter. C: Mary Tudor: The White Queen. P23. University of Washington Press. 1970.
12. 'Il Natale in Cul Ludovico d ivento il More'. 26 December 2007.
13. Richardson, Walter. C: Mary Tudor: The White Queen. P17. University of Washington Press. 1970.
14. Letters and Papers Volume 2. The King's Book of Payments. January 1513.
15. Bietenholz, Peter. G and Deutscher Thomas Brian: Contemporaries of Erasmus: A Biographical Register of the Renaissance and Reformation. Volume 3. P17. University of Toronto Press. 2003.
16. Green, Mary Anne Everett: Lives of the Princesses of England. P4. Volume 5. London. 1854.
17. Richardson, Walter. C.: Mary Tudor: The White Queen. P23. University of Washington Press. 1970.
18. Richardson, Walter. C: Mary Tudor: The White Queen. P34. University of Washington Press. 1970.
19. Perry, Maria: Sisters to the King. P42. André Deutsch. London 2002.

20. Loades, David: Mary Rose Tudor Princess, Queen of France, the extraordinary life of Henry VIII's sister. P42. Amberley Publishing. 2012.
21. Green, Mary Anne Everett: Lives of the Princesses of England. P4. Volume 5. London. 1854.
22. Richardson, Walter. C: Mary Tudor: The White Queen. P40. University of Washington Press. 1970.
23. Penn, Thomas: The Winter King: The Dawn of Tudor England. P285. London. 2011.
24. Cripps-Day, Francis Henry: The History of the Urrament in England and France. P122. London 1918.
25. Penn, Thomas: The Winter King: The Dawn of Tudor England. P289. London. 2011.
26. Sadlack, Erin: The French Queen's Letters. P109. New York. 2011.
27. Calendar of State Papers. Spain. Volume 1. 558.
28. Green, Mary Anne Everett: Lives of the Princesses of England. P10-11. Volume 5. London. 1854.
29. Green, Mary Anne Everett: Lives of the Princesses of England. P13. Volume 5. London. 1854.
30. Green, Mary Anne Everett: Lives of the Princesses of England. P13. Volume 5. London. 1854.
31. Green, Mary Anne Everett: Lives of the Princesses of England. P13. Volume 5. London. 1854.
32. Green, Mary Anne Everett: Lives of the Princesses of England. PP14-15. Volume 5. London. 1854.
33. Mumby, F: The Youth of Henry VIII: A narrative in Contemporary Letters. P116-120. Boston. 1913.
34. Mumby, F: The Youth of Henry VIII: A narrative in Contemporary Letters. P116-120. Boston. 1913.

35. Penn, Thomas: The Winter King: The Dawn of Tudor England. P273. London. 2011.
36. The Will of Henry VII. P38-42.

13 From a Tudor Rose to a French Lily

1. Vergil, P: Anglica Historia. 1555.
2. Richardson, Walter. C.: Mary Tudor: The White Queen. P58. University of Washington Press. 1970.
3. Hutchinson, Robert: Young Henry: The Rise of Henry VIII. P121. London. 2012.
4. Richardson, Walter. C: Mary Tudor: The White Queen. P61. University of Washington Press. 1970.
5. Green, Mary Anne Everett: Lives of the Princesses of England. P16. Volume 5. London. 1854.
6. Letters and Papers, Foreign and Domestic. Volume 1. 202.
7. Letters and Papers, Foreign and Domestic. Volume 1. 2366.
8. Letters and Papers, Foreign and Domestic. Volume 1. 2515.
9. Camden Society: The Chronicle of Calais in the Reigns of Henry VII and Henry VIII to the Year 1540. P66. Great Britain. 1838.
10. Richardson, Walter. C: Mary Tudor: The White Queen. P74. University of Washington Press. 1970.
11. Wilson, Derek: A Brief History of Henry VIII. P62. London. 2009.
12. Richardson, Walter. C: Mary Tudor: The White Queen. P60. University of Washington Press. 1970.
13. Loades, David: Mary Rose Tudor Princess, Queen of France, the extraordinary life of Henry VIII's sister. P64. Amberley Publishing. 2012.

14. Perry, Maria: Sisters to the King. P123. André Deutsch. London 2002.
15. Baumgartner, Frederic J: Louis XII. P1. New York. 1996.
16. Bell, Susan G: The Lost Tapestries of the City of Ladies. P105. University of California Press. 2004.
17. Gibson, Mary Lou: 'Saints for our Times: French Saint endured much torment from her family'. Catholic Spirit. Volume 31. Number 2. 14 October 2015.
18. Vauchez, André and Lapidge, Michael: Encyclopaedia of the Middle Ages A-J. P776. James Clarke and Co Ltd. 2000.
19. Lucien, Merlet and Gombert, Maxime de: Récit des funeralles of Anne de Bretage. Introduction' Natv Press. 2010. (Reproduction)
20. Brown, Cynthia Jane: The Cultural and Political Legacy of Anne de Bretagne: Negotiating Convention in Books and Documents. P185. D. S. Brewer 2010.
21. Wieck, Roger S: 'The Primer of Renée of France' in Peebles. Reprising and Legacy of Renée de France: From Fillede France to Dowager Duchess. P89. Palgrave Macmillan. 2021.
22. Jokinen, A: Louis XII, King of France (1462-1515). The Luminarium Encyclopaedia Project. 2007.
23. Calendar of State Papers. Venice. Volume 2. 505.
24. Letters and Papers, Foreign and Domestic. Volume 1. 3171.
25. Richardson, Walter. C: Mary Tudor: The White Queen. P82. University of Washington Press. 1970.
26. Richardson, Walter. C: Mary Tudor: The White Queen. P82. University of Washington Press. 1970.
27. Calendar of State Papers. Venice. Volume 2. 500.
28. Mumby, F: The Youth of Henry VIII: A narrative in Contemporary Letters. P263-264. Boston. 1913.

29. Loades, David: Mary Rose Tudor Princess, Queen of France, the extraordinary life of Henry VIII's sister. P76. Amberley Publishing. 2012.
30. Richardson, Walter. C: Mary Tudor: The White Queen. P85. University of Washington Press. 1970.
31. Letters and Papers, Foreign and Domestic. Volume 1. 3338.
32. Brown, Mary Croom: Mary Tudor Queen of France. P110. London. 1911.
33. Letters and Papers, Foreign and Domestic. Volume 1. 3294.
34. Letters and Papers, Foreign and Domestic. Volume 1. 3346.
35. Chisholm, Hugh: 'Suffolk. Charles Brandon. 1st Duke of'. Encyclopaedia Britannica. Volume 26. PP25-26. Cambridge University Press. 1911.
36. Dugdale, William: The Baronage of England. Volume 1. P723. 1675.
37. Mumby, F: The Youth of Henry VIII: A narrative in Contemporary Letters. PP310-311. Boston. 1913.
38. Ives, Eric: The Life and Death of Anne Boleyn. P335. Wiley Blackwell. 2005.
39. Perry, Maria: Sisters to the King. P135. André Deutsch. London 2002.
40. Richardson, Walter: Mary Tudor: The White Queen. P91. University of Washington Press. 1970.
41. Richardson, Walter: Mary Tudor: The White Queen. P91. University of Washington Press. 1970.
42. Bridge, John Sergeant Cyprian: A History of France from the Death of Louis II. P255. London. 1921.
43. Calendar of State Papers. Venice. Volume 2. 510.
44. Richardson, Walter. C: Mary Tudor: The White Queen. P96. University of Washington Press. 1970.

45. Richardson, Walter. C: Mary Tudor: The White Queen. P97. University of Washington Press. 1970.

14 *Queen and Duchess*

1. Mumby, F: The Youth of Henry VIII: A narrative in Contemporary Letters. P291. Boston. 1913.
2. Letters and Papers, Foreign and Domestic. Volume 1. 3357.
3. Mumby, F: The Youth of Henry VIII: A narrative in Contemporary Letters. P294. Boston. 1913.
4. Richardson, Walter. C: Mary Tudor: The White Queen. P112. University of Washington Press. 1970.
5. Richardson, Walter. C: Mary Tudor: The White Queen. P112. University of Washington Press. 1970.
6. Green, Mary Anne Everett: Lives of the Princesses of England. P53. Volume 5. London. 1854.
7. Green, Mary Anne Everett: Lives of the Princesses of England. P54-55. Volume 5. London. 1854.
8. Brown, Mary Croom: Mary Tudor, Queen of France. P135. London. 1911.
9. Brown, Mary Croom: Mary Tudor, Queen of France. PP136-137. London. 1911.
10. Green, Mary Anne Everett: Lives of the Princesses of England. P59. Volume 5. London. 1854.
11. Green, Mary Anne Everett: Lives of the Princesses of England. P181. Volume 5. London. 1854.
12. Hutchinson, Robert: Young Henry: The Rise of Henry VIII. P192. London. 2011.
13. Green, Mary Anne Everett: Lives of the Princesses of England. P73. Volume 5. London. 1854.
14. Letters and Papers, Foreign and Domestic. Volume 2. 15.

15. Mumby, F: The Youth of Henry VIII: A narrative in Contemporary Letters. P309-310. Boston. 1913.
16. Letters and Papers, Foreign and Domestic. Volume 2. 24.
17. Richardson, Walter. C: Mary Tudor: The White Queen. P166. University of Washington Press. 1970.
18. Loades, David: Mary Rose Tudor Princess, Queen of France, the extraordinary life of Henry VIII's sister. P111. Amberley Publishing. 2012.
19. Sadlack, Erin: The French Queen's Letters. P237-238. New York. 2011.
20. Mumby, F: The Youth of Henry VIII: A narrative in Contemporary Letters. P310-311. Boston. 1913.
21. Green, Mary Anne Everett: Lives of the Princesses of England. P81-82. Volume 5. London. 1854.
22. Letters and Papers, Foreign and Domestic. Volume 2. 80.
23. Letters and Papers, Foreign and Domestic. Volume 2. 203.
24. Letters and Papers, Foreign and Domestic. Volume 2. 343.
25. Letters and Papers, Foreign and Domestic. Volume 2. 827.
26. Loades, David: Mary Rose Tudor Princess, Queen of France, the extraordinary life of Henry VIII's sister. P114. Amberley Publishing. 2012.
27. Savoye, De Louise de.: Duchesse d' Angouleme. P397. Journal
28. Richardson, Walter. C.: Mary Tudor: The White Queen. P185. University of Washington Press. 1970.

15 *From Cloth of Gold to Castle Green*

1. Sadlack, Erin: The French Queen's Letters. P309. New York. 2011.
2. Loades David: Mary Rose Tudor Princess, Queen of France, the extraordinary life of Henry VIII's sister. P117. Amberley Publishing. 2012.

3. Smith, Terence Paul, Watson, Bruce, Martin, Claire and Williams, David: Suffolk Place Southwark London: A Tudor Palace and its Terracotta Architectural Decoration. Post Medieval Archaeology. Volume 48. Issue 1. 2014.
4. Loades, David: Mary Rose Tudor Princess, Queen of France, the extraordinary life of Henry VIII's sister. PP131-132. Amberley Publishing. 2012.
5. Richardson, Walter. C: Mary Tudor: The White Queen. P195. University of Washington Press. 1970.
6. Sadlack, Erin: The French Queen's Letters. P353. New York. 2011
7. Loades, David: Mary Rose Tudor Princess, Queen of France, the extraordinary life of Henry VIII's sister. P131. Amberley Publishing. 2012.
8. Richardson, Walter. C: Mary Tudor: The White Queen. P225. University of Washington Press. 1970.
9. Green, Mary Anne Everett: Lives of the Princesses of England. P113. Volume 5. London. 1854.
10. Green, Mary Anne Everett: Lives of the Princesses of England. P114. Volume 5. London. 1854.
11. Green, Mary Anne Everett: Lives of the Princesses of England. P114. Volume 5. London. 1854.
12. Purse, Amanda Harvey: The Boleyns: From the Tudors to the Windsors. Amberley Publishing. 2022.
13. Loades, David: Mary Rose Tudor Princess, Queen of France, the extraordinary life of Henry VIII's sister. P163. Amberley Publishing. 2012.
14. Green, Mary Anne Everett: Lives of the Princesses of England. P121. Volume 5. London. 1854.
15. Green, Mary Anne Everett: Lives of the Princesses of England. P121-122. Volume 5. London. 1854.

16. Letters and Papers, Foreign and Domestic. Volume 2. 4469.
17. Perry, Maria: Sisters to the King. P201. André Deutsch. London 2002
18. Sadlack, Erin: The French Queen's Letters. P344. New York. 2011.
19. Richardson, Walter. C: Mary Tudor: The White Queen. PP228-229. University of Washington Press. 1970.
20. Calendar of State Papers. Venice. Volume 3. 50.
21. Richardson, Walter. C: Mary Tudor: The White Queen. P230. University of Washington Press. 1970.
22. Calendar of State Papers. Venice. Volume 3. 50.
23. Gunn, Steven: Charles Brandon. P60. Amberley Publishing. 2015.
24. Calendar of State Papers. Venice. Volume 3. 84.
25. Calendar of State Papers. Venice. Volume 3. 69.
26. Purse, Amanda Harvey: The Boleyns: From the Tudors to the Windsors. Amberley Publishing. 2022.
27. Ives, Eric: The Life and Death of Anne Boleyn. P37. Blackwell Publishing. 2005.
28. Ives, Eric: The Life and Death of Anne Boleyn. P38. Blackwell Publishing. 2005.
29. Loades, David: Mary Rose Tudor Princess, Queen of France, the extraordinary life of Henry VIII's sister. P164. Amberley Publishing. 2012
30. Oxford Dictionary of National Biography of Charles Brandon.
31. Wilson, Derek: A Brief History of Henry VIII. P124. London. 2009.
32. Loades, David: Mary Rose Tudor Princess, Queen of France, the extraordinary life of Henry VIII's sister. P132. Amberley Publishing. 2012.

33. Gunn, Steven: Charles Brandon. P67. Amberley Publishing. 2015.
34. Loades, David: Mary Rose Tudor Princess, Queen of France, the extraordinary life of Henry VIII's sister. P172-173. Amberley Publishing. 2012.
35. Wooding, Lucy: Henry VIII. P121. Oxen. 2015.
36. Betteridge, Thomas and Freeman, Thomas: Henry VIII and History of England. 2012.
37. Green, Mary Anne Everett: Lives of the Princesses of England. P241-242. Volume 5. London. 1854.
38. Loades, David: Mary Rose Tudor Princess, Queen of France, the extraordinary life of Henry VIII's sister. P153. Amberley Publishing. 2012.
39. Letters and Papers, Foreign and Domestic. Volume 4. 1431.
40. Loades, David: Mary Rose Tudor Princess, Queen of France, the extraordinary life of Henry VIII's sister. P153. Amberley Publishing. 2012.
41. Sadlack, Erin: The French Queen's Letters. PP475-476. New York. 2011.
42. Calendar of State Papers. Venice. Volume 4. 761.
43. Perry, Maria: Sisters to the King. P267. André Deutsch. London 2002.
44. Sadlack, Erin: The French Queen's Letters. P403. New York. 2011.
45. Loades, David: Mary Rose Tudor Princess, Queen of France, the extraordinary life of Henry VIII's sister. PP173-173. Amberley Publishing. 2012.
46. Loades, David: Mary Rose Tudor Princess, Queen of France, the extraordinary life of Henry VIII's sister. P189. Amberley Publishing. 2012.

47. Sadlack, Erin: The French Queen's Letters. P407-408. New York. 2011.
48. Loades, David: Mary Rose Tudor Princess, Queen of France, the extraordinary life of Henry VIII's sister. 191-192. Amberley Publishing. 2012.
49. De Lisle, Leanda: Tudor The Family Story. P283-284. London. 2013.
50. Emerson, Kathy Lynn: A who's who of Tudor Women. www.kateemersonhistorical.com.
51. Letters and Papers. Foreign and Domestic. Volume 21. PP313-348.

BIBLIOGRAPHY

(n.d.). Retrieved from www.revealingrichardiii.com.

(n.d.). Retrieved from ScottishChurches.org.uk.

(n.d.). Retrieved from www.enfarchsoc.org. Enfield Archaeological Society.

(n.d.). Retrieved from www.historicenvironment.scot .

(n.d.). *Garrett MS. 168.* . Manuscripts Division. Department of Rare Books and Special Collections. Princeton University.

'Enfield, Manors'. (n.d.). *A History of the County of Middlesex.*

14:14, C. o. (1960). London: Held at Her Majesty's Stationary Office.

(n.d.). 23. *Calendar of State Papers. Venice. Volume 2. 505.*

(1877). *Accounts of the Treasurer of Scotland. Volume I.* Edinburgh.

(1483). *Acts of Sovereigns and other Supreme Authorities, Louis XI, King*. London: British Library.

Amin, N. (2020). *Henry VII and the Tudor Pretenders: Simnel, Warbeck and Warwick*. Amberley Publishing.

Anglo, S. (1960-1961). 'The British History in Early Tudor Propaganda'. *Bulletin of the John Ryland's Library* .

Anstis, J. (1724). *The Register of the Most Noble Order of the Garter, from its Cover in Black Velvet usually called the Black Book*. London.

Ashdown Hill, J. (2016). *Eleanor Talbot: The Secret Queen*. Stroud.

Ashdown Hill, J. (2016). *The Private of Edward IV*. Stroud.

Ashdown-Hill, J. (2019). *Elizabeth Widville, Lady Grey*. Pen and Sword History.

Backhouse, J. (1995). *'Illuminated Manuscripts Associated with Henry VII and Members of his Immediate Family' in the Reign of Henry VII*. Stamford: 1993 Harlaxton Symposium.

Bain, J. (1888). *Calendar of Document Relating to Scotland 1357-1509*. Edinburgh.

Bain, J. (1890). *Hamilton Papers* . Edinburgh.

Baldwin, D. (2007). *The Lost Prince: The Survival of Richard of York* . Stoud.

Barker, J. (2012). *Conquest: The English Kingdom of France 1417-1450*. Harvard University Press.

Barker., 1. F. (n.d.). *Manuscript MS 2M6*. . London: Held at College of Arms. Queen Victoria Street.

Baumgartner, F. J. (1996). *Louis XII*. New York.

Bell, S. G. (2004). *The Lost Tapestries of the City of Ladies*. University of California Press.

Bennett, M. (1987). *Lambert Simnel and the Battle of Stoke.* New York: St Martin's Press.

Bentley, S. (1831). *Excerpa Historica or Illustrations of English History III.* London.

Bietenholz, P. G. (2003). *Contemporaries of Erasmus: A Biographical Register of the Renaissance and Reformation.* University of Toronto Press .

(n.d.). *BL Add. MS 5001.* London: British Library.

(n.d.). *BL Royal MS 14 EIII.* London.: British Library.

(n.d.). *BL Royal MS 16 FII.*

Borman, T. (2017). *The Private Lives of the Tudors.* . Hodder.

Breverton, T. (2014). *Jasper Tudor Dynasty Maker.* Amberley Publishing.

Brewer, E. J. (1920). *Letters and Papers: Foreign and Domestic – Henry VIII.* London.

Brown, C. J. (2010). *The Cultural and Political Legacy of Anne de Bretagne: Negotiating Convention in Books and Documents.* D. S. Brewer.

Buchanan, P. (1985). *Margaret Tudor: Queen of Scots.* Edinburgh: Scottish Academic Press Ltd.

Buck, G. (1979). *The History of Richard the Third. 1619* . Gloucester: Alan Sutton.

(n.d.). *Calendar of Patent Rolls 1467-1477.*

(n.d.). *Calendar of Patent Rolls. Edward IV. 1461-1467.*

(n.d.). *Calendar of Patient Rolls 1476-1485. Numbers 1036, 1037 and 1038.* . Held within British History Online. .

(n.d.). *Calendar of State Papers. Spain. Volume 1. 558.*

(n.d.). *Calendar of State Papers. Venice. Volume 2. 500.*

Calendar of State Papers. Venice. Volume 2. 510. (n.d.).

(n.d.). *Calendar of State Papers. Venice. Volume 3. 50.*

('July 1498'.). *Calendar of State Papers: Spain.*

(n.d.). *Calendar of the Close Rolls Henry VII 1485-1500.* London: Preserved in the Public Record Office.

Campbell, W. (1873). *Materials for a History of the Reign of Henry VII.* London: Original Documents Preserved in the Public Record Office. 1:6. Longman and Turbner.

Chapman, A. a. (1999). The Medieval Abbey of St James (Part 1)'. The Former Express Lift Site, Northampton. . *Northamptonshire Archaeology.* .

Chapman, H. (1969). *The Sisters of Henry VIII.* Bath: Jonathan Cape Ltd.

Chisholm, H. (1911). 'Suffolk. Charles Brandon. 1st Duke of'. *Encyclopaedia Britannica.* Cambridge University Press.

Chrimes, S. B. (1999). *Henry VII.* Yale University Press.

Clark, D. (2007). *Barnet 1471: Death of a Kingmaker.* Pen and Sword.

Clarke, P. D. (2005). 'English Royal Marriage and the Papal Penitentiary in the Fifteenth Century'. *English Historical Review.*

Cokayne, G. E. (1916). *The Complete Peerage. Vol IV.* London: St Catherine Press.

Crawford, A. (1992). *Howard Household Books.* Stroud.

Cripps-Day, F. H. (1918). *The History of the Urrament in England and France.* London.

Croom Brown, M. (1911). *Mary Tudor, Queen of France.* London.

Cyprian Bridge, J. S. (1921). *A History of France from the Death of Louis II.* London.

Davis, R. (1843). *Extracts from the Municipal Records of the City of York.* London.

Decommines, Philip Lord Of Argenton (1855). *The Memoirs of Philip de Commines.* London: Lord of Argenton Books.

De Lisle, L. (2013). *Tudor, The Family Story.* London.

Dodd, G. a. (2008). *The Reign of Henry IV: Rebellion and Survival 1403-1413*. York Medieval Press.

Drummond, W. (1745). *History of Scotland*. London.

Du Chesne, A. (1631). *Histoire généalogique de la maison royale de Dreux et de quelaues autres familles Illustres qui en sont descendues parfemnes*. S. Cramoisy.

DuBoulay, F. R. (n.d.). *Registrum Thomas Bourchier Cantuariensis Archbishop AD 1454-1486* . Held at Lambeth Palace Library. .

Dunbar, J. G. (1999). *Scottish Royal Palaces*. East Linton.

(n.d.). *E 404/81/1. 31 December 1491 and 20 July 1492.* . London: Held at the National Archives.

(1495). *E 404/82. Warrant* . Held at the National Archives.

Edwards, R. (1983). The Itinerary of King Richard III. *Richard III Society*.

Ellis, H. (1824). *Original Letters*. London: Harding, Triphook and Lepard.

Emerson, K. L. (n.d.). *A Who's Who of Tudor Women*. Retrieved from www.kateemersonhistorical.com .

Everett Green, M. A. (1846). *Letters of Royal Illustrious Ladies of Great Britain*. London: H. Colburn.

Everett Green, M. A. (1857). *Lives of the Princesses of England from the Norman Conquest*. London.

Fabian, R. (1811). *The New Chronicles of England and France*. London.

Fahy, C. (1960). 'The Marriage of Edward IV and Elizabeth Woodville: A New Italian Source'. *English Historical Review*.

Fitzroy, C. a. (2000). *Grafton Regis: The History of a Northamptonshire Village*. Merton Priory Press.

Gairdner, J. (1880). Three Fifteen Century Chronicles. *Camden Society*.

Gairdner, J. (1904). *The Paston Letter: III*. London.

Gairdner, J. (n.d.). *The Paston Letters* (Vol. 1).

Gairdner., J. (1493-1494). *E 404/81/3. Warrants Letters and Papers Illustrative of the Reigns of Richard III and Henry VII.* London: Held at the National Archives.

Gibson, M. L. (2015). 'Saints for our Times: French Saint endured much torment from her family'. *Catholic Spirit*.

Goodwin, G. (2013). *Fatal Rivalry: Flodden 1513*. London.

Grose, F. a. (1807). *The Antiquarian Repertory: A Miscellaneous Assemblage of Topography, History, Biography, Customs and Manners.*

Grummitt, D. (2008). *The Calais Garrison, War and Military Service in England 1436-1558*. The Boydell Press.

Guicciardini, F. (1984). *History of Italy*. Princeton University.

Gunn, S. a. (2009). *Arthur Tudor, Prince of Wales: Life, Death and Commemoration*. Woodbridge.

Haigh, P. (2014). *From Wakefield to Towton*. Pen and Sword Military.

Hall, E. (1889). *Hall's Chronicle, containing the History of England*. London.

Hammond, P. W. (1985). *Richard III: The Road to Bosworth* . London.

Hanham, A. (1987). 'Sir George Buck and Princess Elizabeth's letter: A problem in Detection'. *Ricardian*.

Hannay, R. K. (1932). *Acts of the Lords of Council in Public Affairs*. Edinburgh.

Harris, M. D. (1907). *The Coventry Leet Book or Mayor's Register*. Eary English Text Society.

Harthan, J. (1977). *The Book of Hours: With a Historical Survey and Commentary by John Harthan*. New York : Crowell.

Harvey, N. L. (1975). *The Rose and the Thorn.* New York: Macmillan.

Hay Fleming, D. a. (1936). *Register of the Privy Seal 1542-1548.* Edinburgh.

(n.d.). *Henry VIII: September 1513.* British History Online.

Henry, E. (1970). *Original Letters, Illustrative of English History. Second Series.* New York: AMS Press.

Henry, W. (1840). *Illustrations of Ancient State and Chivalry.* London: From Manuscripts in the Ashmolean Museum.

Hepburn, W. (2023). *The Household and Court of James IV of Scotland.* Boydell.

Hight, J. (n.d.). *Britain's Tree Story.* London: National Trust.

History of Mote Park . (n.d.). Retrieved from Moteparkfellowship.org.uk .

Horrox, R. (2004). Grey Sir Richard. *Oxford Dictionary of National Biography.*

Hutchinson, R. (2012). *Young Henry: The Rise of Henry VIII.* London.

Ives, E. (2005). *The Life and Death of Anne Boleyn.* Wiley Blackwell.

Jobson, A. W. (1893). *'Lovell, Thomas'. Dictionary of National Biography.* London.

Jokinen, A. (2007). *Louis XII, King of France (1462-1515).* The Luminarium Encyclopaedia Project.

Kendall, P. M. (2002). *Richard the Third.* W. W Norton and Company.

Kingsford, C. L. (1905). *Vitellus Axvi in the Chronicles of London.* Oxford: Clarendon Press.

Kingsford, C. L. (1913). *English Historical Literature in the Fifteen Century.* Oxford.

Kipling, G. (1990). *The Receyt of the Lady Kateryne.* Oxford University Press.

L., L. J. (2005). *The Last Medieval Queens: English Queenship. 1445-1503.* Oxford University Press.

Laynesmith, J. L. (2017). *The Fifteenth Century XV: Writing Records and Rhetoric.* Boydell Press.

Legg, L. G. (1901). *English Coronation Records.* London.

Leland, J. (1774). *De Rebus Brittanicus Collectanea.* London.

Leslie, B. J. (1830). *The History of Scotland: From the Death of King James I in the Year M.CCCC.XXXVI, to the year M.D.LXI* . Bannatyne Club.

(1513). *Letters and Papers Volume 2. The King's Book of Payments. January.*

(n.d.). *Letters and Papers, Foreign and Domestic. Henry VII.*

Lindsay, M. (1986). *The Castles of Scotland.* London: Constable.

Loades, D. (2012). *Mary Rose Tudor Princess, Queen of France, the Extraordinary Life of Henry VIII's Sister.* Amberley Publishing.

Lucien, M. (2010. (Reproduction)). *Récit des funeralles of Anne de Bretage. Introduction'.* Natv Press.

Samuel Stebbing (2018). *A Genealogical History of the Kings and Queens of England and Monarchs. From Conquest.* Gale Print Editions.

Madden, F. (1834). *Genealogical and Historical Notes in Ancient Calendars.* Collected Topographical et Genealogical.

Mancini, D. (1984). *The Usurpation of Richard III.* Sutton Publishing Ltd.

Marshall, R. K. (1977). *Mary of Guise.* London: Harper Collins.

Marshall, R. K. (2003). *Scottish Queens: 1034-1714.* Tuckwell Press Ltd.

McKisack, M. (1959). *The Fourteenth Century: 1307-1399*. Oxford University Press .

Mervin, B. (2014). *Enquiring History: Tudor Rebellions 1485-1603*. Hodder Education.

Meyer, C. J. (2016). *The Tudors: The Complete Story of England's Most Notorious Dynasty.* New York.

Middleton, R. (2003). *Manuscript of the Lancelot-Grail Cycle in England and Wales: Some books and their owners in a companion to the Lancelot-Grail cycle*. Woodbridge.

Monstrelet. (1857-62). *La Chronique d'Enguerian de: En Deux Livres Avec Pieces Justificatives 1400 – 1444*. Pans.

More, T. (1924). *The History of King Richard III*. University Press.

Morrison, E. (2003). *Luminating the Renaissance: The Triumph of Flemish Manuscript Painting in Europe* . Getty Museum.

Mumby, F. (1913). *The Youth of Henry VIII: A narrative in Contemporary Letters*. Boston.

Myers, A. R. (1959). *The Household of Edward IV: The Black Book and the Ordinance of 1478*. Manchester University Press.

Neillands, R. (2001). *The Hundred Years War.* Routledge.

Nicolas, N. H. (1830). *Privy Purse Expenses of Elizabeth of York: Wardrobe Accounts of Edward IV.* London.

Okerlund, A. (2005). *Elizabeth Wydville: The Slandered Queen.* Tempus Publishing.

Paton, H. (1957). *Accounts of the Masters of Work*. Edinburgh.

Penn, T. (2011). *The Winter King: The Dawn of Tudor England.* London: Penguin.

Perry, M. (1998). *Sisters to the King*. London: Andre Deutsch Ltd.

(n.d.). *Proceedings and Ordinances of the Privy Council. (POPC).*

Pronay, N. a. (1986). *The Crowland Chronicle Continuations 1459-1486*. London.

Pugh, T. B. (1988). *Henry V and the Southampton Plot of 1415*. Alan Sutton.

Purse, A. H. (2022). *The Boleyns: From the Tudors to the Windsors*. Amberley Publishing .

(1882). *Register of the Privy Council of Scotland*. Edinburgh.

Richardson, W. C. (1970). *Mary Tudor: The White Queen*. University of Washington Press.

Rosser, G. (1989). *Medieval Westminster 1200-1540*. Oxford Clarendon Press.

(1832). *Rotuli Parliamentorium. 6: 288*. London.

Sadlack, E. (2011). *The French Queen's Letters*. New York.

Sadler, J. (2011). *Towton: The Battle of Palm Sunday Field 1461*. Pen and Sword Military.

Salmon, M. (2022). *Medieval Syphilis and Treponemal Disease*. Amsterdam University Press.

(n.d.). *SC 1/45/236*. Held at The National Archives.

Scarisbrick, J. J. (1997). *Henry VIII*. Yale University Press.

Scofield, C. (1923). *The Life and Reign of Edward the Fourth*. London.

Scott, K. L. (1996). *Later Gothic Manuscripts 1390-1490: Survey of Manuscripts Illuminated in the British Isles*. London.

Scott, R. M. (1982). *Robert the Bruce, King of the Scots*. Edinburgh.

Searle, W. G. (1867). *The History of the Queens College of St Margaret and St Bernard in the University of Cambridge. 1446-1560*. Cambridge University Press.

Sheerin, J. (2002, 26 September). 'Medieval Skeletons are found at palace' . *Independent*.

Shepherd, R. (2012). *Westminster: A Biography From the Earliest Times to the Present*. A&C Black.

Smith, G. (1935). *The Coronation of Elizabeth Wydeville.* London.

Smith, T. P. (2014). 'Suffolk Place, Southwark London: A Tudor Palace and its Terracotta Architectural Decoration'. *Post Medieval Archaeology.*

Squires, A. (2002). *The Greys: A Long and Noble Line.* Silk Press Books.

St Michael's Church. (n.d.). Retrieved from UndiscoveredScotland.co.uk.

Starkey, D. (2009). *Henry: The Prince who would Turn Tyrant.* Harper Press.

Stevens, J. (1961). *Music and Poetry in the Early Tudor Court.* London: Methien and co.

Stickland, A. (1868). *Lives of the Tudor Princesses.* London: Longmans, Green and Co.

Stone, J. (1902). *The Chronicle of John Stone: Monk of Christ Church 1415-1471.* Cambridge: Antiquarian Society.

Stow, J. (1598). *Survey of London: Cripplegate Ward.*

Stride, P. a. (2013). 'Henry VIII, McLeod syndrome and Jacquetta's curse'. *The Journal of the Royal College of Physicians of Edinburgh.*

Sutton, A. F. (1983). *The Coronation of Richard III: The Extant Documents.* Gloucester: Alan Sutton.

Sutton, A. F.-F. (2005). 'The Royal Funerals of the House of York at Windsor'. *Richard III Society.*

Tait, J. (n.d.). 'Plantagenet, Edward'. *Dictionary of National Biography.* London: Smith, Elder and Co .

Taylor, I. A. (1913). *The Life of James IV.* London: Wentworth Press.

The Chronicle of Calais in the Reigns of Henry VII and Henry VIII to the Year 1540. (1838). Camden Society.

(n.d.). *The Will of Henry VII.*

Thomas, A. H. (1938). *The Great Chronicle of London* . London: Held at Guildhall Library.

Tout, T. (n.d.). 'Mortimer, Edmund Earl of March and Ulster'. *Dictionary of National Biography.* London: Smith, Elder and Co.

Tuetey, A. (1881). *Journal d'un bourgeois de Paris, 1405–1449.* Rome and Paris, Public Manuscripts. Champion.

Vauchez, A. Ed. (2000). *Encyclopaedia of the Middle Ages*. James Clarke and Co Ltd.

Vergil, P. (1950). *The Anglica Historia of Polydore Vergil AD 1485-1537*. London: Royal Historical Society.

Vergil, P. E. (1844). *Three books of Polydore Vergil's English History, comprising the reigns of Henry VI, Edward IV and Richard III.*

Vischer-Fuchs, S. (1996). 'The Reburial of Richard, Duke of York 21-30 July 1476'. *Richard III Society*, 19.

Watkins, S. B. (2017). *Margaret Tudor: Queen of Scots: The Life of Henry VIII's Sister.* Chronos Books .

Weir, A. (2008). *Princes in the Tower.* Vintage.

Weir, A. (2009). *The Wars of the Roses: Lancaster and York.* Ballantine Books.

Westminster Abbey Archives. (n.d.). Retrieved from www.westminster-abbey.org. .

Wieck, R. S. (2021). 'The Primer of Renée of France' in Peebles. *Reprising and Legacy of Renée de France: From Fille de France to Dowager Duchess*. Palgrave Macmillan.

William, D. (1675). *The Baronage of England.*

Williams, E. C. (1963). *My Lord Bedford 1389-1435, Being a Life of John of Lancaster, first Duke of Bedford, brother of Henry V and Regent of France.* Longman's, Green and Co Ltd.

Williamson, J. A. (1961). *The Tudor Age.* D. McKay Co.

Wilson, D. (2009). *A Brief History of Henry VIII.* London.

Wolffe, B. P. (2001). *Henry VI. Yale Monarchs.* London: Yale University Press.

Woolgar, C. (1999). *The Great Household in Late Medieval England.* Yale.

Wroe, A. (2004). *Perkin.* Vintage.

Young, J. (n.d.). *The Fyancells of Margaret, Eldest Daughter of Henry VII* as quoted in *Leland: Collectanea,* Volume four. Oxford.

INDEX